M000082281

ISBN 1-932051-15-5

9 781932 051155

51295

codeflesh

codeflesh
by joe casey and charlie adlard

published by
ait/planet lar
2034 47th avenue
san francisco, ca 94116

first edition: november 2003
isbn: 1-932051-15-5

10 9 8 7 6 5 4 3 2 1

copyright © 2003 joe casey and charlie adlard. All rights reserved.

lettered by richard starkings and comicraft

book design by whiskey island

originally published as
double image #1-5 by image comics and *double take* #6-8 by funkotron

no part of this publication may be reproduced, stored in any
retrieval system, or transmitted, in any form or by any means
(except for short excerpts as part of a review) without prior
written permission of the publisher, nor be otherwise circulated
in any form of binding or cover other than that in which it is
published.

printed and bound in canada by quebecor printing, inc.

ISBN 1-932051-15-5

9 781932 051155

51295

codeflesh

joe casey

charlie adlard

richard starkings and comicraft

san francisco

introduction

I *hate Larry Young.* I hate that bearded, bespectacled, baseball-cap-wearin' sumbitch for one reason: He's publishing *Codeflesh* and I'm not.

I *hate Joe Casey.* I hate him because as a writer, he's bold, compelling, aggressive, and ultimately... just bold. Here's a guy who comes on to characters such as Superman or The X-Men and has no fucking qualms about turning them on their Kryptonian or mutated ears. To hell with convention, to hell what you think you know. Joe Casey has no fear of coming into your comic book house, eating your Bugaloos-lunch-boxed lunch, and destroying your precious X-Men. Hell, just imagine what the kid could do if someone took the restraints off; if he went wild and free-balling on something new, something bold, something where nothing fenced him in. Something like, oh, I dunno... maybe *Codeflesh.*

I *hate Charlie Adlard, too.* I hate him because he explodes my stereotype of the dour, taciturn, ever-gloomy British. He's bright, cheery, and always quick with a joke. Hell, his teeth are even okay. And if that doesn't explode your typical Limey stereotype, I don't know what will. He's also one of the more talented artists on the scene, a stylist with a million styles. He's the perfect comics chameleon, able to adapt to any situation, any mood, any environment, and make it his own.

Oh, yeah -- speaking of that environment, here's your "high concept": Cameron Daltrey is a bail bondsman with an adrenaline problem. He writes bonds for the high-risk guys, criminals who he knows will skip. Daltrey specializes in supervillains.

When the scummiest of the scum invariably bolt, Daltrey doesn't hire a bounty hunter. He's his *own* bounty hunter. He puts on a funky, UPC-code-lookin' mask, and brings 'em back alive, himself. All much to the chagrin of his girlfriend, who's unaware of his double life, and knows only that Cameron is never there when he says he's going to be. But he can't stop. He's addicted to the rush, addicted to knowing he's going up against a stone-cold killer a million times more powerful than he is. He knows that every time he goes after a skip, the odds are stacked horribly against him. If someone's coming back in a body bag -- always a possibility -- the smart money says it'll be Cameron Daltrey. He's the highest-stakes gambler there is. His chips are his life, and he pushes them to the middle of the table every night.

That having been said, for me, the book isn't even *about* Cameron Daltrey. The real star of the show is the setting -- a sleazy area of Northeast Los Angeles where the people have just enough money to be dangerous, but are just a little too poor to move out. In this neighborhood, some months, crack comes before rent. Some months, you crack someone to make the rent. What happens if you take a wrong turn off of Hyperion Boulevard in Silver Lake? What's really happening in those old, old mansions up on the hill in Los Feliz? Do dead bodies really turn up in the canyons of Griffith Park? This book knows. Codeflesh knows. And the answers are anything but pretty.

Word to the wise and something to look forward to: These motherfuckers -- Casey and Adlard -- bring down the house like no one you've ever *seen*. The final story in this collection once again breaks every convention of comics, yet emerges as one of the most commanding and lyrical stories you'll ever find in the medium. **Straight up and true: It's the freshest, most invigorating, boldest thing I've seen in comics in the last five years.** It's 12 pages of pure comic poetry. I gotta -- I *really* gotta -- stop short of saying "It's a work worthy of Will Eisner." Eisner is the Old Master. None may even stand in his shadow. But this is close. *Damn* close.

Enough standard intro hype and heaping of praise. In the interest of balance and fair play, a list of criticisms: 1) I don't like the title. *Codeflesh?* What's it **mean?** Sounds like a hospital drama on FOX. 2) I don't get the mask. Just don't get it.

In retrospect, having looked back at the words I've typed to this point, I really don't know what the hell I'm doing here. I'm probably the worst guy on Earth to write an intro to this. I hate Joe Casey. Hate Charlie Adlard. Hate *Codeflesh*.

But most of all, I hate Larry Young.

No offense.

Jim McLauchlin
October 2003

— *Jim McLauchlin is the editor-in-chief of Top Cow Productions, and a convention organizer for the Wizard World conventions. He's a frequent contributor to magazines such as* Playboy *and* FHM. *He hates cats. And Larry Young.*

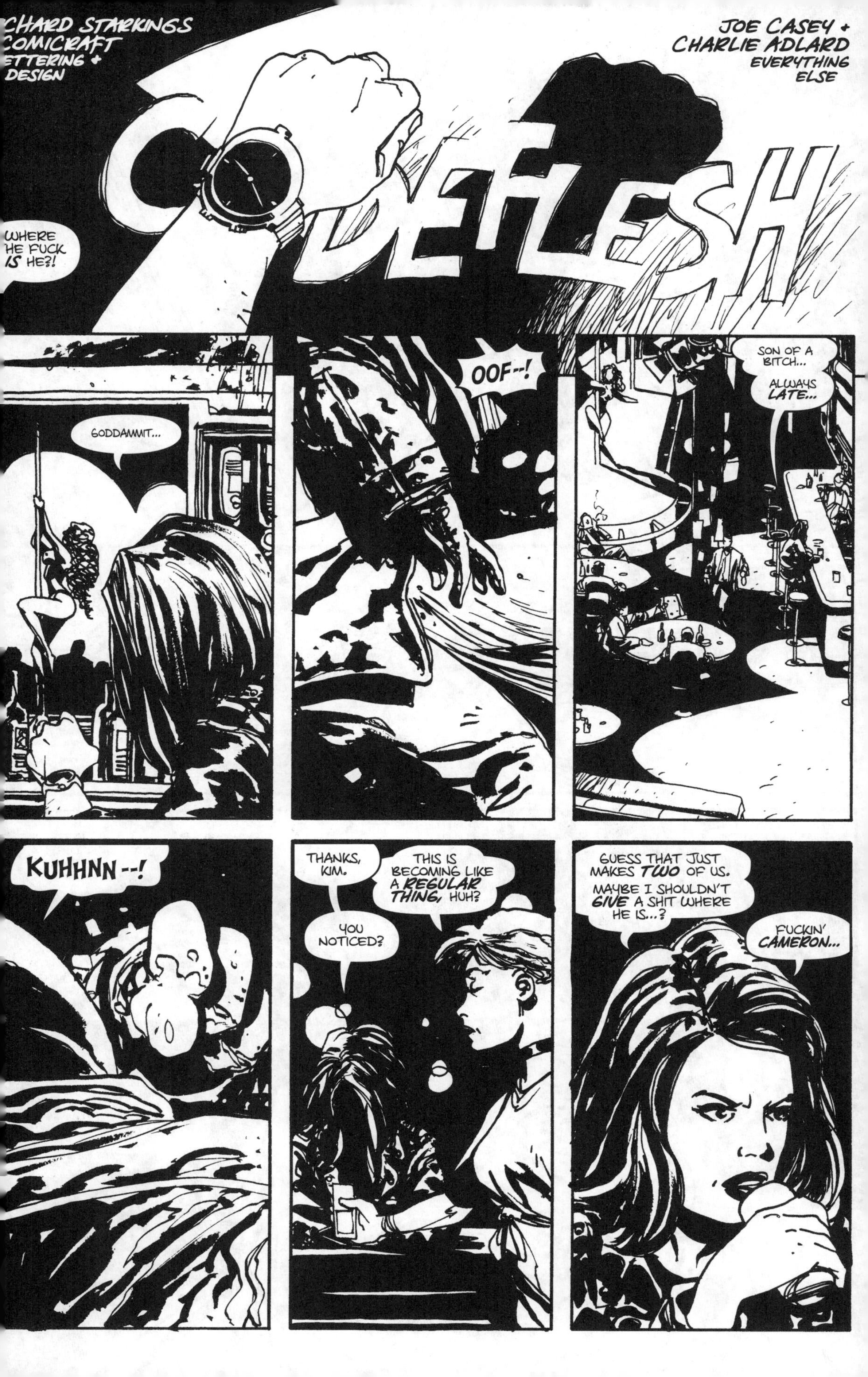

CHARD STARKINGS
COMICRAFT
ETTERING +
DESIGN
JOE CASEY +
CHARLIE ADLARD
EVERYTHING
ELSE
WHERE
HE FUCK
IS HE?!
DEFLESH
GODDAMMIT...
OOF--!
SON OF A
BITCH...
ALWAYS
LATE...
KUHHNN--!
THANKS,
KIM.
THIS IS
BECOMING LIKE
A REGULAR
THING, HUH?
YOU
NOTICED?
GUESS THAT JUST
MAKES TWO OF US.
MAYBE I SHOULDN'T
GIVE A SHIT WHERE
HE IS...?
FUCKIN'
CAMERON...

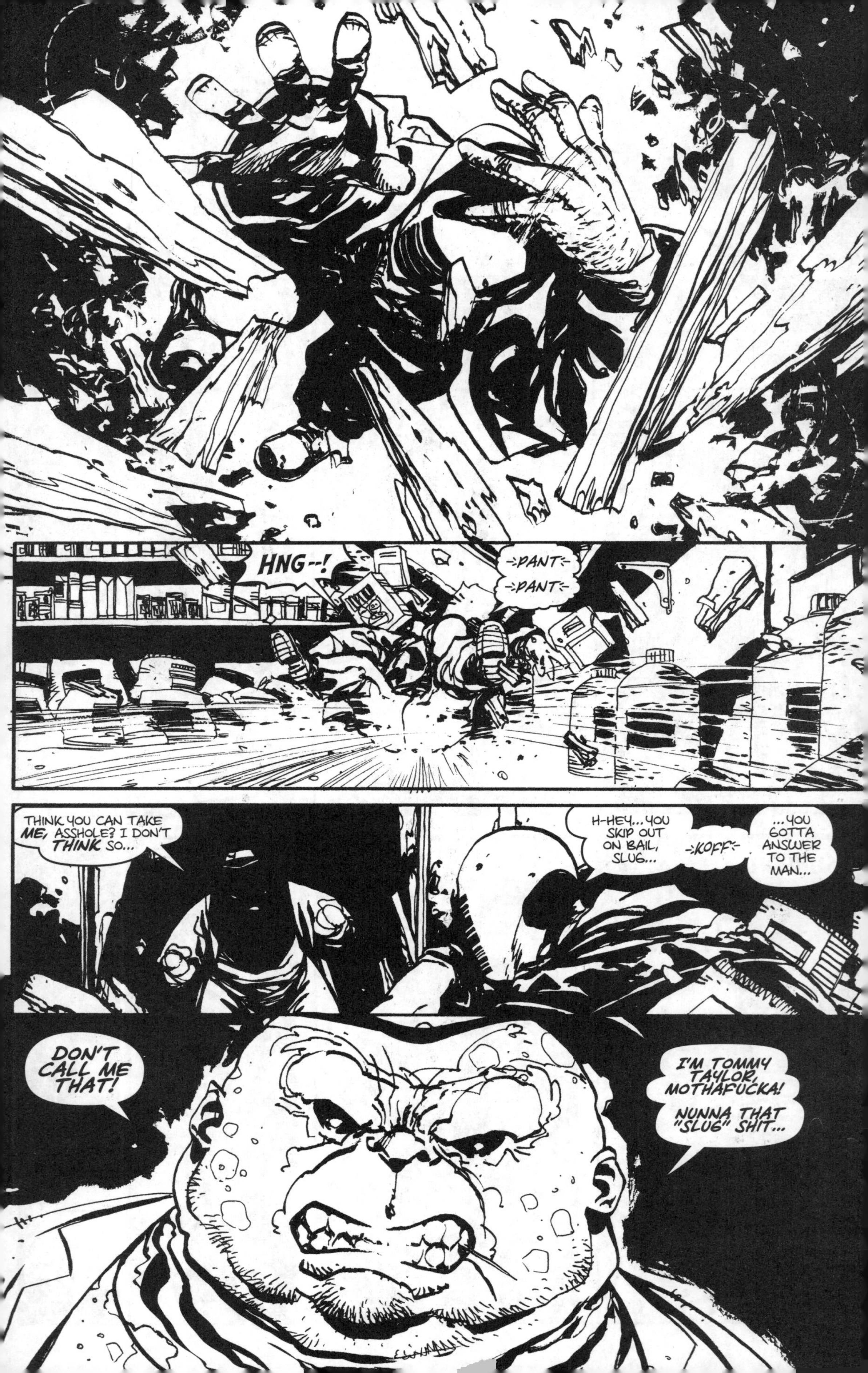
HNG--!
-PANT-
-PANT-
THINK YOU CAN TAKE *ME*, ASSHOLE? I DON'T *THINK* SO...
H-HEY... YOU SKIP OUT ON BAIL, SLUG...
-KOFF-
...YOU GOTTA ANSWER TO THE MAN...
DON'T CALL ME THAT!
I'M TOMMY TAYLOR, MOTHAFUCKA!
NUNNA THAT "SLUG" SHIT...

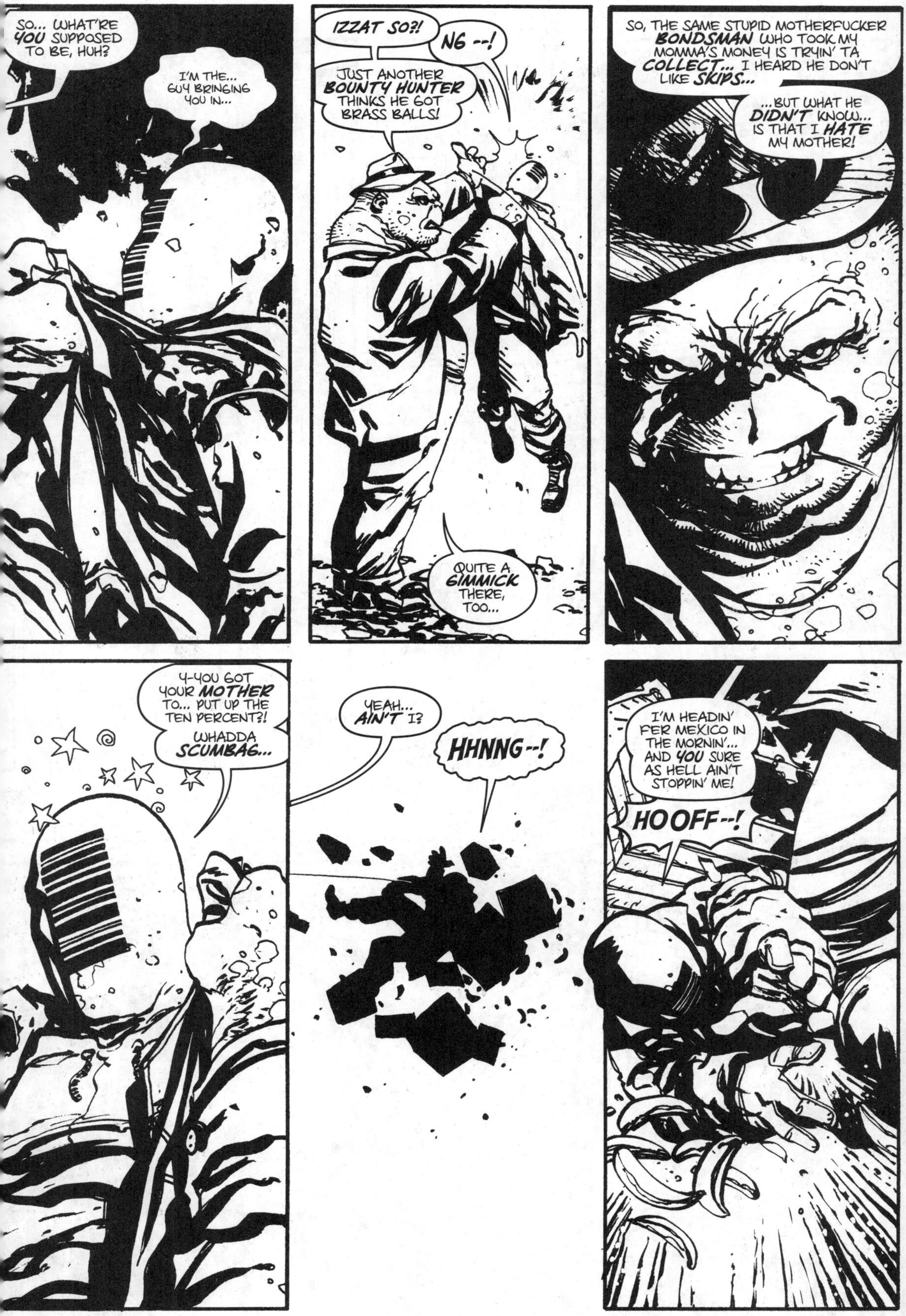
SO... WHAT'RE YOU SUPPOSED TO BE, HUH?
I'M THE... GUY BRINGING YOU IN...
IZZAT SO?!
JUST ANOTHER BOUNTY HUNTER THINKS HE GOT BRASS BALLS!
NG --!
QUITE A GIMMICK THERE, TOO...
SO, THE SAME STUPID MOTHERFUCKER BONDSMAN WHO TOOK MY MOMMA'S MONEY IS TRYIN' TA COLLECT... I HEARD HE DON'T LIKE SKIPS...
...BUT WHAT HE DIDN'T KNOW... IS THAT I HATE MY MOTHER!
Y-YOU GOT YOUR MOTHER TO... PUT UP THE TEN PERCENT?!
WHADDA SCUMBAG...
YEAH... AIN'T I?
HHNNG--!
I'M HEADIN' FER MEXICO IN THE MORNIN'... AND YOU SURE AS HELL AIN'T STOPPIN' ME!
HOOFF--!

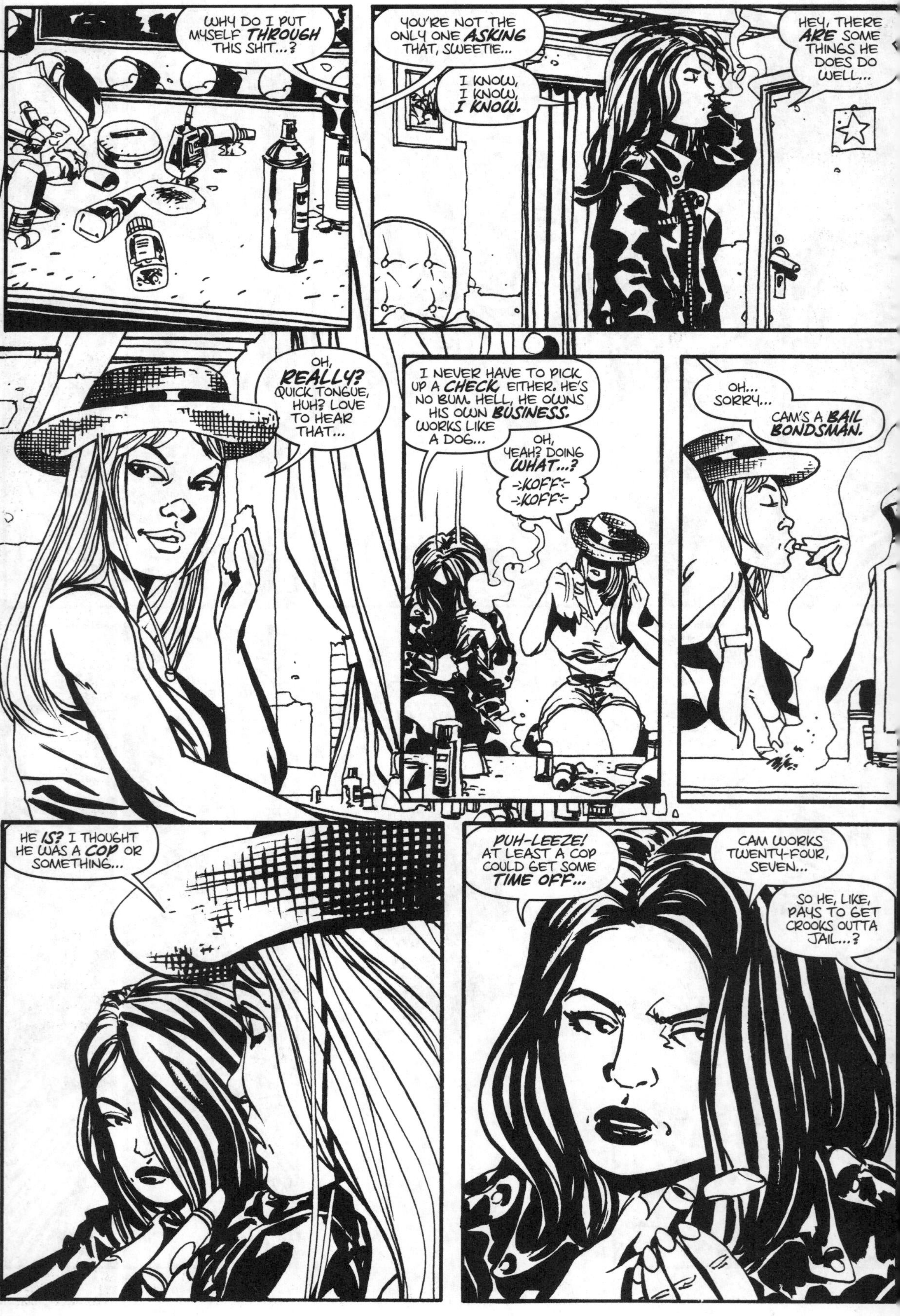
WHY DO I PUT MYSELF THROUGH THIS SHIT...?
YOU'RE NOT THE ONLY ONE ASKING THAT, SWEETIE...
I KNOW, I KNOW, I KNOW.
HEY, THERE ARE SOME THINGS HE DOES DO WELL...
OH, REALLY? QUICK TONGUE, HUH? LOVE TO HEAR THAT...
I NEVER HAVE TO PICK UP A CHECK, EITHER. HE'S NO BUM. HELL, HE OWNS HIS OWN BUSINESS. WORKS LIKE A DOG...
OH, YEAH? DOING WHAT...? -KOFF- -KOFF-
OH... SORRY...
CAM'S A BAIL BONDSMAN.
HE IS? I THOUGHT HE WAS A COP OR SOMETHING...
PUH-LEEZE! AT LEAST A COP COULD GET SOME TIME OFF...
CAM WORKS TWENTY-FOUR, SEVEN...
SO HE, LIKE, PAYS TO GET CROOKS OUTTA JAIL...?

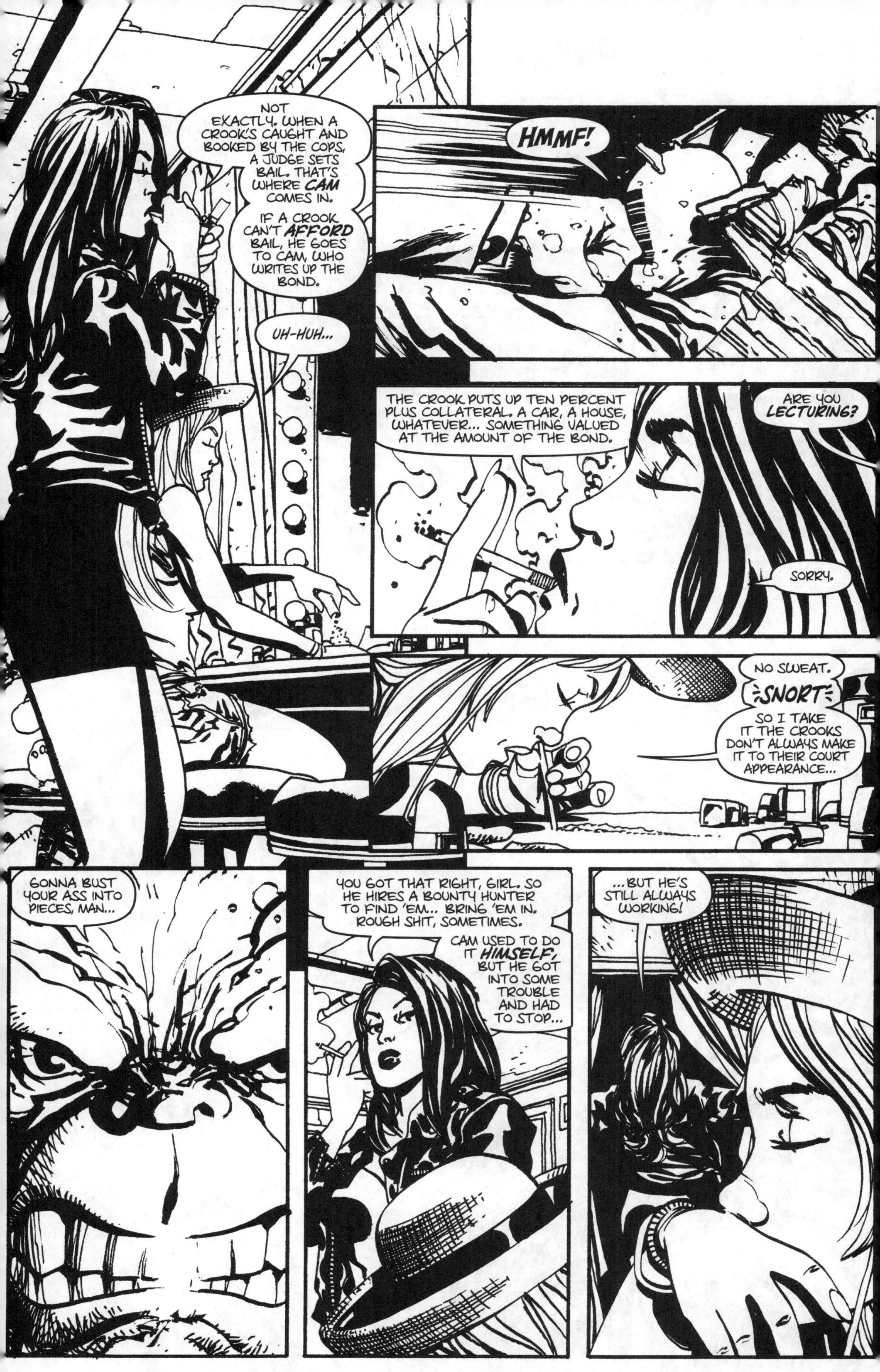
NOT EXACTLY. WHEN A CROOK'S CAUGHT AND BOOKED BY THE COPS, A JUDGE SETS BAIL. THAT'S WHERE CAM COMES IN.
IF A CROOK CAN'T AFFORD BAIL, HE GOES TO CAM, WHO WRITES UP THE BOND.
UH-HUH...
HMMF!
THE CROOK PUTS UP TEN PERCENT PLUS COLLATERAL. A CAR, A HOUSE, WHATEVER... SOMETHING VALUED AT THE AMOUNT OF THE BOND.
ARE YOU LECTURING?
SORRY.
NO SWEAT.
SNORT
SO I TAKE IT THE CROOKS DON'T ALWAYS MAKE IT TO THEIR COURT APPEARANCE...
GONNA BUST YOUR ASS INTO PIECES, MAN...
YOU GOT THAT RIGHT, GIRL. SO HE HIRES A BOUNTY HUNTER TO FIND 'EM... BRING 'EM IN. ROUGH SHIT, SOMETIMES.
CAM USED TO DO IT HIMSELF, BUT HE GOT INTO SOME TROUBLE AND HAD TO STOP...
...BUT HE'S STILL ALWAYS WORKING!

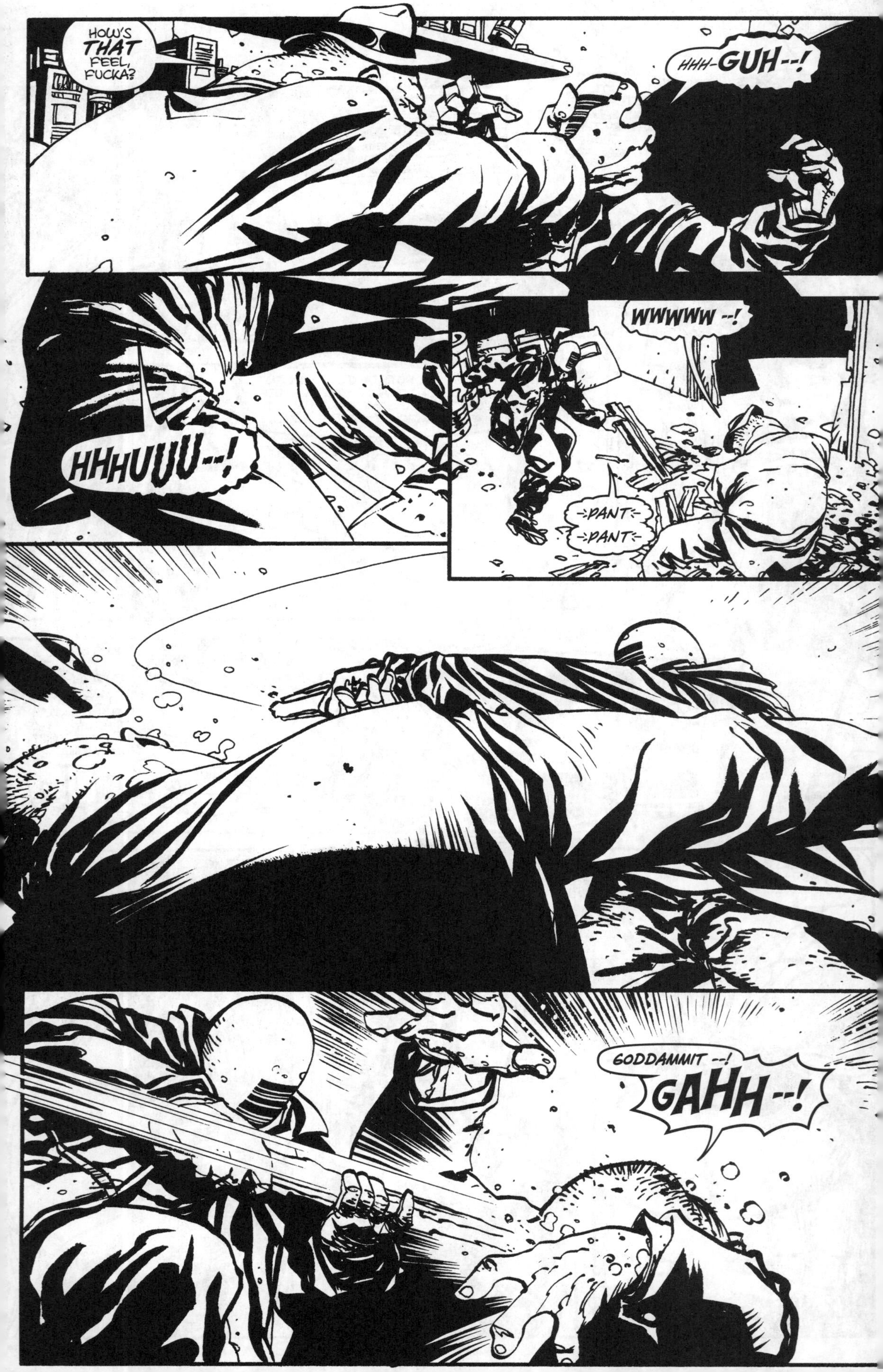
HOW'S THAT FEEL, FUCKA?
HHH-GUH--!
HHHUUU--!
WWWWW--!
-PANT-
-PANT-
GODDAMMIT--!
GAHH--!

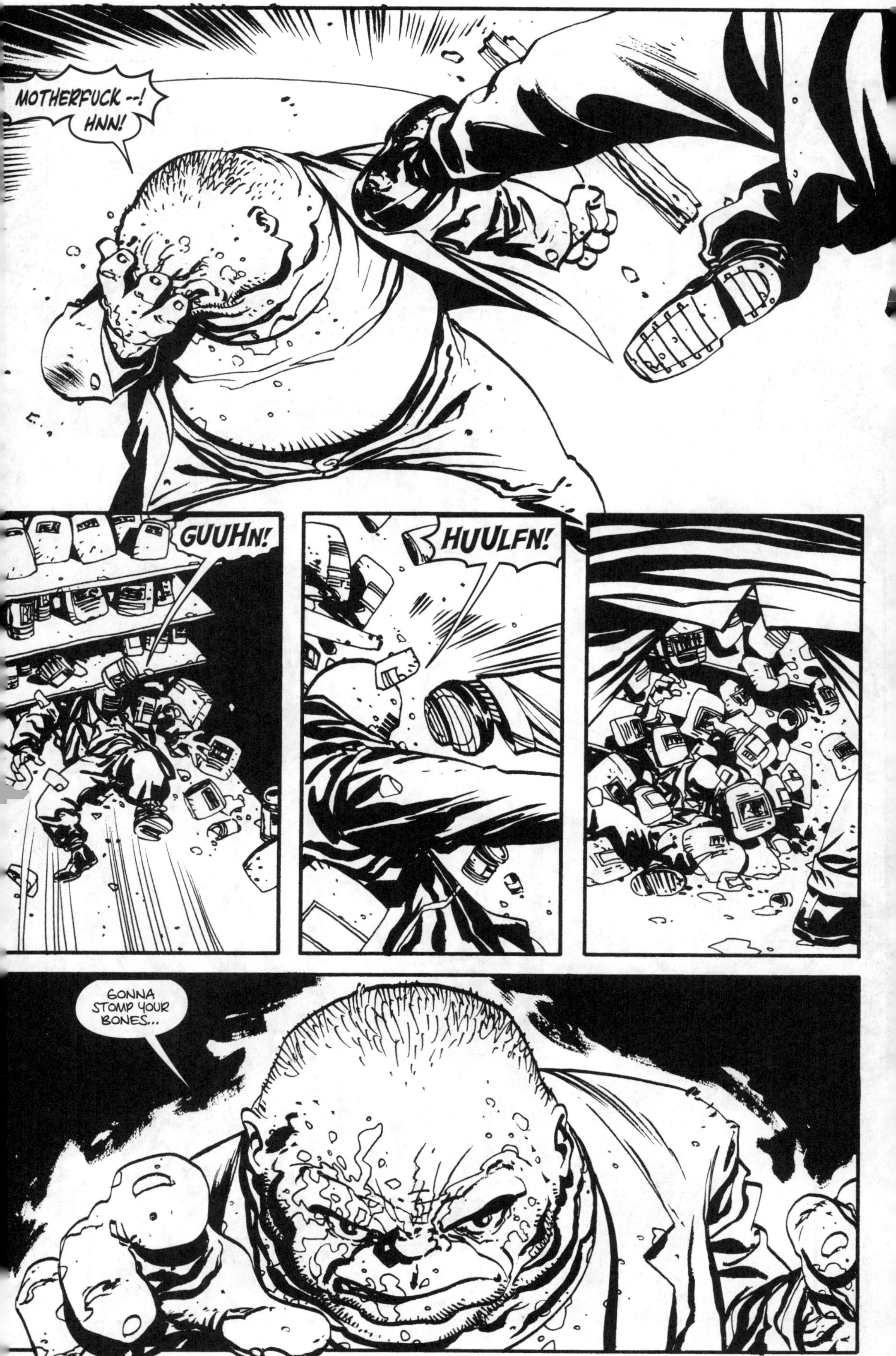
MOTHERFUCK --! HNN!
GUUHn!
HUULFN!
GONNA STOMP YOUR BONES...

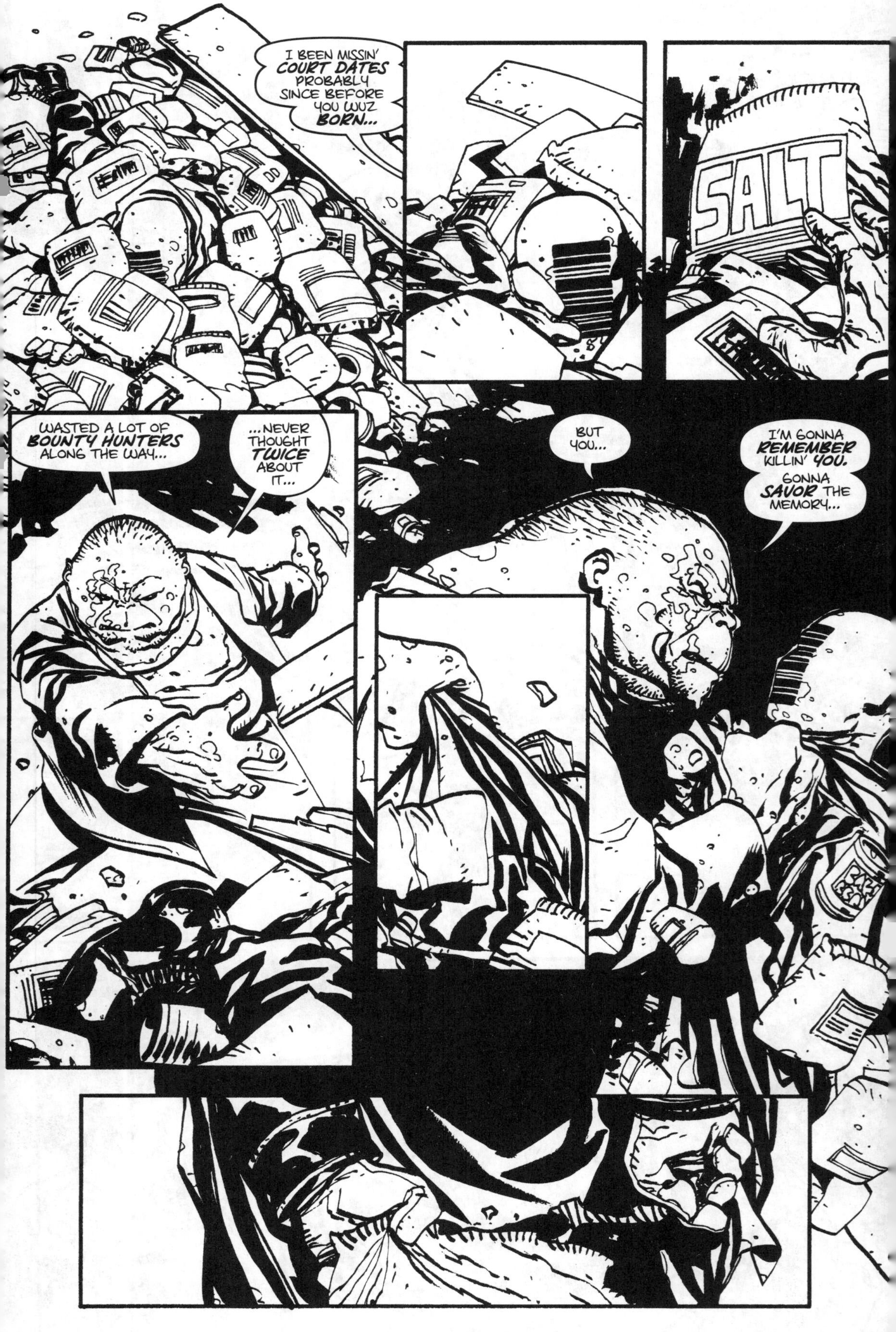
I BEEN MISSIN' COURT DATES PROBABLY SINCE BEFORE YOU WUZ BORN...
SALT
WASTED A LOT OF BOUNTY HUNTERS ALONG THE WAY...
...NEVER THOUGHT TWICE ABOUT IT...
BUT YOU...
I'M GONNA REMEMBER KILLIN' YOU. GONNA SAVOR THE MEMORY...

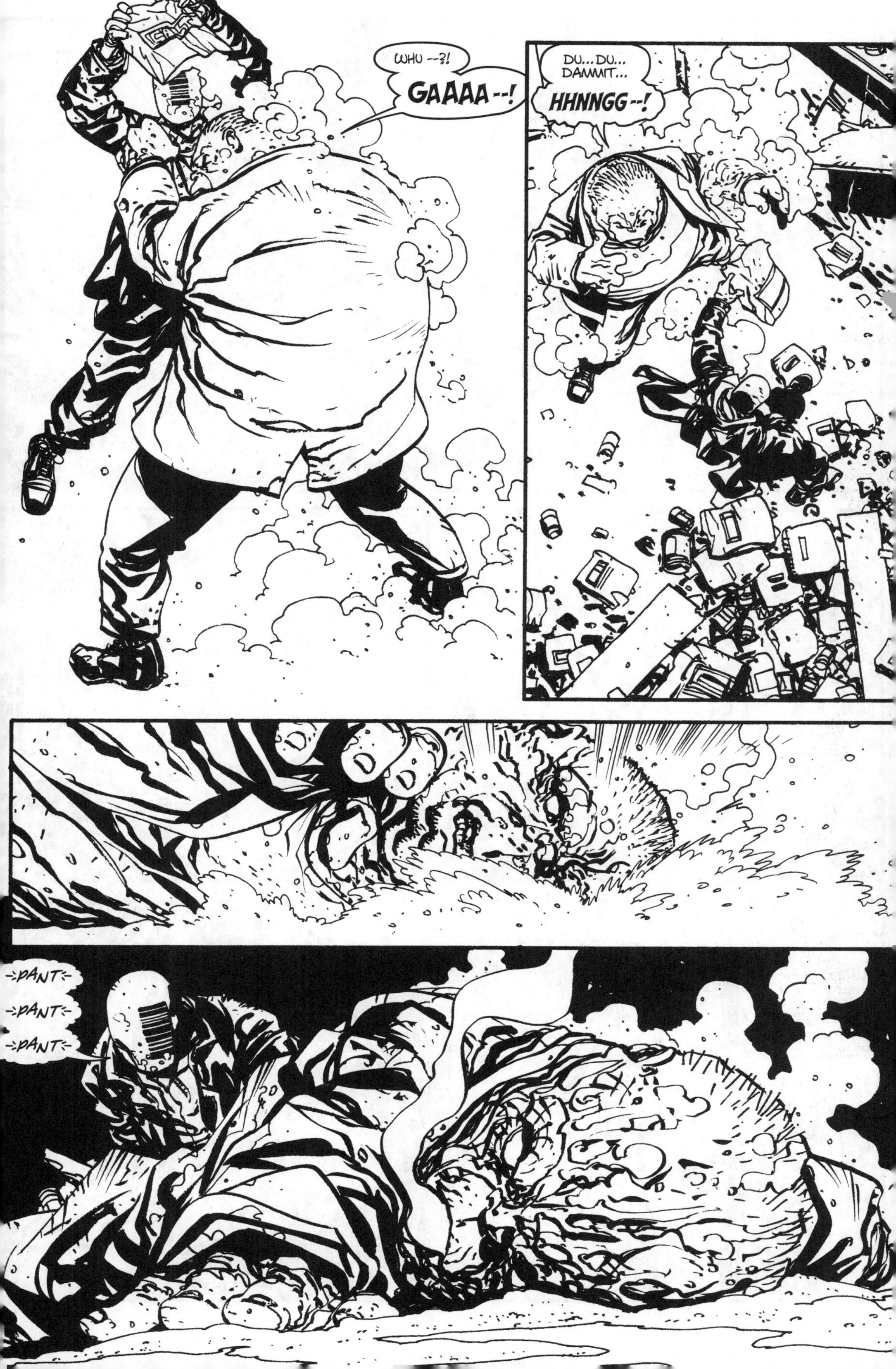
WHU --?!
GAAAA --!
DU...DU...
DAMMIT...
HHNNGG --!
-PANT-
-PANT-
-PANT-

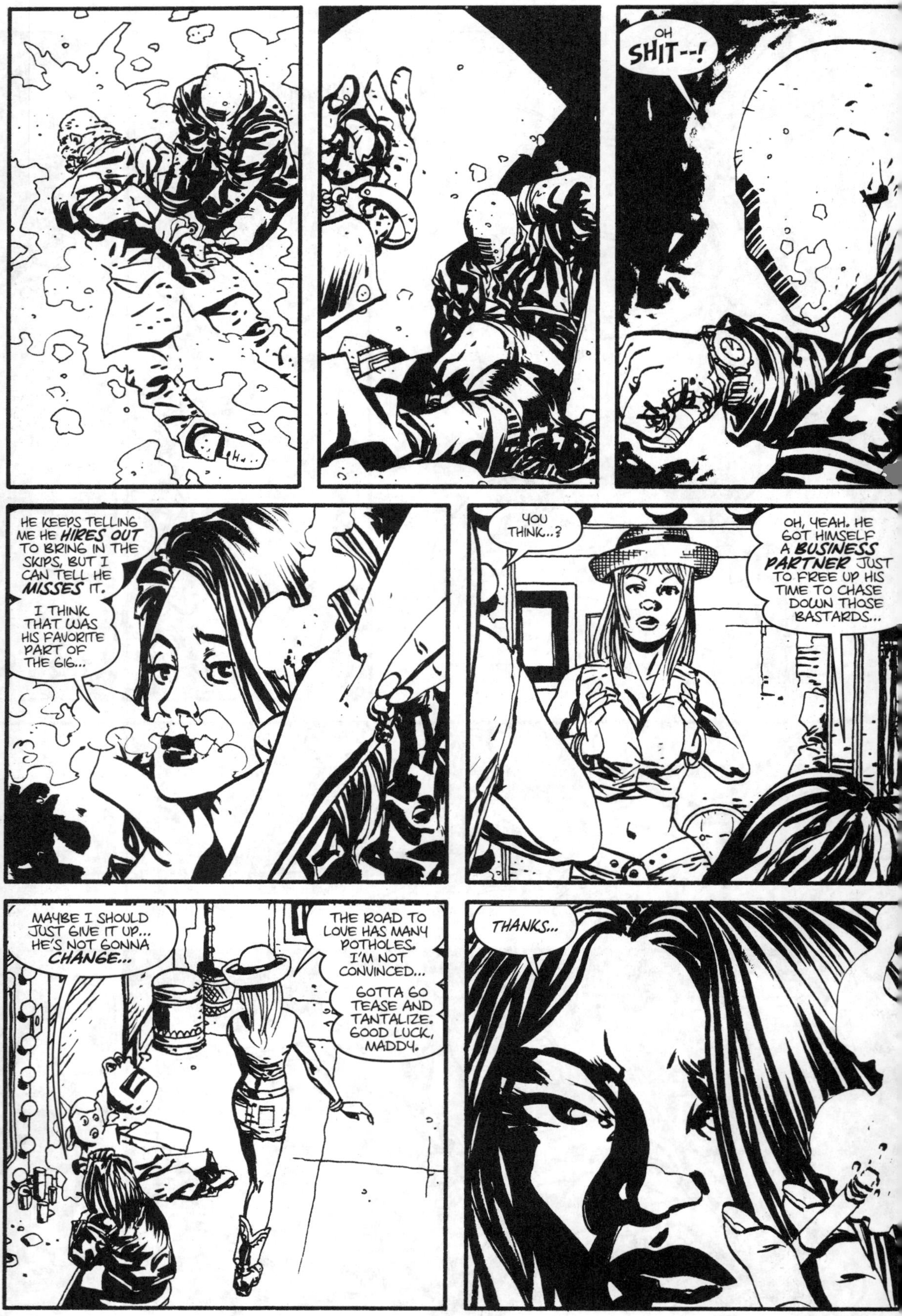
OH
SHIT--!
HE KEEPS TELLING ME HE HIRES OUT TO BRING IN THE SKIPS, BUT I CAN TELL HE MISSES IT.
I THINK THAT WAS HIS FAVORITE PART OF THE GIG...
YOU THINK...?
OH, YEAH. HE GOT HIMSELF A BUSINESS PARTNER JUST TO FREE UP HIS TIME TO CHASE DOWN THOSE BASTARDS...
MAYBE I SHOULD JUST GIVE IT UP... HE'S NOT GONNA CHANGE...
THE ROAD TO LOVE HAS MANY POTHOLES. I'M NOT CONVINCED...
GOTTA GO TEASE AND TANTALIZE. GOOD LUCK, MADDY.
THANKS...

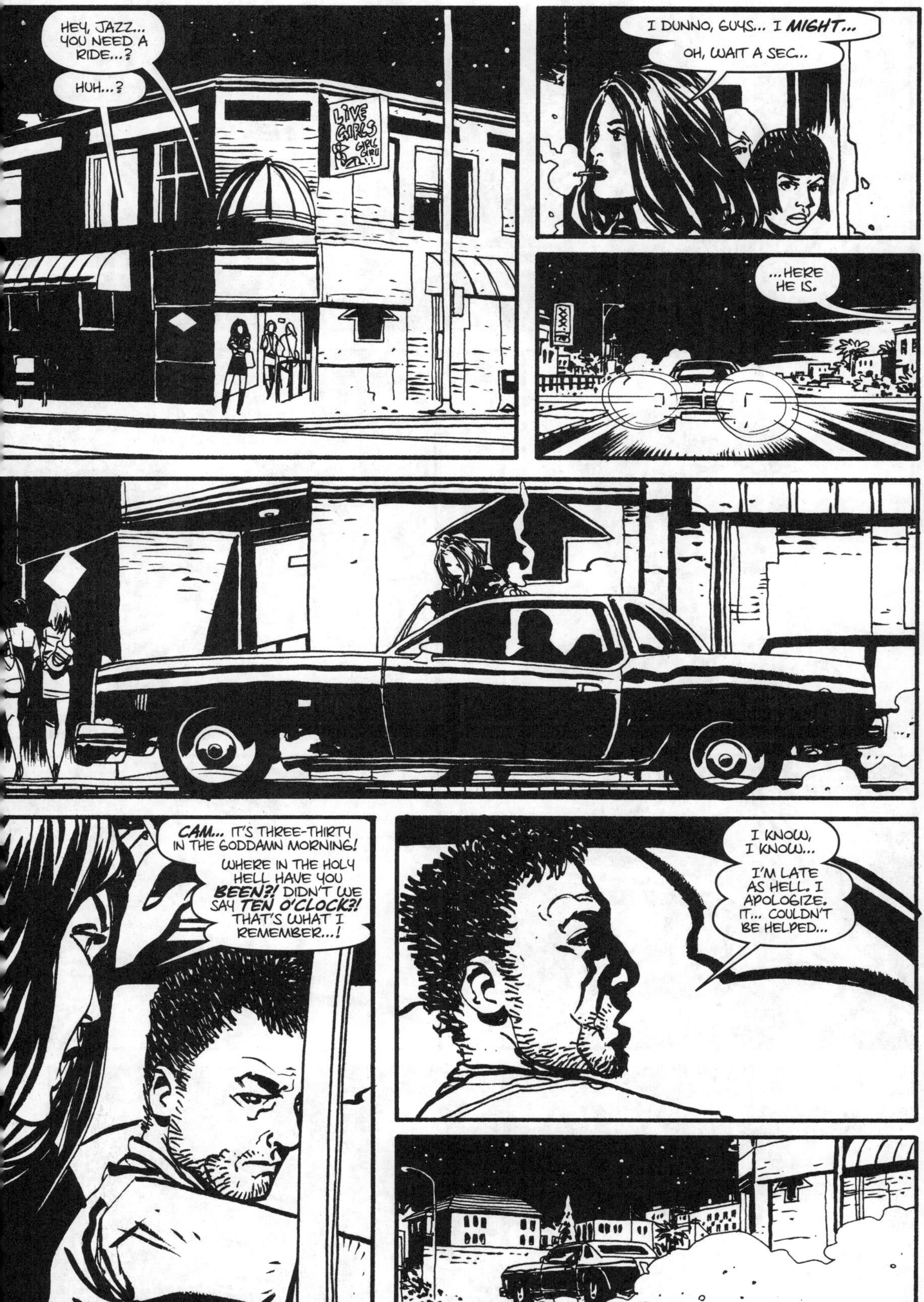

HEY, JAZZ... YOU NEED A RIDE...?
HUH...?
LIVE GIRLS
I DUNNO, GUYS... I **MIGHT**...
OH, WAIT A SEC...
...HERE HE IS.
XXX
CAM... IT'S THREE-THIRTY IN THE GODDAMN MORNING!
WHERE IN THE HOLY HELL HAVE YOU **BEEN?!** DIDN'T WE SAY **TEN O'CLOCK?!** THAT'S WHAT I REMEMBER...!
I KNOW, I KNOW...
I'M LATE AS HELL. I APOLOGIZE. IT... COULDN'T BE HELPED...

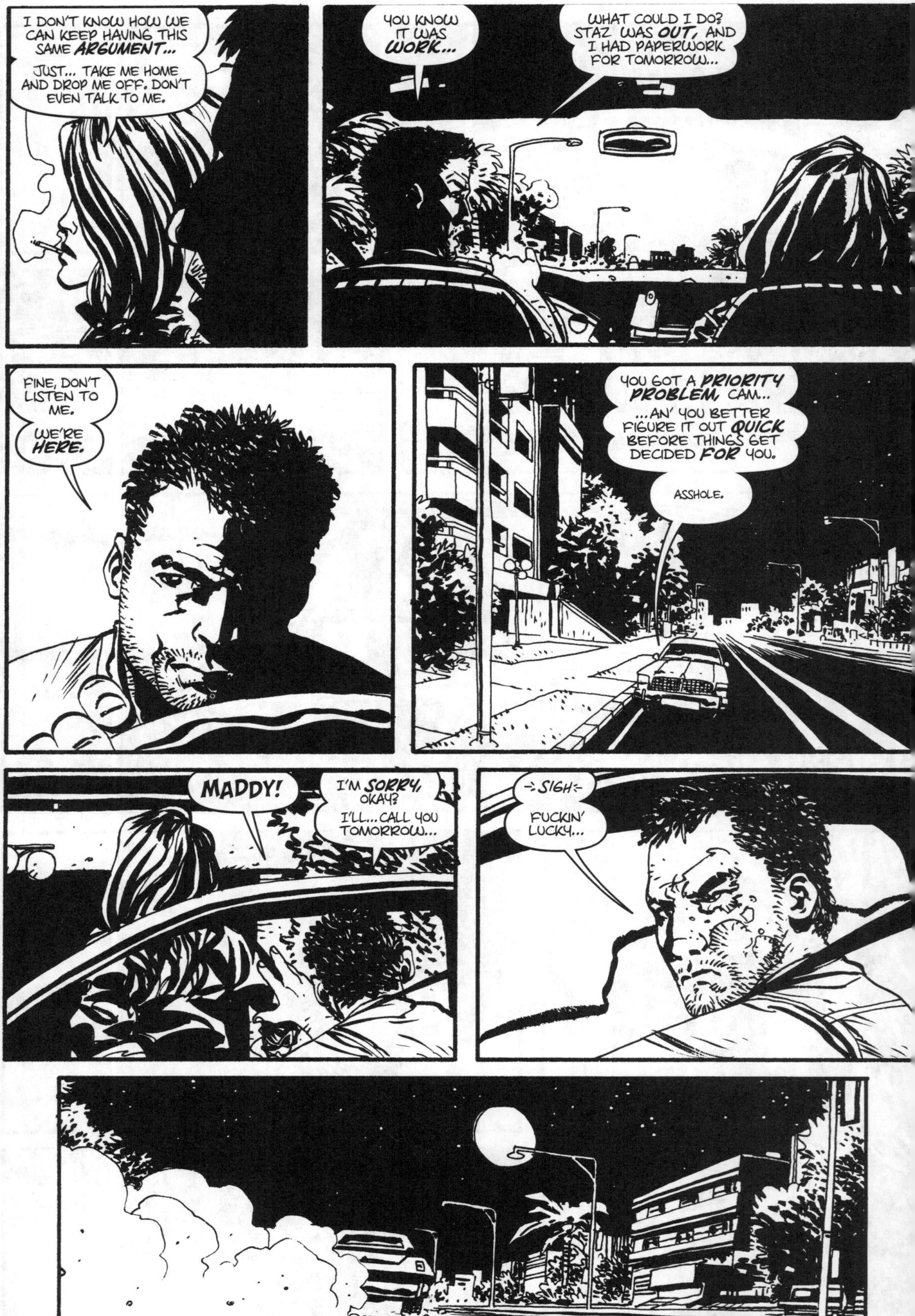
I DON'T KNOW HOW WE CAN KEEP HAVING THIS SAME ARGUMENT...
JUST... TAKE ME HOME AND DROP ME OFF. DON'T EVEN TALK TO ME.
YOU KNOW IT WAS WORK...
WHAT COULD I DO? STAZ WAS OUT, AND I HAD PAPERWORK FOR TOMORROW...
FINE, DON'T LISTEN TO ME.
WE'RE HERE.
YOU GOT A PRIORITY PROBLEM, CAM...
...AN' YOU BETTER FIGURE IT OUT QUICK BEFORE THINGS GET DECIDED FOR YOU.
ASSHOLE.
MADDY!
I'M SORRY, OKAY?
I'LL...CALL YOU TOMORROW...
-SIGH-
FUCKIN' LUCKY...

Something stirred in the darkness.
The sound of something heavy slithering
in slow movements across the floor. Labored
breathing pushed out by mutated lungs.
Through his mask, Cameron recognized
the musty smell of moist, decaying flesh...

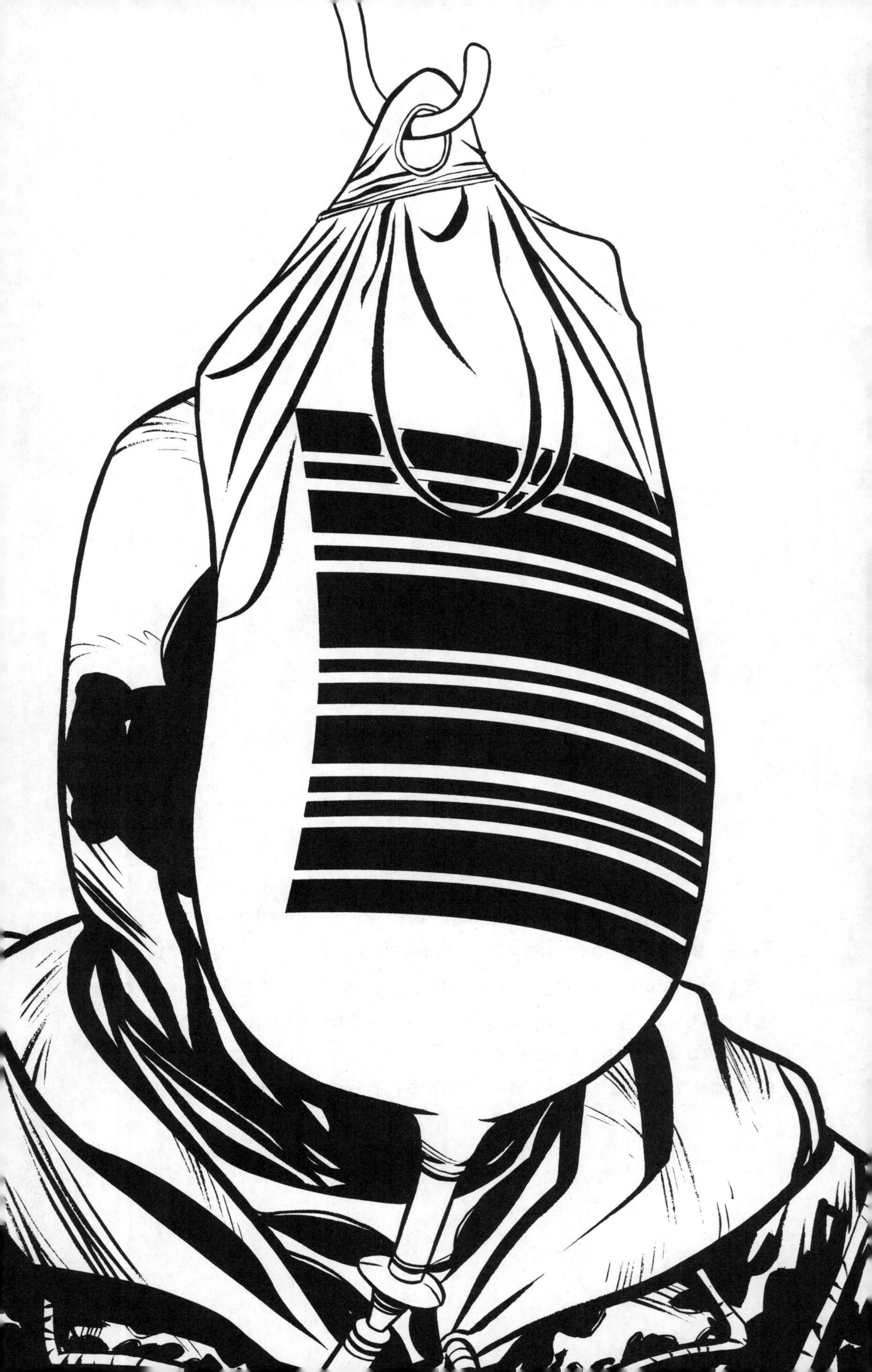

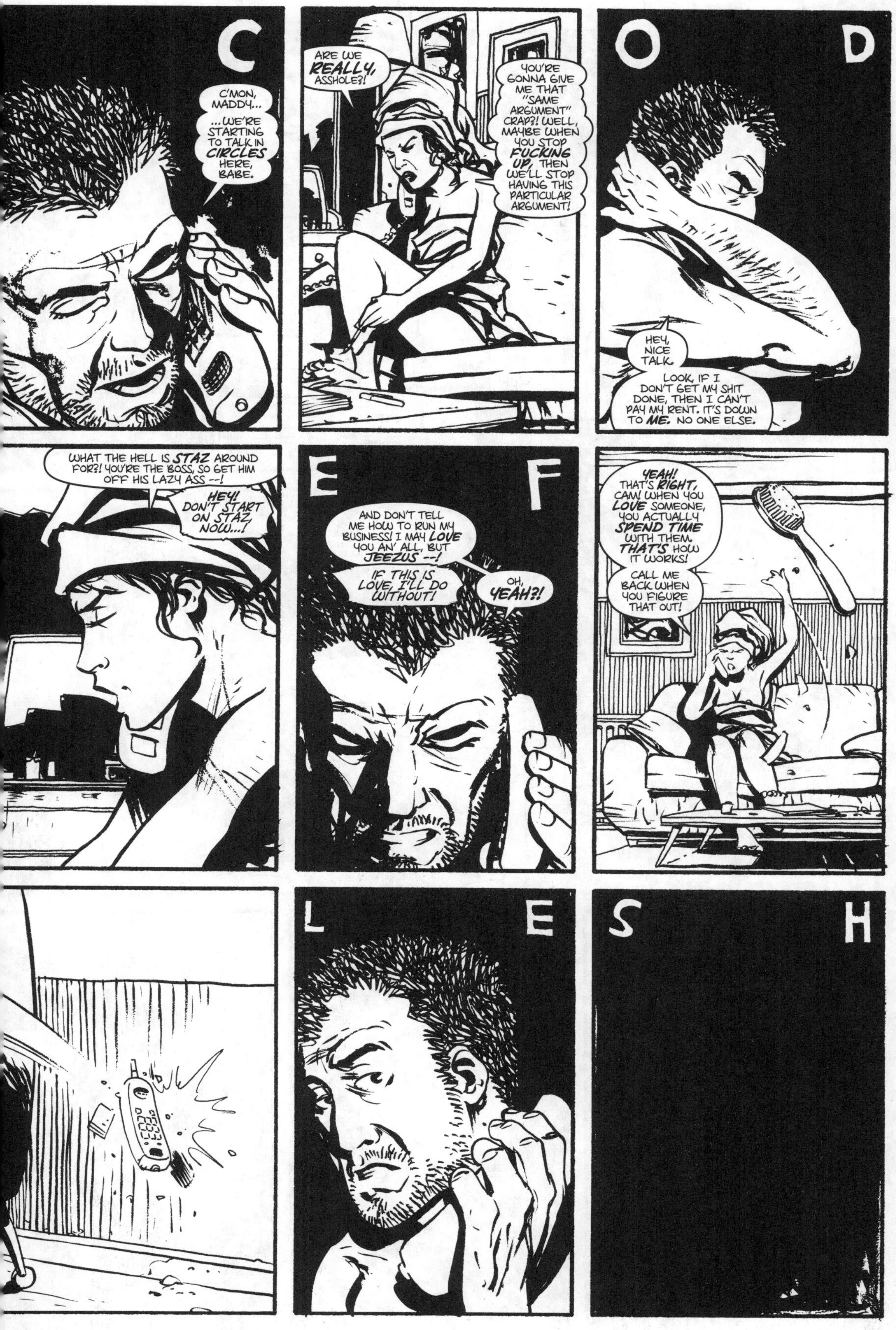
C
C'MON, MADDY...
...WE'RE STARTING TO TALK IN CIRCLES HERE, BABE.
ARE WE REALLY, ASSHOLE?!
YOU'RE GONNA GIVE ME THAT "SAME ARGUMENT" CRAP?! WELL, MAYBE WHEN YOU STOP FUCKING UP, THEN WE'LL STOP HAVING THIS PARTICULAR ARGUMENT!
O
D
HEY, NICE TALK.
LOOK, IF I DON'T GET MY SHIT DONE, THEN I CAN'T PAY MY RENT. IT'S DOWN TO ME. NO ONE ELSE.
WHAT THE HELL IS STAZ AROUND FOR?! YOU'RE THE BOSS, SO GET HIM OFF HIS LAZY ASS --!
HEY! DON'T START ON STAZ, NOW...!
E
F
AND DON'T TELL ME HOW TO RUN MY BUSINESS! I MAY LOVE YOU AN' ALL, BUT JEEZUS --!
IF THIS IS LOVE, I'LL DO WITHOUT!
OH, YEAH?!
YEAH! THAT'S RIGHT, CAM! WHEN YOU LOVE SOMEONE, YOU ACTUALLY SPEND TIME WITH THEM. THAT'S HOW IT WORKS!
CALL ME BACK WHEN YOU FIGURE THAT OUT!
L
E
S
H

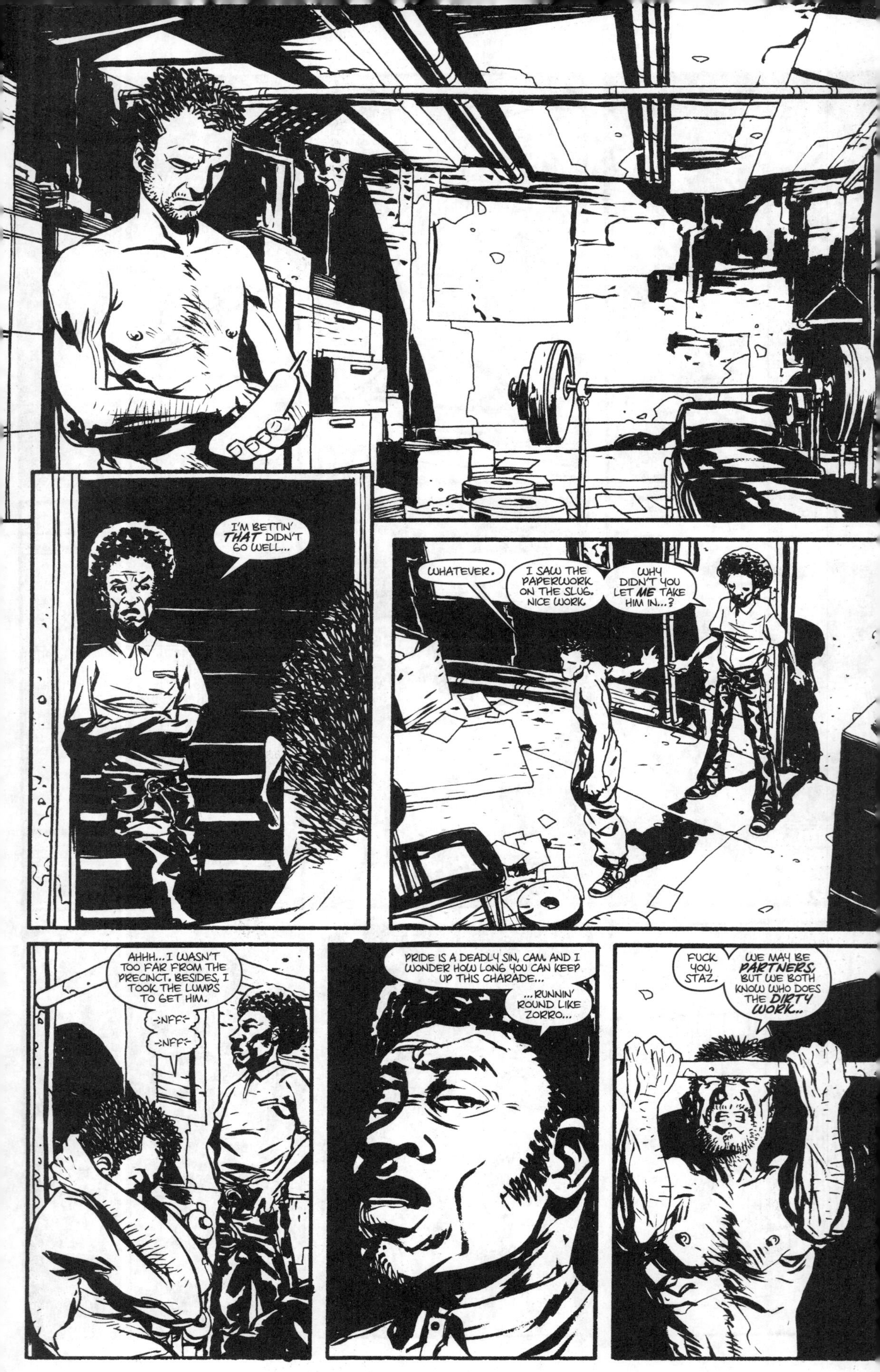
I'M BETTIN' THAT DIDN'T GO WELL...
WHATEVER.
I SAW THE PAPERWORK ON THE SLUG. NICE WORK.
WHY DIDN'T YOU LET ME TAKE HIM IN...?
AHHH...I WASN'T TOO FAR FROM THE PRECINCT. BESIDES, I TOOK THE LUMPS TO GET HIM.
-NFF-
-NFF-
PRIDE IS A DEADLY SIN, CAM. AND I WONDER HOW LONG YOU CAN KEEP UP THIS CHARADE...
...RUNNIN' ROUND LIKE ZORRO...
FUCK YOU, STAZ.
WE MAY BE PARTNERS, BUT WE BOTH KNOW WHO DOES THE DIRTY WORK...

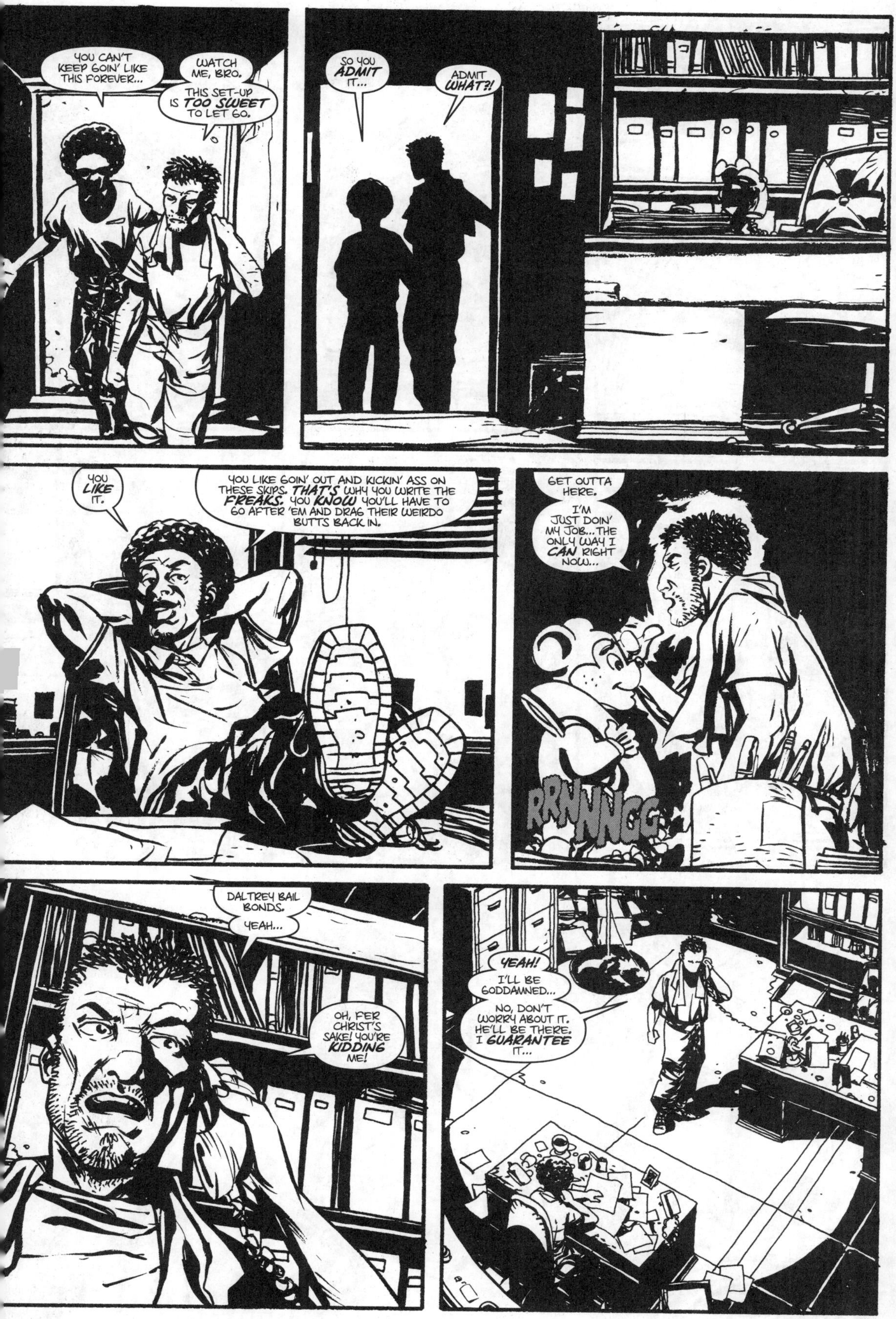
YOU CAN'T KEEP GOIN' LIKE THIS FOREVER...
WATCH ME, BRO.
THIS SET-UP IS TOO SWEET TO LET GO.
SO YOU ADMIT IT...
ADMIT WHAT?!
YOU LIKE IT.
YOU LIKE GOIN' OUT AND KICKIN' ASS ON THESE SKIPS. THAT'S WHY YOU WRITE THE FREAKS. YOU KNOW YOU'LL HAVE TO GO AFTER 'EM AND DRAG THEIR WEIRDO BUTTS BACK IN.
GET OUTTA HERE.
I'M JUST DOIN' MY JOB... THE ONLY WAY I CAN RIGHT NOW...
RRNNNGG
DALTREY BAIL BONDS.
YEAH...
OH, FER CHRIST'S SAKE! YOU'RE KIDDING ME!
YEAH!
I'LL BE GODDAMNED...
NO, DON'T WORRY ABOUT IT. HE'LL BE THERE. I GUARANTEE IT...

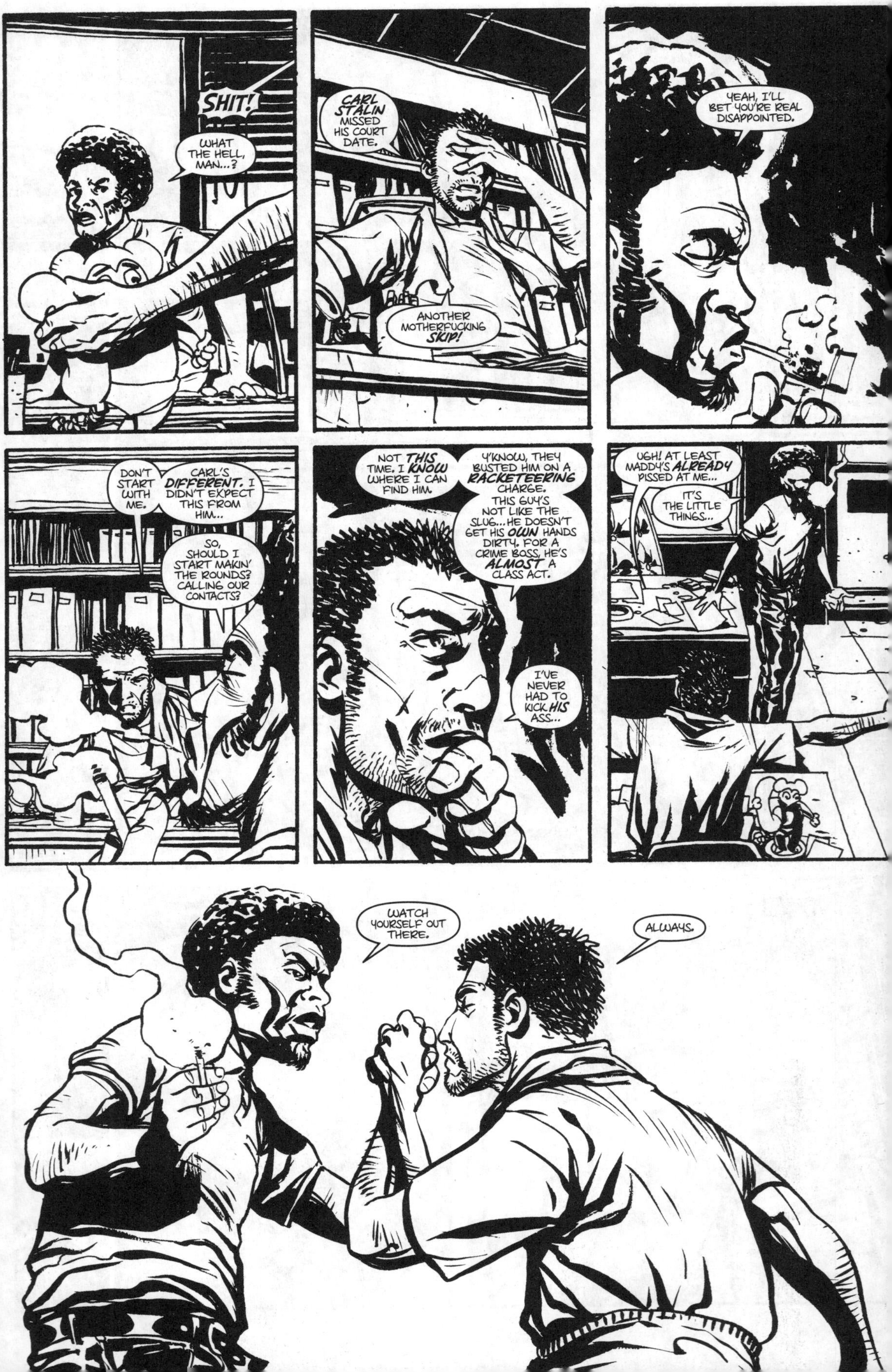
SHIT!
WHAT THE HELL, MAN...?
CARL STALIN MISSED HIS COURT DATE.
ANOTHER MOTHERFUCKING SKIP!
YEAH, I'LL BET YOU'RE REAL DISAPPOINTED.
DON'T START WITH ME.
CARL'S DIFFERENT. I DIDN'T EXPECT THIS FROM HIM...
SO, SHOULD I START MAKIN' THE ROUNDS? CALLING OUR CONTACTS?
NOT THIS TIME. I KNOW WHERE I CAN FIND HIM.
Y'KNOW, THEY BUSTED HIM ON A RACKETEERING CHARGE. THIS GUY'S NOT LIKE THE SLUG... HE DOESN'T GET HIS OWN HANDS DIRTY. FOR A CRIME BOSS, HE'S ALMOST A CLASS ACT.
I'VE NEVER HAD TO KICK HIS ASS...
UGH! AT LEAST MADDY'S ALREADY PISSED AT ME...
IT'S THE LITTLE THINGS...
WATCH YOURSELF OUT THERE.
ALWAYS.

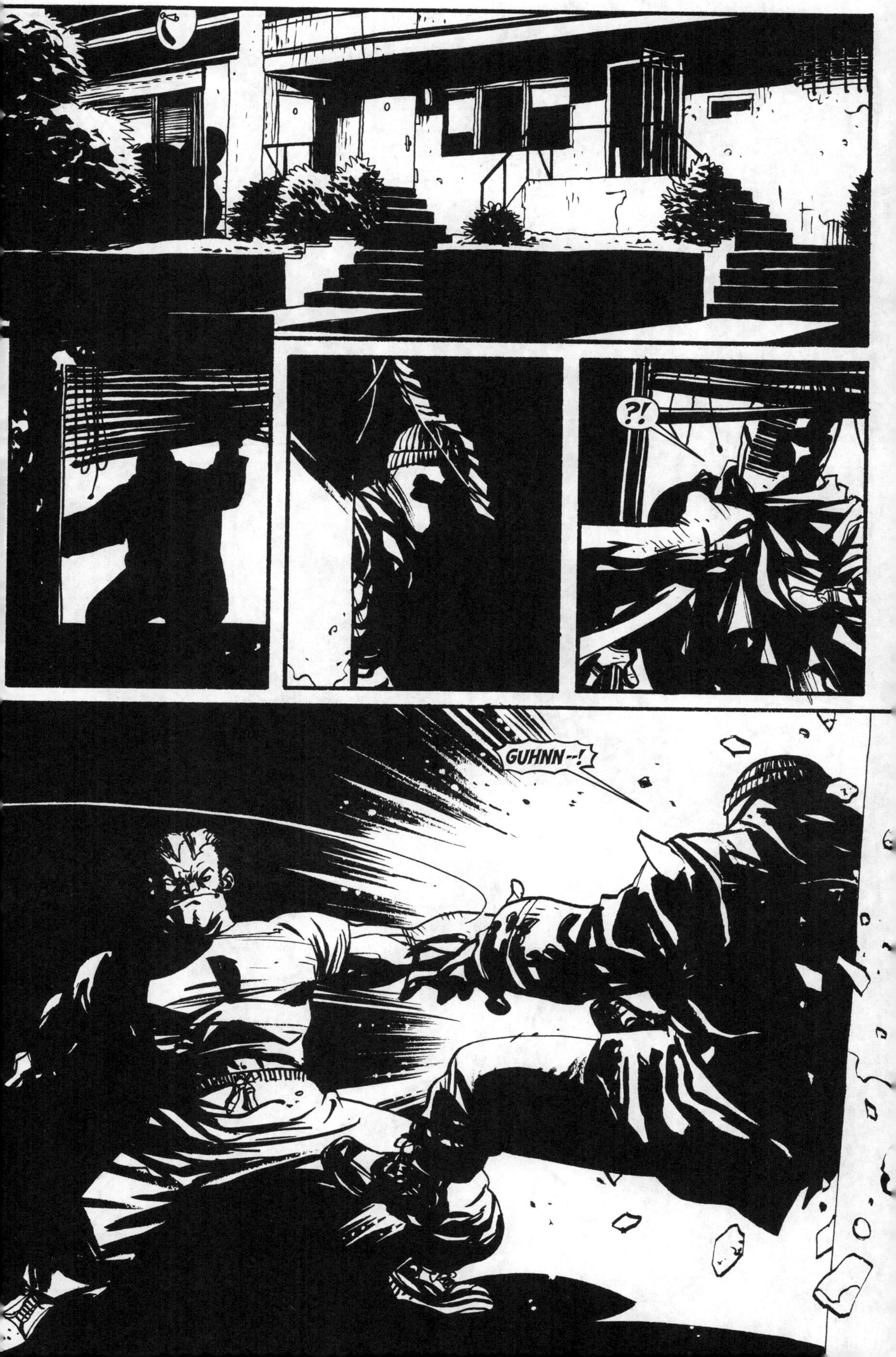
?!
GUHNN--!

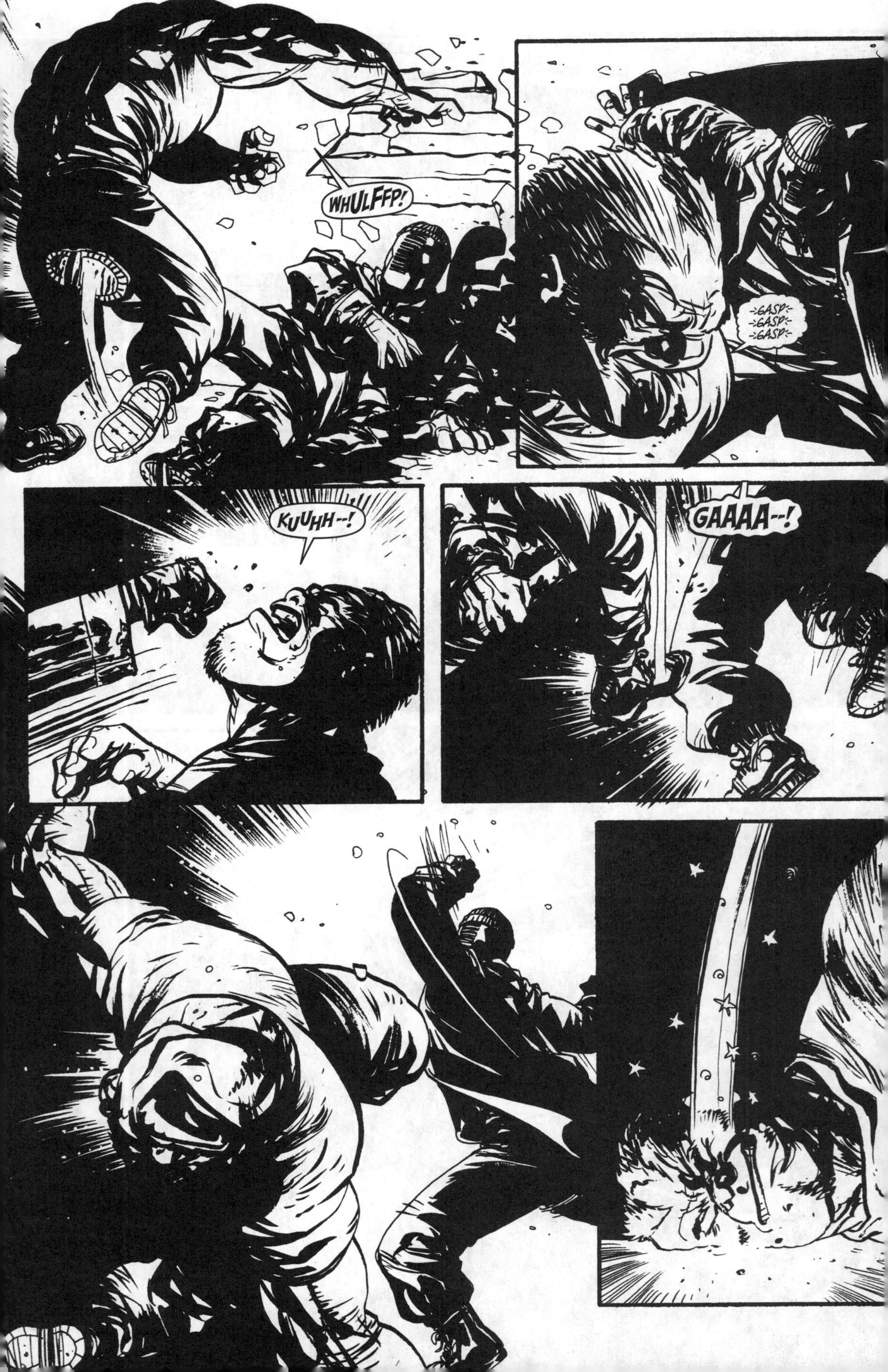

WHULFFP!
GASP GASP GASP
KUUHH--!
GAAAA--!

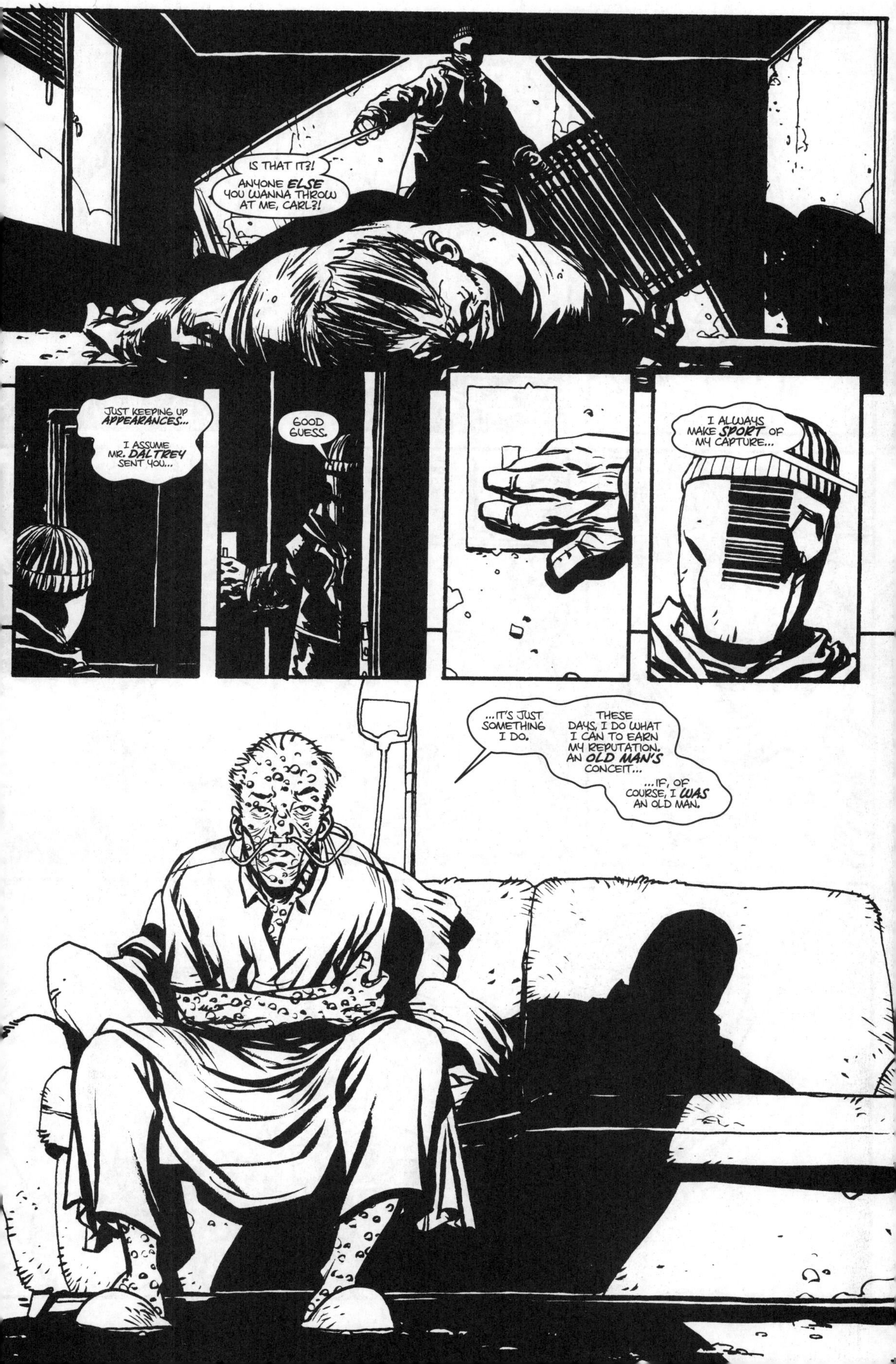
IS THAT IT?!
ANYONE ELSE YOU WANNA THROW AT ME, CARL?!
JUST KEEPING UP APPEARANCES...
I ASSUME MR. DALTREY SENT YOU...
GOOD GUESS.
I ALWAYS MAKE SPORT OF MY CAPTURE...
...IT'S JUST SOMETHING I DO.
THESE DAYS, I DO WHAT I CAN TO EARN MY REPUTATION. AN OLD MAN'S CONCEIT...
...IF, OF COURSE, I WAS AN OLD MAN.

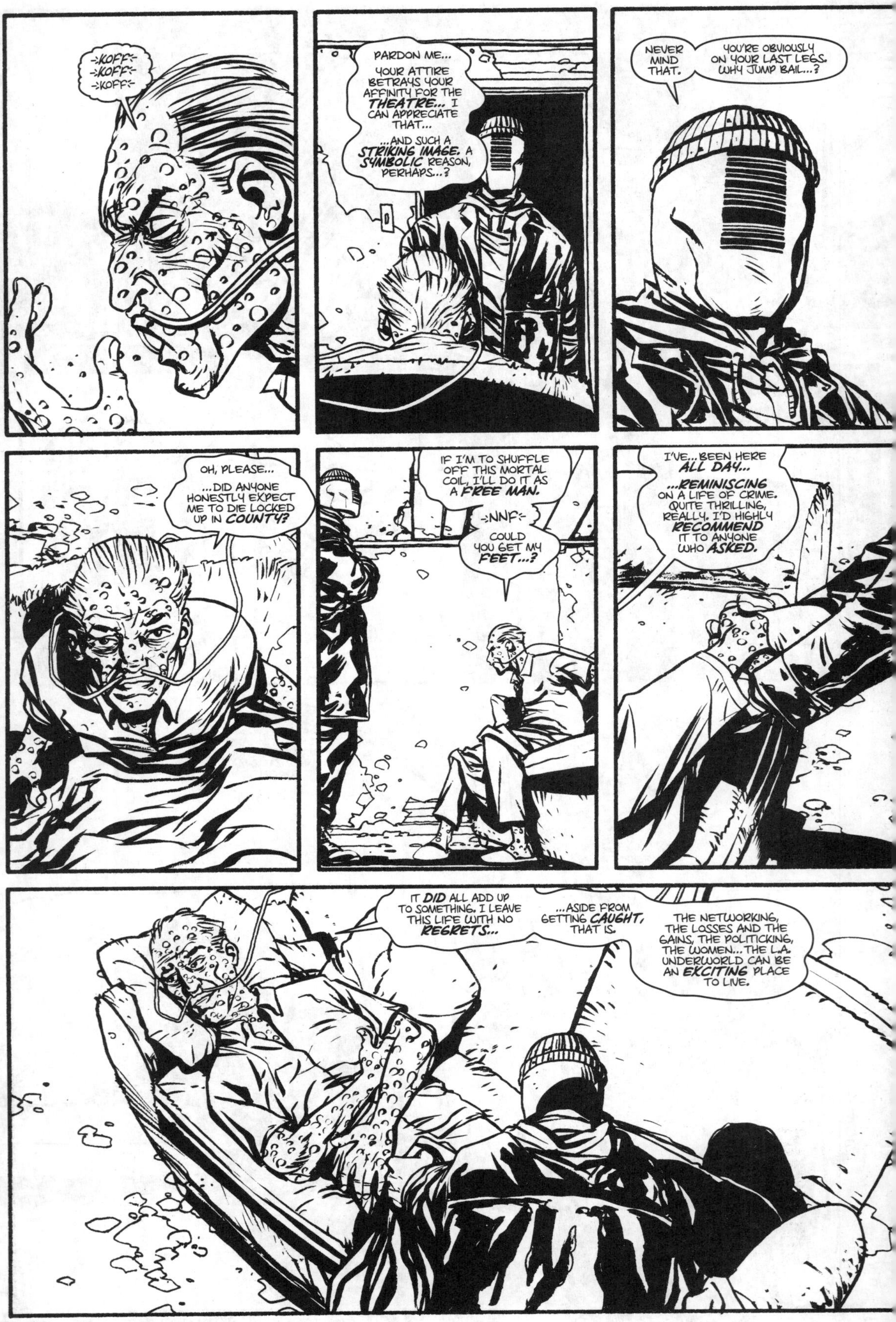
-KOFF- -KOFF- -KOFF
PARDON ME... YOUR ATTIRE BETRAYS YOUR AFFINITY FOR THE THEATRE... I CAN APPRECIATE THAT...
...AND SUCH A STRIKING IMAGE. A SYMBOLIC REASON, PERHAPS...?
NEVER MIND THAT.
YOU'RE OBVIOUSLY ON YOUR LAST LEGS. WHY JUMP BAIL...?
OH, PLEASE...
...DID ANYONE HONESTLY EXPECT ME TO DIE LOCKED UP IN COUNTY?
IF I'M TO SHUFFLE OFF THIS MORTAL COIL, I'LL DO IT AS A FREE MAN.
-NNF-
COULD YOU GET MY FEET...?
I'VE... BEEN HERE ALL DAY...
...REMINISCING ON A LIFE OF CRIME. QUITE THRILLING, REALLY. I'D HIGHLY RECOMMEND IT TO ANYONE WHO ASKED.
IT DID ALL ADD UP TO SOMETHING. I LEAVE THIS LIFE WITH NO REGRETS...
...ASIDE FROM GETTING CAUGHT, THAT IS.
THE NETWORKING, THE LOSSES AND THE GAINS, THE POLITICKING, THE WOMEN... THE L.A. UNDERWORLD CAN BE AN EXCITING PLACE TO LIVE.

I HAD A GOOD RUN. *TEN YEARS* OF SHITS AND GIGGLES. LOTS OF ROBBERIES. LOVED PLANNING THOSE HEISTS.

IT WAS A WORLD THAT *TOOK ME* IN...

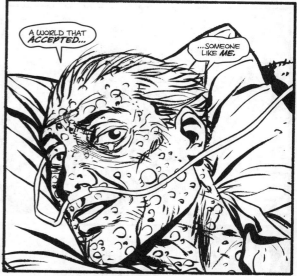

A WORLD THAT *ACCEPTED*...

...SOMEONE LIKE *ME*.

I SUPPOSE THAT'S WHY I ALWAYS CAME TO *YOU*, MR. DALTREY...

...YOU'RE A FREAK LIKE *ME*.

FUCKIN' HELL--!

OH, GOOD HEAVENS. DO YOU TAKE ME FOR AN *IDIOT?*

I KNOW YOUR HISTORY. I FIGURED YOU'D FIND A WAY TO KEEP A HAND IN THE *PHYSICAL* SIDE OF YOUR WORK.

BUT THIS *MASQUERADE*...

...HOW LONG CAN YOU POSSIBLY *KEEP* THIS SECRET?

I ASSUME FROM YOUR *REACTION* THAT I'M THE ONLY ONE WHO HAS PIERCED YOUR DISGUISE.

GODDAMMIT.

FEAR NOT, MR. DALTREY. I WON'T BE TAKING *THIS* PARTICULAR PIECE OF INFO ANYWHERE...

...EXCEPT, PERHAPS, TO *HELL.*

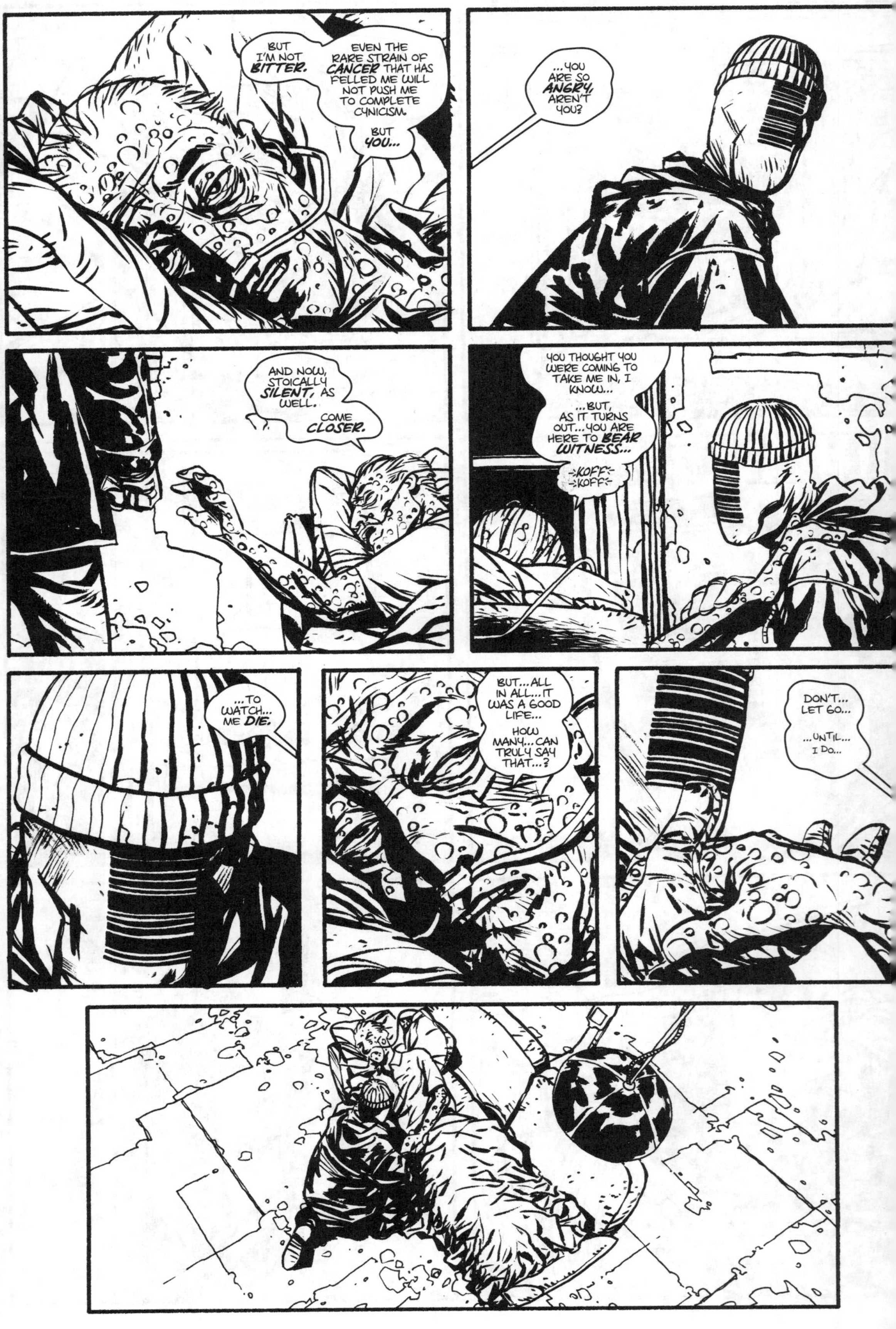
BUT I'M NOT **BITTER.**
EVEN THE RARE STRAIN OF **CANCER** THAT HAS FELLED ME WILL NOT PUSH ME TO COMPLETE CYNICISM.
BUT **YOU...**
...YOU ARE SO **ANGRY,** AREN'T YOU?
AND NOW, STOICALLY **SILENT,** AS WELL.
COME **CLOSER.**
YOU THOUGHT YOU WERE COMING TO TAKE ME IN, I KNOW...
...BUT, AS IT TURNS OUT...YOU ARE HERE TO **BEAR WITNESS...**
KOFF KOFF
...TO WATCH... ME **DIE.**
BUT...ALL IN ALL...IT WAS A GOOD LIFE...
HOW MANY...CAN TRULY SAY THAT...?
DON'T... LET GO...
...UNTIL... I DO...

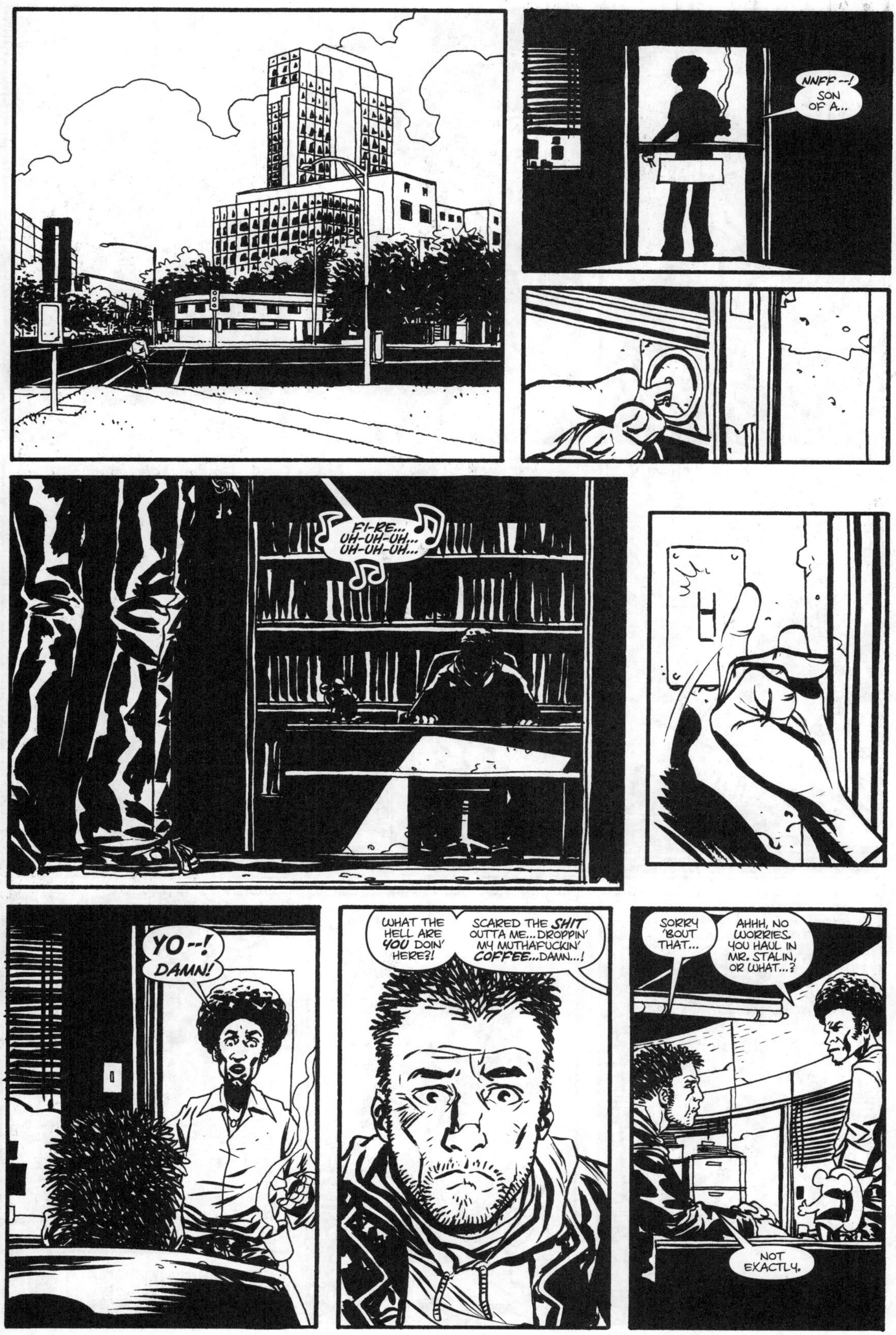
NNFF --! SON OF A...
FI-RE... UH-UH-UH... UH-UH-UH...
YO--! DAMN!
WHAT THE HELL ARE YOU DOIN' HERE?!
SCARED THE SHIT OUTTA ME...DROPPIN' MY MUTHAFUCKIN' COFFEE...DAMN...!
SORRY 'BOUT THAT...
AHHH, NO WORRIES. YOU HAUL IN MR. STALIN, OR WHAT...?
NOT EXACTLY.

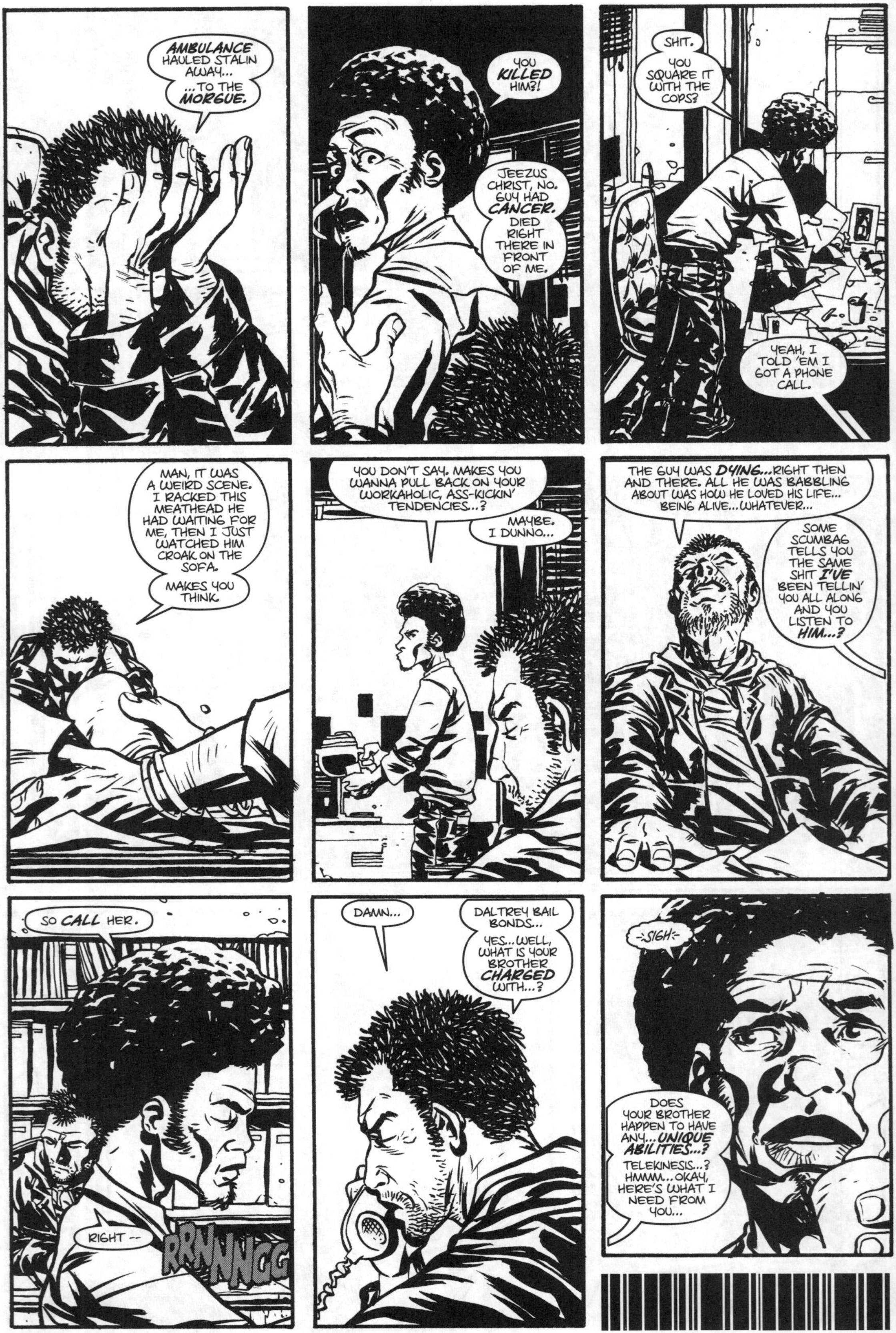

AMBULANCE HAULED STALIN AWAY... ...TO THE MORGUE.
YOU KILLED HIM?!
JEEZUS CHRIST, NO. GUY HAD CANCER. DIED RIGHT THERE IN FRONT OF ME.
SHIT.
YOU SQUARE IT WITH THE COPS?
YEAH, I TOLD 'EM I GOT A PHONE CALL.
MAN, IT WAS A WEIRD SCENE. I RACKED THIS MEATHEAD HE HAD WAITING FOR ME, THEN I JUST WATCHED HIM CROAK ON THE SOFA.
MAKES YOU THINK.
YOU DON'T SAY. MAKES YOU WANNA PULL BACK ON YOUR WORKAHOLIC, ASS-KICKIN' TENDENCIES...?
MAYBE. I DUNNO...
THE GUY WAS DYING...RIGHT THEN AND THERE. ALL HE WAS BABBLING ABOUT WAS HOW HE LOVED HIS LIFE... BEING ALIVE...WHATEVER...
SOME SCUMBAG TELLS YOU THE SAME SHIT I'VE BEEN TELLIN' YOU ALL ALONG AND YOU LISTEN TO HIM...?
SO CALL HER.
RIGHT --
RRNNNGG
DAMN...
DALTREY BAIL BONDS...
YES...WELL, WHAT IS YOUR BROTHER CHARGED WITH...?
-SIGH-
DOES YOUR BROTHER HAPPEN TO HAVE ANY...UNIQUE ABILITIES...?
TELEKINESIS...? HMMM...OKAY, HERE'S WHAT I NEED FROM YOU...

The old man shifted his weight.
A wet sputter escaped from his lips.
The revelations were coming fast and furious.
The sounds of traffic outside... an aural
backdrop to the urban morality play careening
headlong toward its final curtain call.

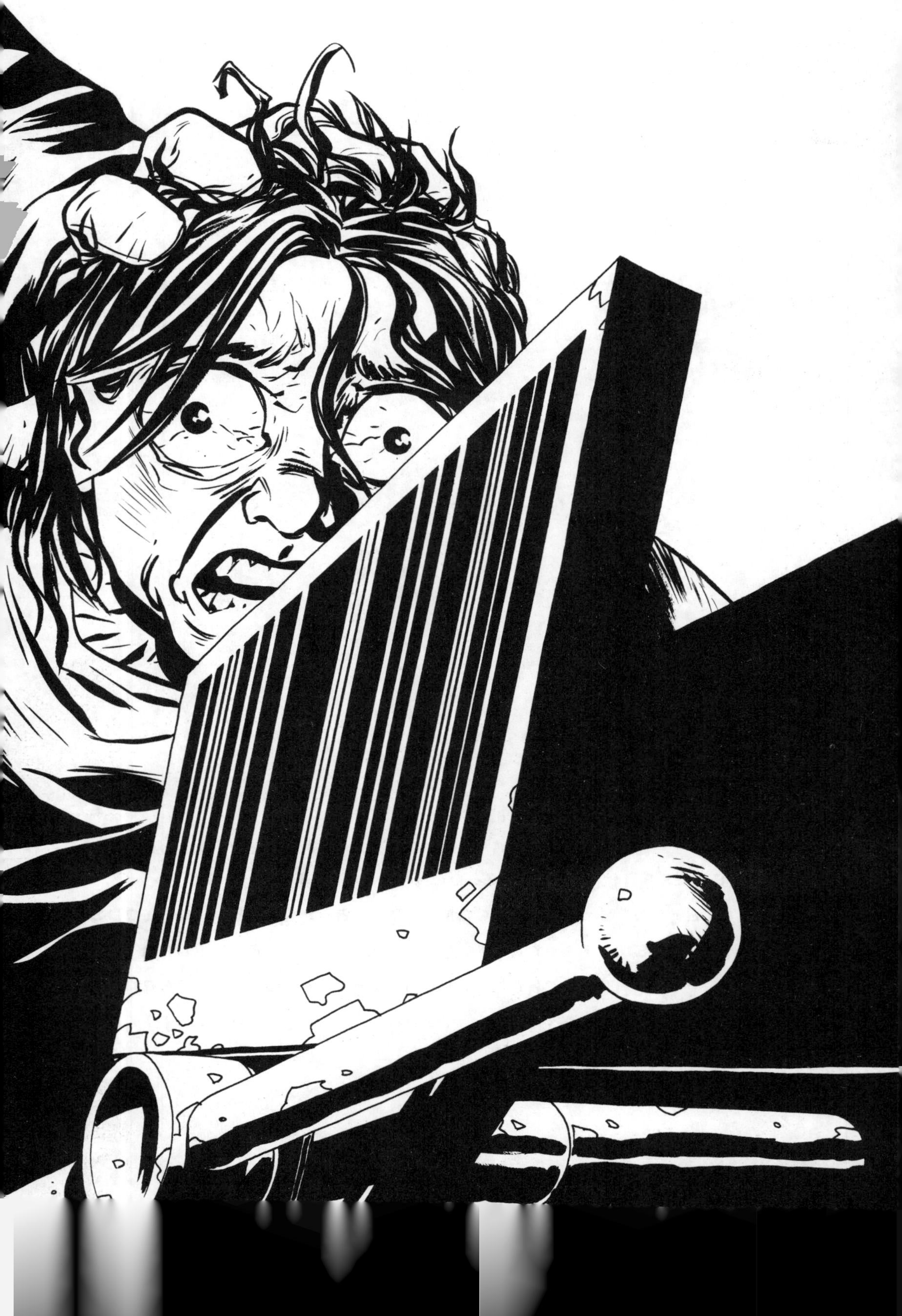

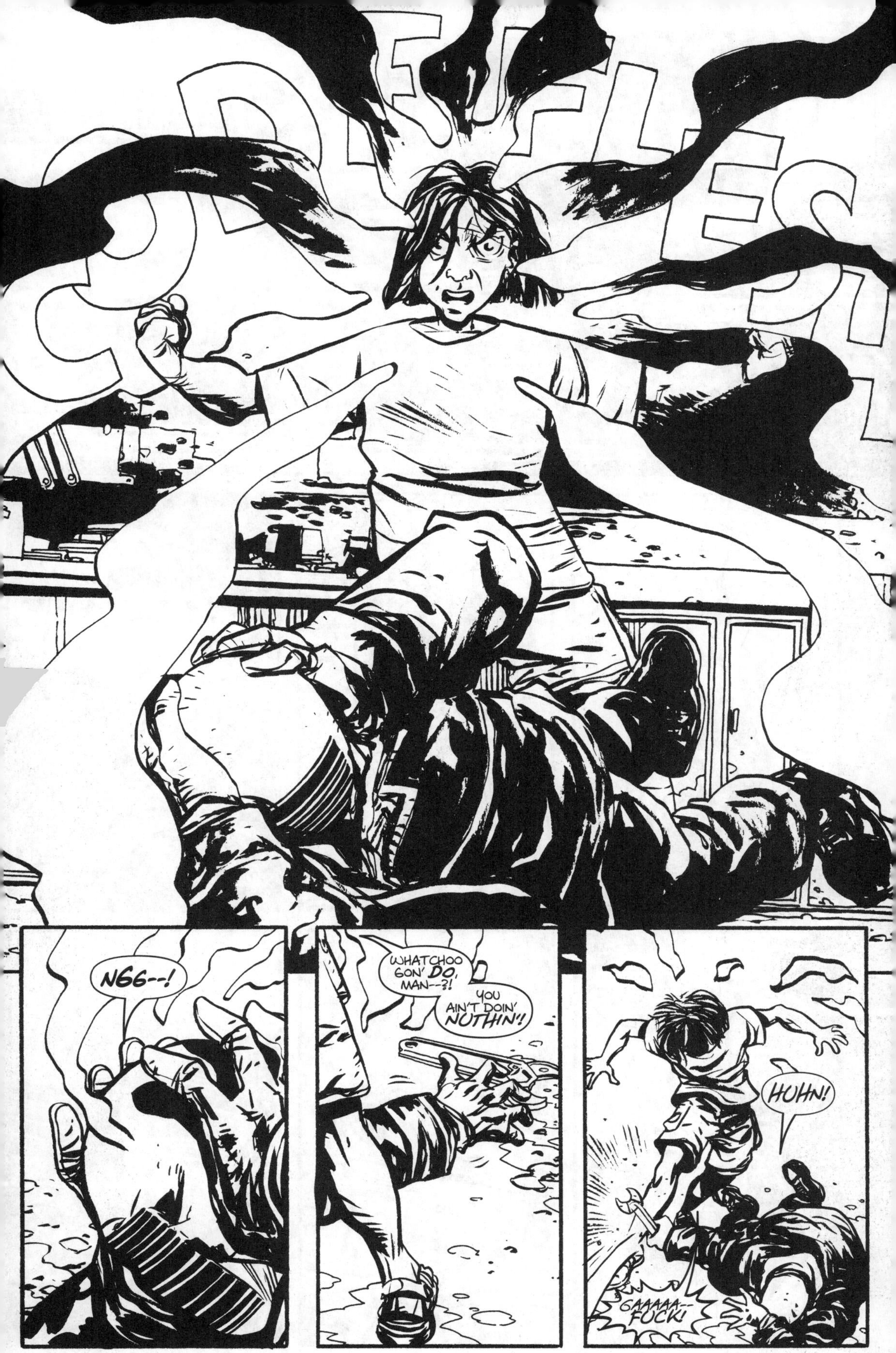

NGG--!
WHATCHOO GON' DO, MAN--?!
YOU AIN'T DOIN' NUTHIN'!
HUHN!
GAAAAA--FUCK!

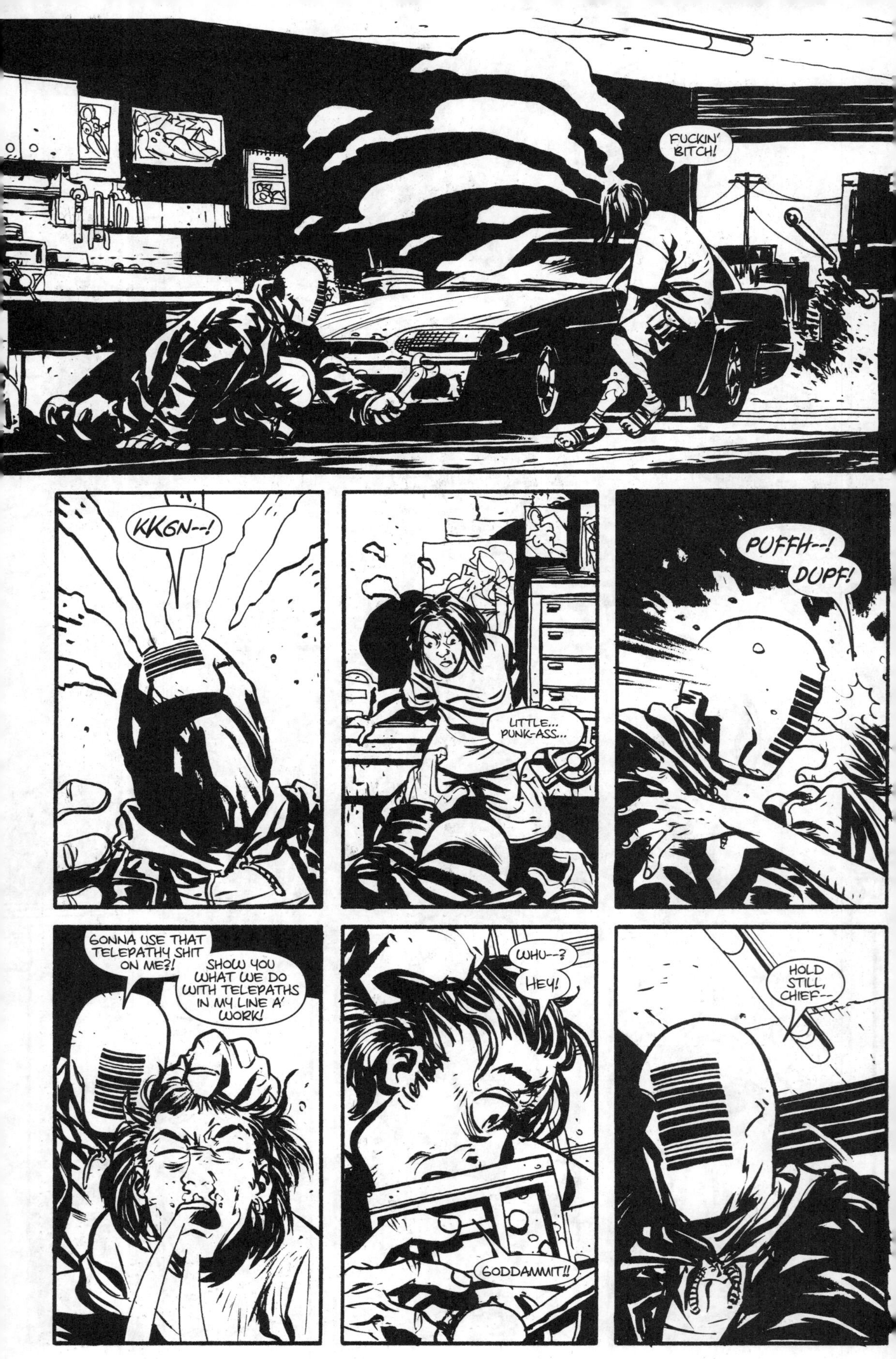
FUCKIN' BITCH!
KKGN--!
LITTLE... PUNK-ASS...
PUFFH--!
DUPF!
GONNA USE THAT TELEPATHY SHIT ON ME?!
SHOW YOU WHAT WE DO WITH TELEPATHS IN MY LINE A' WORK!
WHU--?
HEY!
GODDAMMIT!!
HOLD STILL, CHIEF--

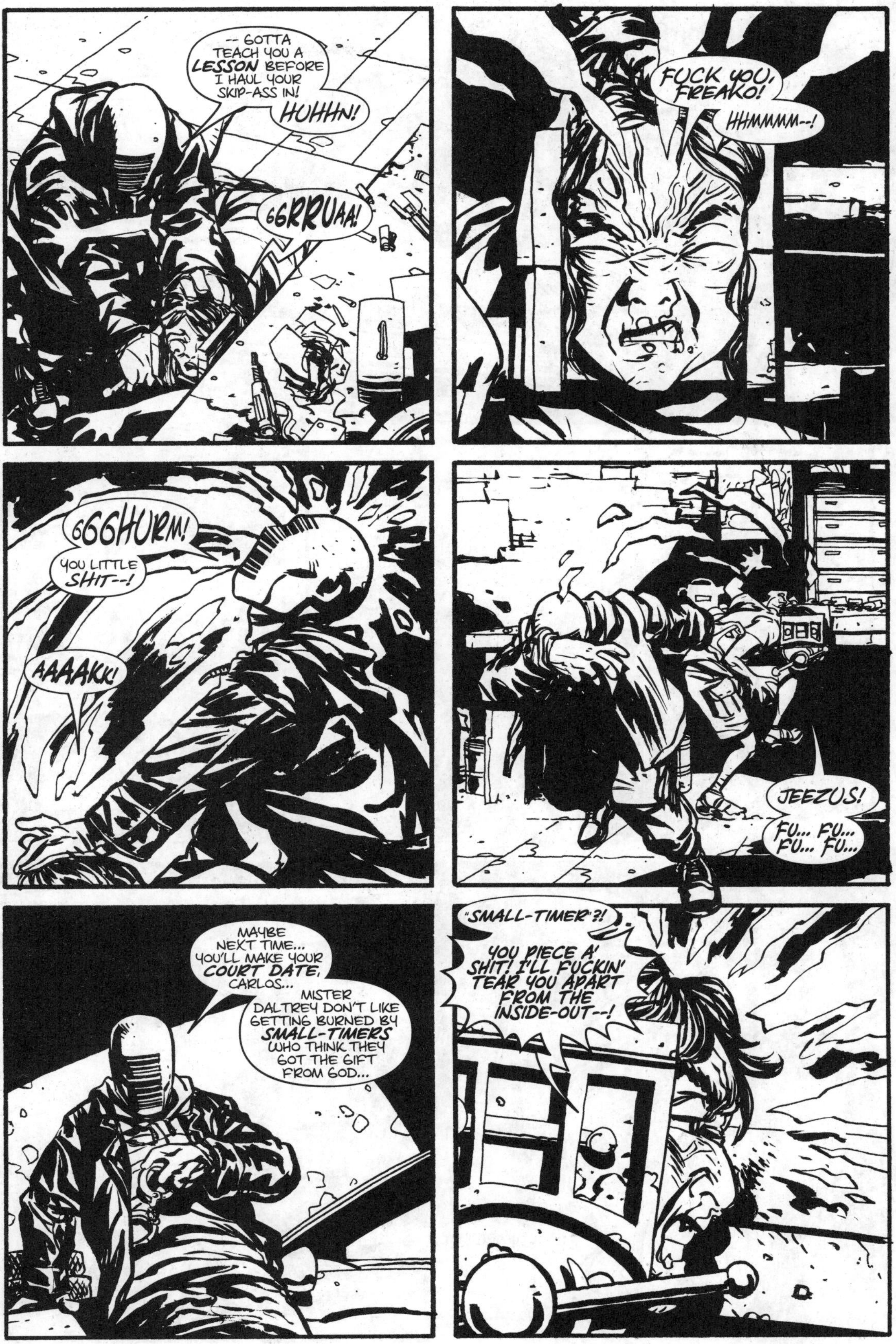

-- GOTTA TEACH YOU A LESSON BEFORE I HAUL YOUR SKIP-ASS IN!
HUHHN!
GGRRUAA!
FUCK YOU, FREAKO!
HHMMMM--!
GGGHURM!
YOU LITTLE SHIT--!
AAAAKK!
JEEZUS!
FU... FU... FU... FU...
MAYBE NEXT TIME... YOU'LL MAKE YOUR COURT DATE, CARLOS...
MISTER DALTREY DON'T LIKE GETTING BURNED BY SMALL-TIMERS WHO THINK THEY GOT THE GIFT FROM GOD...
"SMALL-TIMER"?!
YOU PIECE A' SHIT! I'LL FUCKIN' TEAR YOU APART FROM THE INSIDE-OUT--!

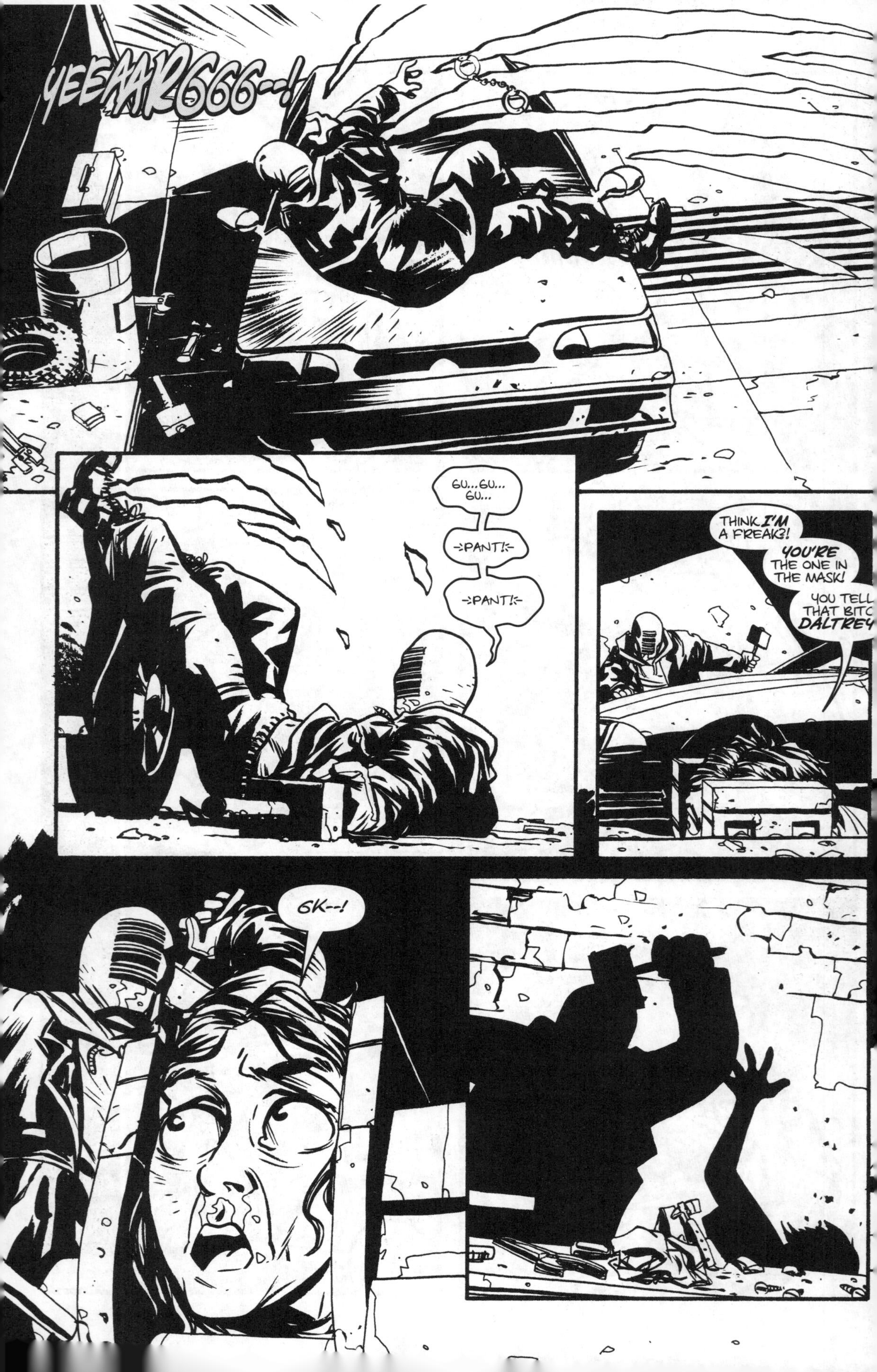
YEEAARGGG--!
GU...GU...
GU...
-PANT!-
-PANT!-
THINK I'M A FREAK?!
YOU'RE THE ONE IN THE MASK!
YOU TELL THAT BITC
DALTREY
GK--!

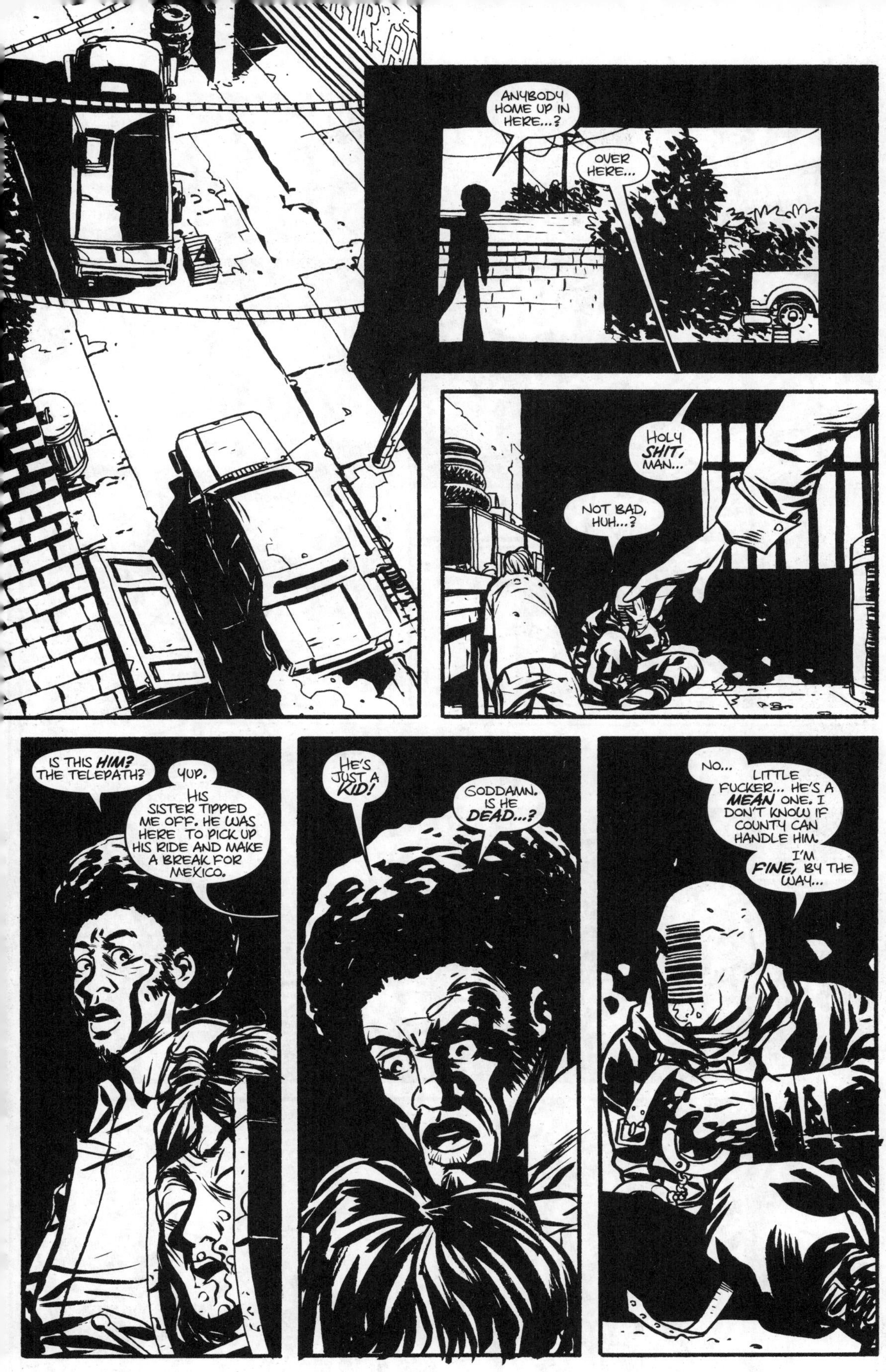
ANYBODY HOME UP IN HERE...?
OVER HERE...
HOLY SHIT, MAN...
NOT BAD, HUH...?
IS THIS HIM? THE TELEPATH?
YUP.
HIS SISTER TIPPED ME OFF. HE WAS HERE TO PICK UP HIS RIDE AND MAKE A BREAK FOR MEXICO.
HE'S JUST A KID!
GODDAMN. IS HE DEAD...?
NO... LITTLE FUCKER... HE'S A MEAN ONE. I DON'T KNOW IF COUNTY CAN HANDLE HIM.
I'M FINE, BY THE WAY...

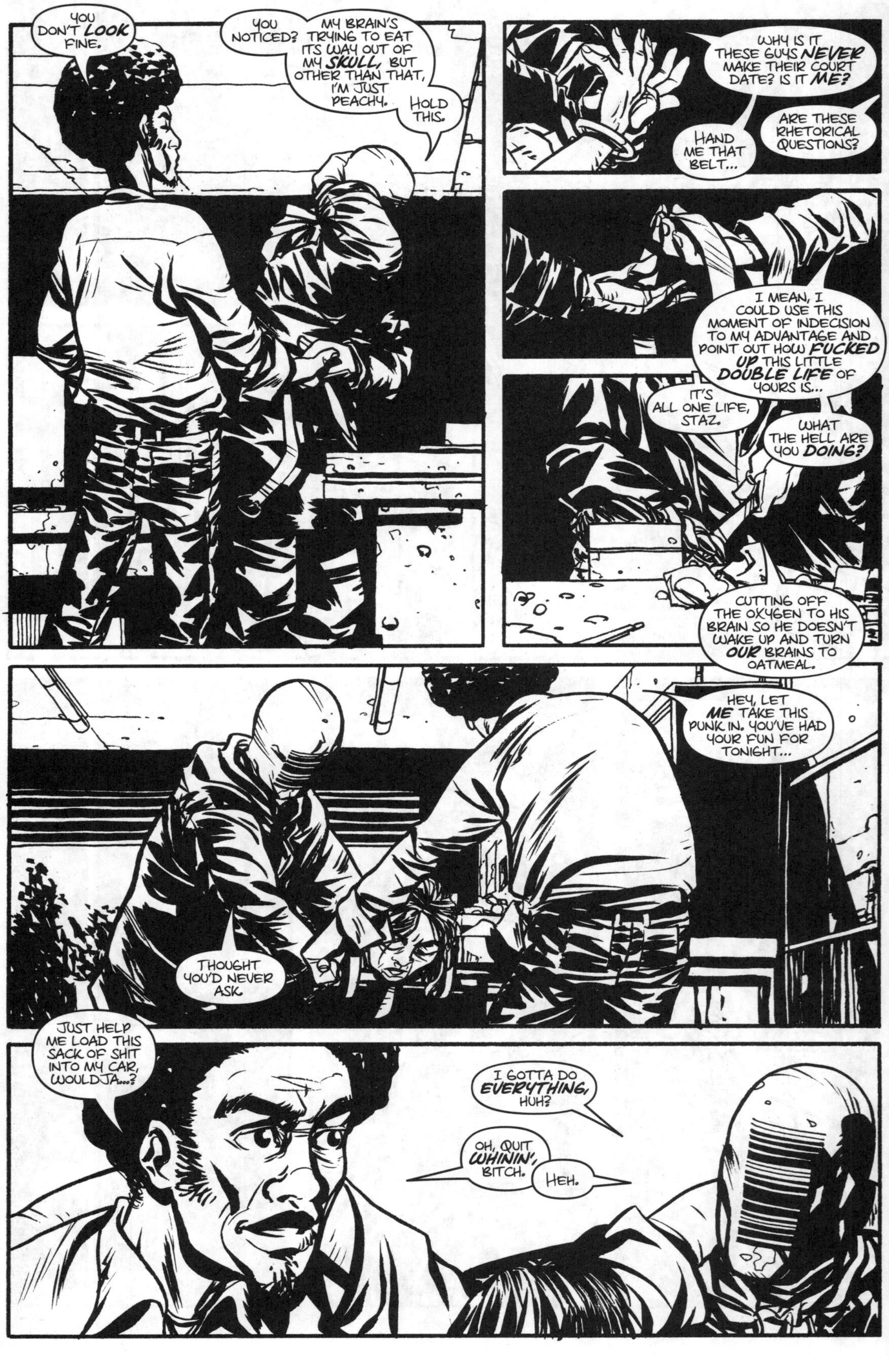

YOU DON'T LOOK FINE.
YOU NOTICED? MY BRAIN'S TRYING TO EAT ITS WAY OUT OF MY SKULL, BUT OTHER THAN THAT, I'M JUST PEACHY.
HOLD THIS.
WHY IS IT THESE GUYS NEVER MAKE THEIR COURT DATE? IS IT ME?
HAND ME THAT BELT...
ARE THESE RHETORICAL QUESTIONS?
I MEAN, I COULD USE THIS MOMENT OF INDECISION TO MY ADVANTAGE AND POINT OUT HOW FUCKED UP THIS LITTLE DOUBLE LIFE OF YOURS IS...
IT'S ALL ONE LIFE, STAZ.
WHAT THE HELL ARE YOU DOING?
CUTTING OFF THE OXYGEN TO HIS BRAIN SO HE DOESN'T WAKE UP AND TURN OUR BRAINS TO OATMEAL.
HEY, LET ME TAKE THIS PUNK IN. YOU'VE HAD YOUR FUN FOR TONIGHT...
THOUGHT YOU'D NEVER ASK.
JUST HELP ME LOAD THIS SACK OF SHIT INTO MY CAR, WOULDJA...?
I GOTTA DO EVERYTHING, HUH?
OH, QUIT WHININ', BITCH.
HEH.

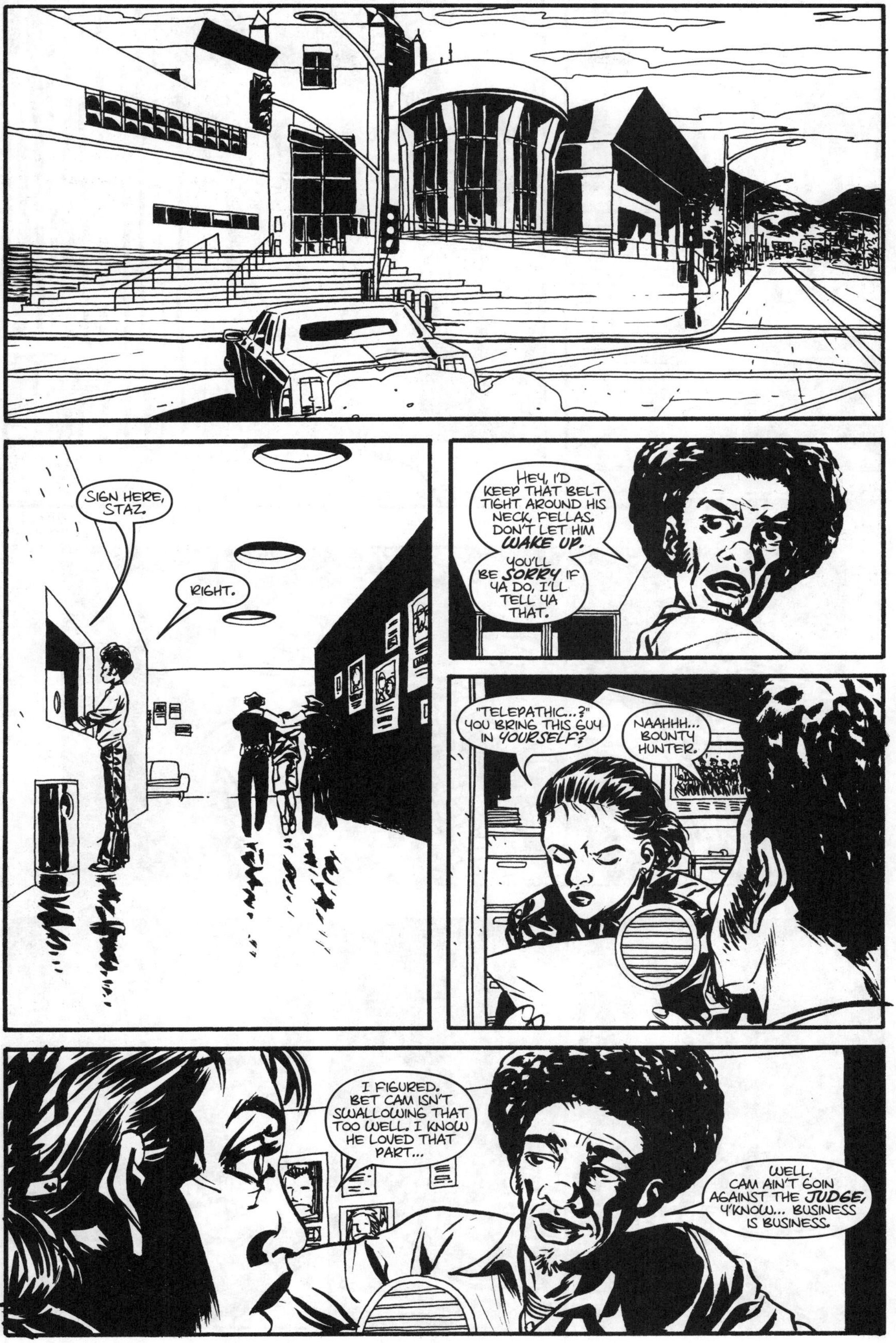
SIGN HERE, STAZ.
RIGHT.
HEY, I'D KEEP THAT BELT TIGHT AROUND HIS NECK, FELLAS. DON'T LET HIM WAKE UP.
YOU'LL BE SORRY IF YA DO, I'LL TELL YA THAT.
"TELEPATHIC...?" YOU BRING THIS GUY IN YOURSELF?
NAAHHH... BOUNTY HUNTER.
I FIGURED. BET CAM ISN'T SWALLOWING THAT TOO WELL. I KNOW HE LOVED THAT PART...
WELL, CAM AIN'T GOIN AGAINST THE JUDGE, Y'KNOW... BUSINESS IS BUSINESS.

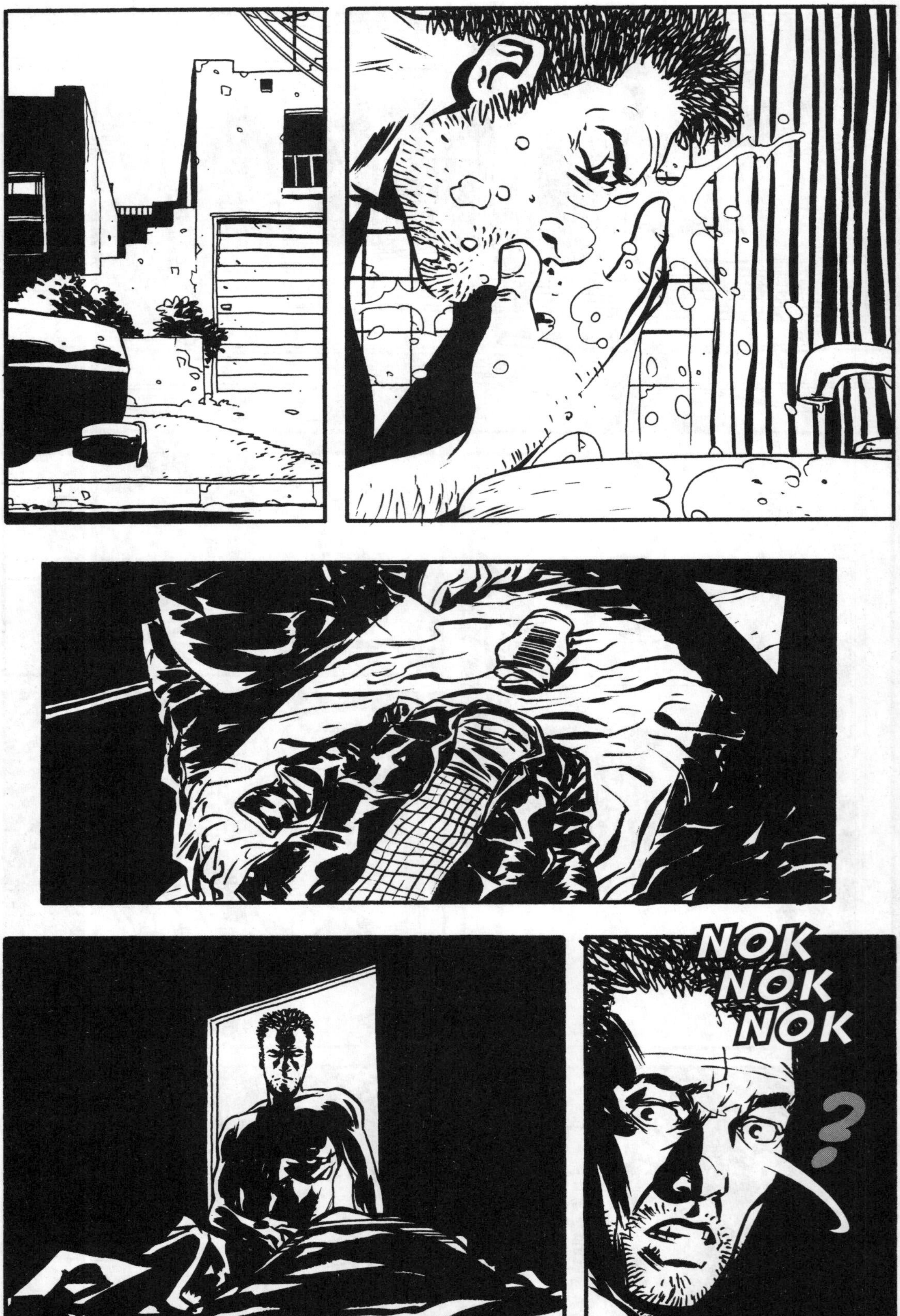
NOK
NOK
NOK
?

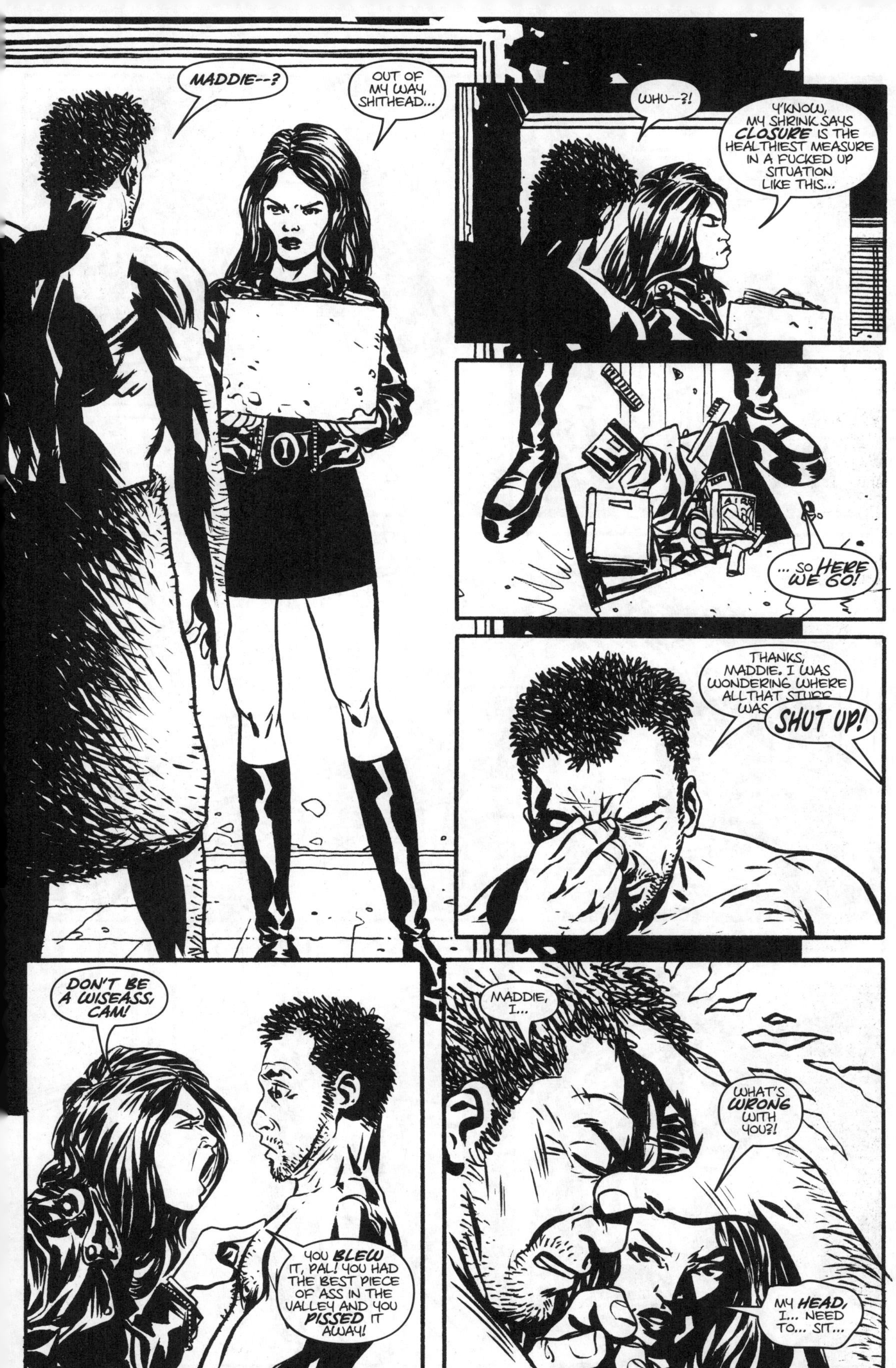
MADDIE--?
OUT OF MY WAY, SHITHEAD...
WHU--?!
Y'KNOW, MY SHRINK SAYS CLOSURE IS THE HEALTHIEST MEASURE IN A FUCKED UP SITUATION LIKE THIS...
...SO HERE WE GO!
THANKS, MADDIE. I WAS WONDERING WHERE ALLTHAT STUFF WAS...
SHUT UP!
DON'T BE A WISEASS, CAM!
YOU BLEW IT, PAL! YOU HAD THE BEST PIECE OF ASS IN THE VALLEY AND YOU PISSED IT AWAY!
MADDIE, I...
WHAT'S WRONG WITH YOU?!
MY HEAD, I... NEED TO... SIT...

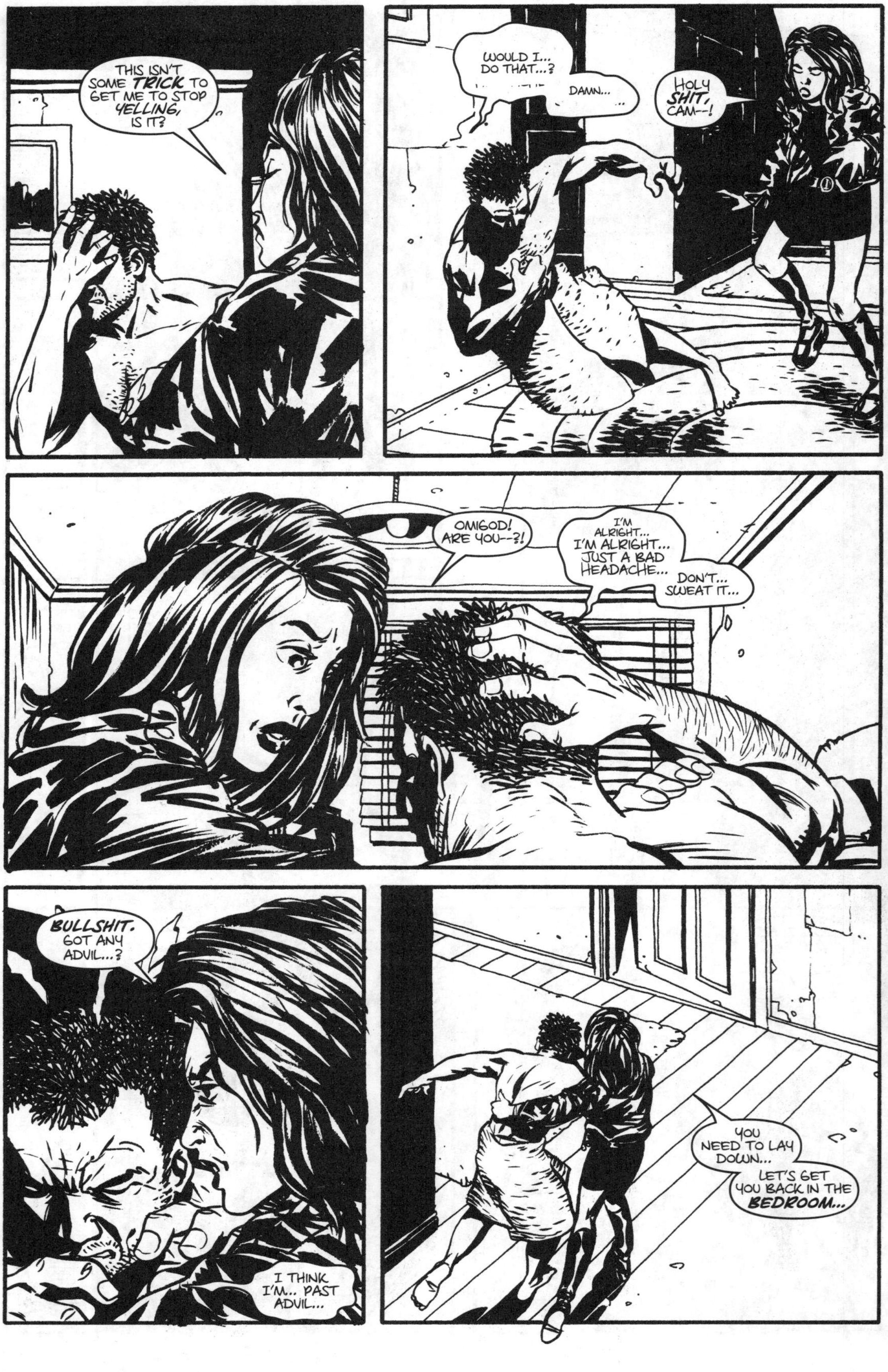
THIS ISN'T SOME TRICK TO GET ME TO STOP YELLING, IS IT?
WOULD I... DO THAT...?
DAMN... ...
HOLY SHIT, CAM--!
OMIGOD! ARE YOU--?!
I'M ALRIGHT... I'M ALRIGHT... JUST A BAD HEADACHE...
DON'T... SWEAT IT...
BULLSHIT. GOT ANY ADVIL...?
I THINK I'M... PAST ADVIL...
YOU NEED TO LAY DOWN...
LET'S GET YOU BACK IN THE BEDROOM...

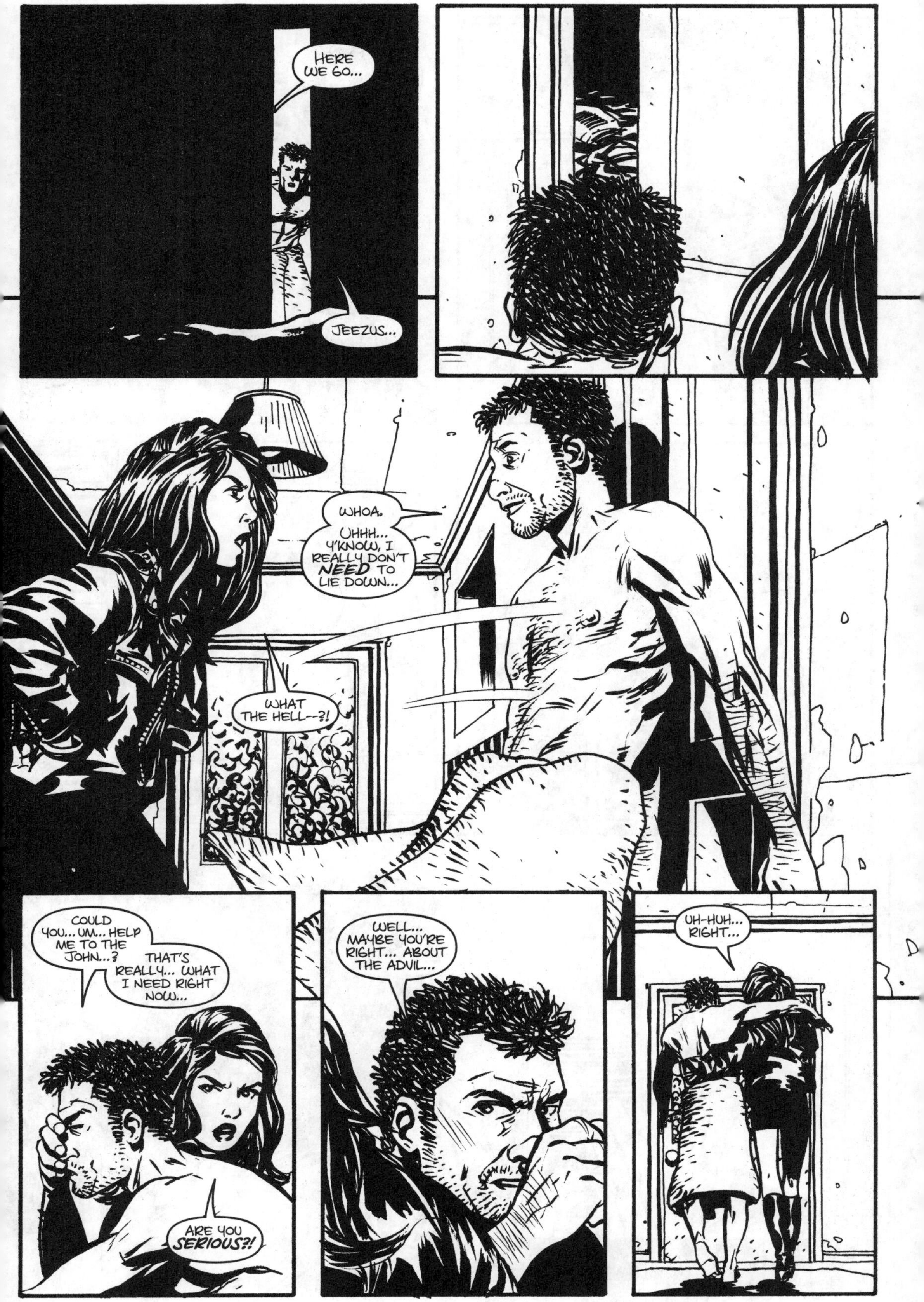
HERE WE GO...
JEEZUS...
WHOA. UHHH... Y'KNOW, I REALLY DON'T NEED TO LIE DOWN...
WHAT THE HELL--?!
COULD YOU...UM...HELP ME TO THE JOHN...?
THAT'S REALLY... WHAT I NEED RIGHT NOW...
ARE YOU SERIOUS?!
WELL... MAYBE YOU'RE RIGHT... ABOUT THE ADVIL...
UH-HUH... RIGHT...

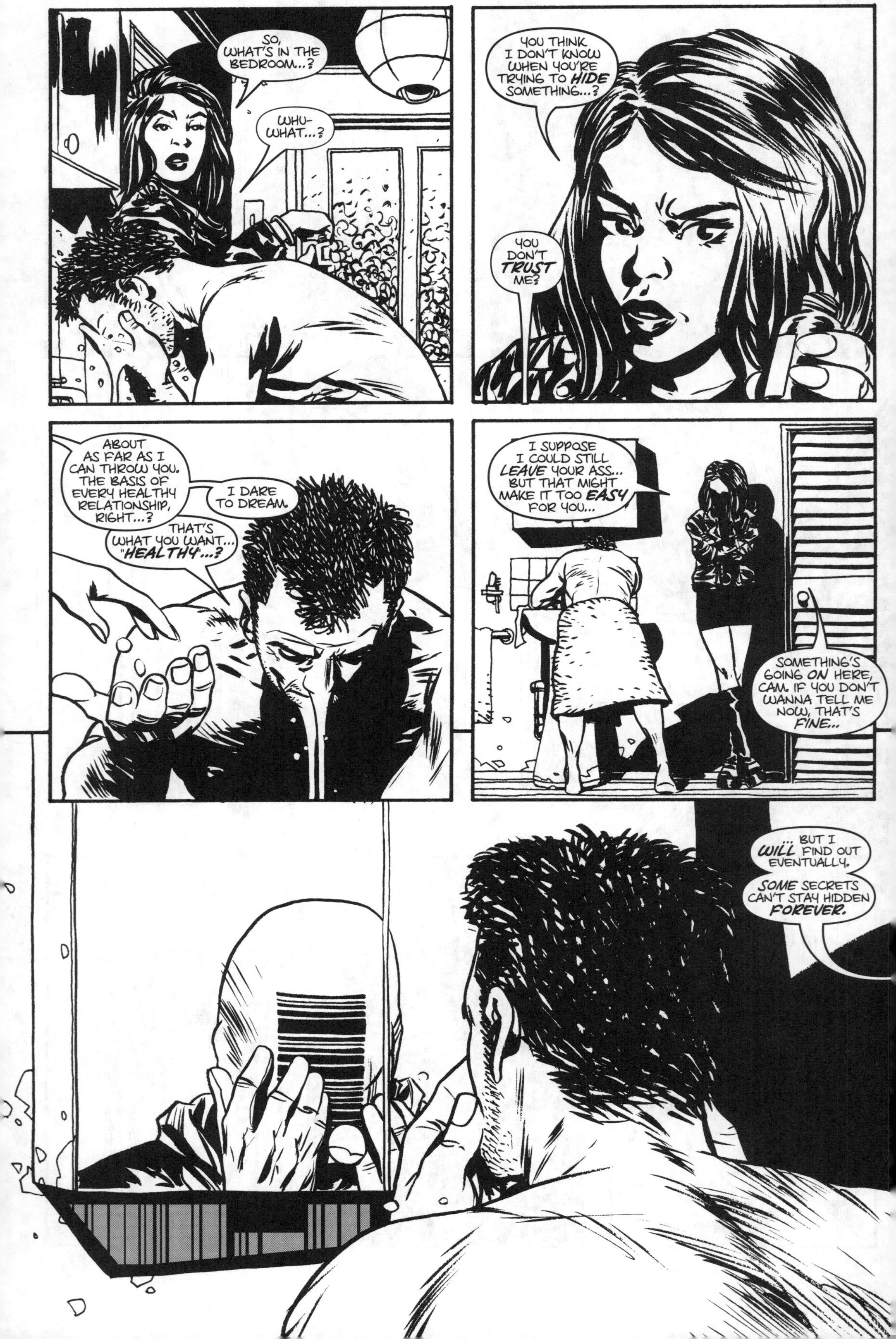
SO, WHAT'S IN THE BEDROOM...?
WHU-WHAT...?
YOU THINK I DON'T KNOW WHEN YOU'RE TRYING TO HIDE SOMETHING...?
YOU DON'T TRUST ME?
ABOUT AS FAR AS I CAN THROW YOU. THE BASIS OF EVERY HEALTHY RELATIONSHIP, RIGHT...?
I DARE TO DREAM.
THAT'S WHAT YOU WANT... "HEALTHY"...?
I SUPPOSE I COULD STILL LEAVE YOUR ASS... BUT THAT MIGHT MAKE IT TOO EASY FOR YOU...
SOMETHING'S GOING ON HERE, CAM. IF YOU DON'T WANNA TELL ME NOW, THAT'S FINE...
... BUT I WILL FIND OUT EVENTUALLY.
SOME SECRETS CAN'T STAY HIDDEN FOREVER.

It was not unlike a dagger being plunged
into the center of his brain. He clawed at
his own head, desperate to remove this
intangible thing. The kid smiled through
his own pain. The mental magnifying glass
inching closer to the burning insect...

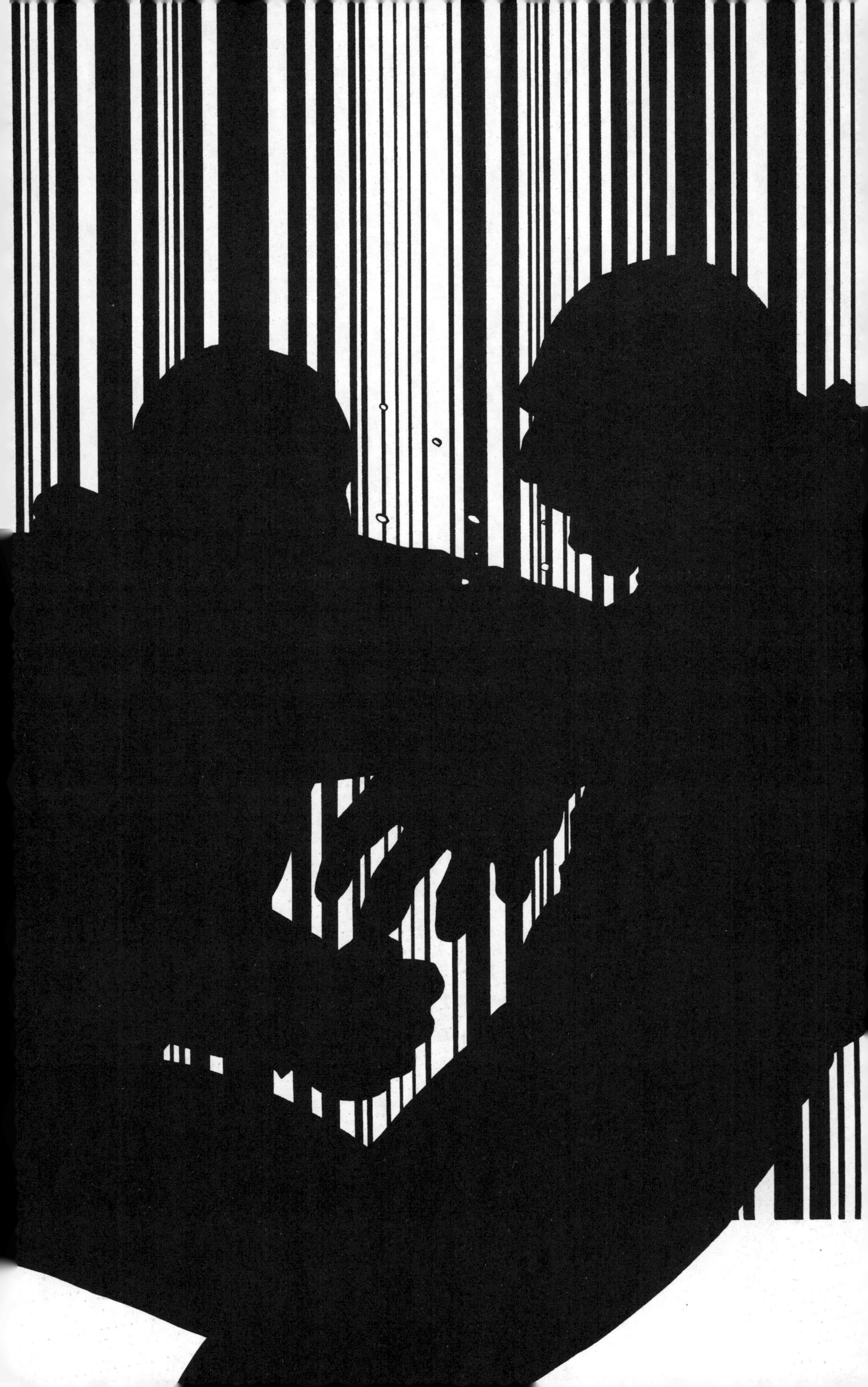

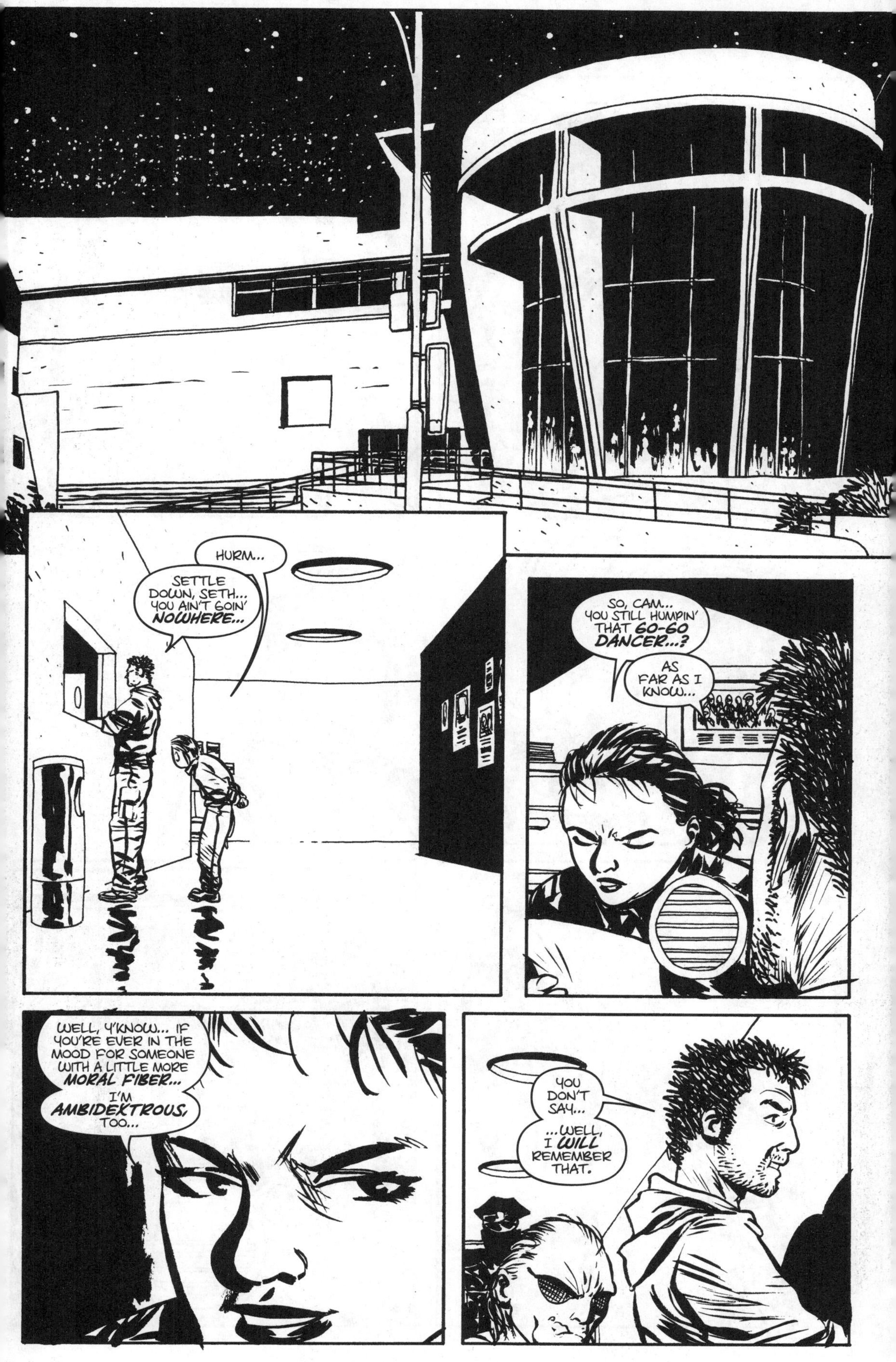

HURM...
SETTLE DOWN, SETH... YOU AIN'T GOIN' NOWHERE...
SO, CAM... YOU STILL HUMPIN' THAT GO-GO DANCER...?
AS FAR AS I KNOW...
WELL, Y'KNOW... IF YOU'RE EVER IN THE MOOD FOR SOMEONE WITH A LITTLE MORE MORAL FIBER...
I'M AMBIDEXTROUS, TOO...
YOU DON'T SAY...
...WELL, I WILL REMEMBER THAT.

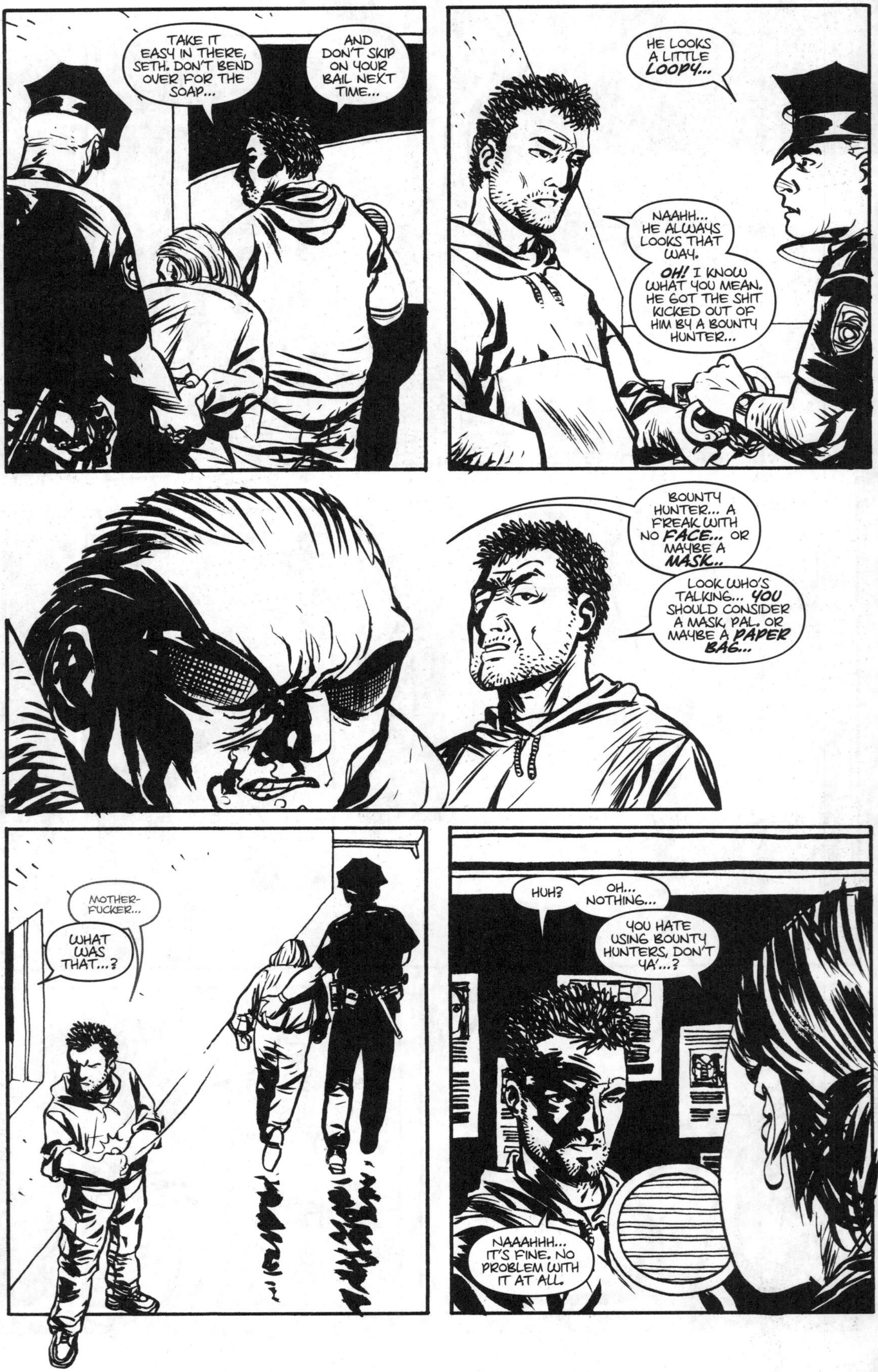
TAKE IT EASY IN THERE, SETH. DON'T BEND OVER FOR THE SOAP...
AND DON'T SKIP ON YOUR BAIL NEXT TIME...
HE LOOKS A LITTLE LOOPY...
NAAHH... HE ALWAYS LOOKS THAT WAY.
OH! I KNOW WHAT YOU MEAN. HE GOT THE SHIT KICKED OUT OF HIM BY A BOUNTY HUNTER...
BOUNTY HUNTER... A FREAK WITH NO FACE... OR MAYBE A MASK...
LOOK WHO'S TALKING... YOU SHOULD CONSIDER A MASK, PAL. OR MAYBE A PAPER BAG...
MOTHER-FUCKER...
WHAT WAS THAT...?
HUH?
OH... NOTHING...
YOU HATE USING BOUNTY HUNTERS, DON'T YA'...?
NAAAHHH... IT'S FINE. NO PROBLEM WITH IT AT ALL.

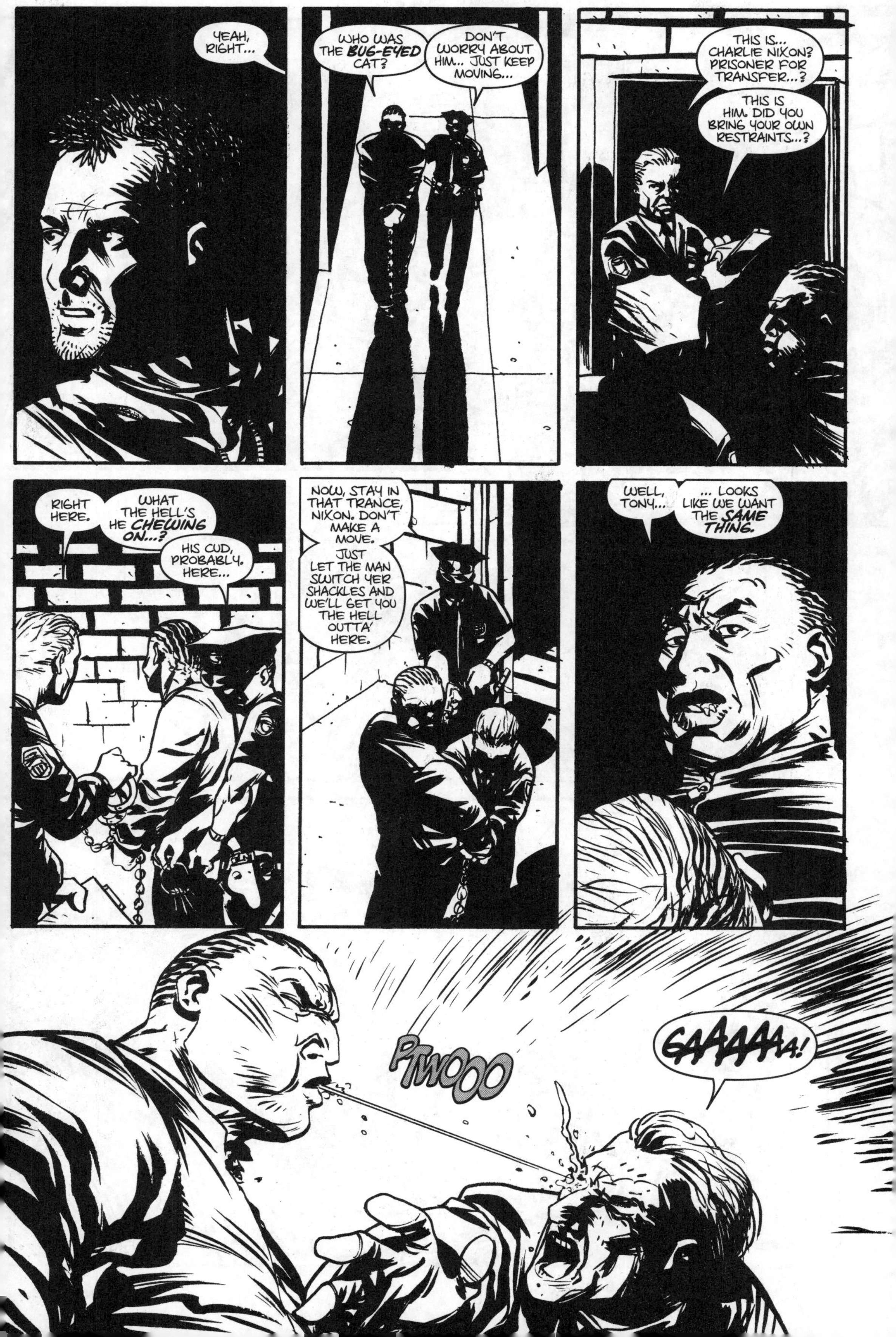
YEAH, RIGHT...
WHO WAS THE BUG-EYED CAT?
DON'T WORRY ABOUT HIM... JUST KEEP MOVING...
THIS IS... CHARLIE NIXON? PRISONER FOR TRANSFER...?
THIS IS HIM. DID YOU BRING YOUR OWN RESTRAINTS...?
RIGHT HERE.
WHAT THE HELL'S HE CHEWING ON...?
HIS CUD, PROBABLY. HERE...
NOW, STAY IN THAT TRANCE, NIXON. DON'T MAKE A MOVE.
JUST LET THE MAN SWITCH YER SHACKLES AND WE'LL GET YOU THE HELL OUTTA' HERE.
WELL, TONY...
... LOOKS LIKE WE WANT THE SAME THING.
PTWOOO
GAAAAAA!

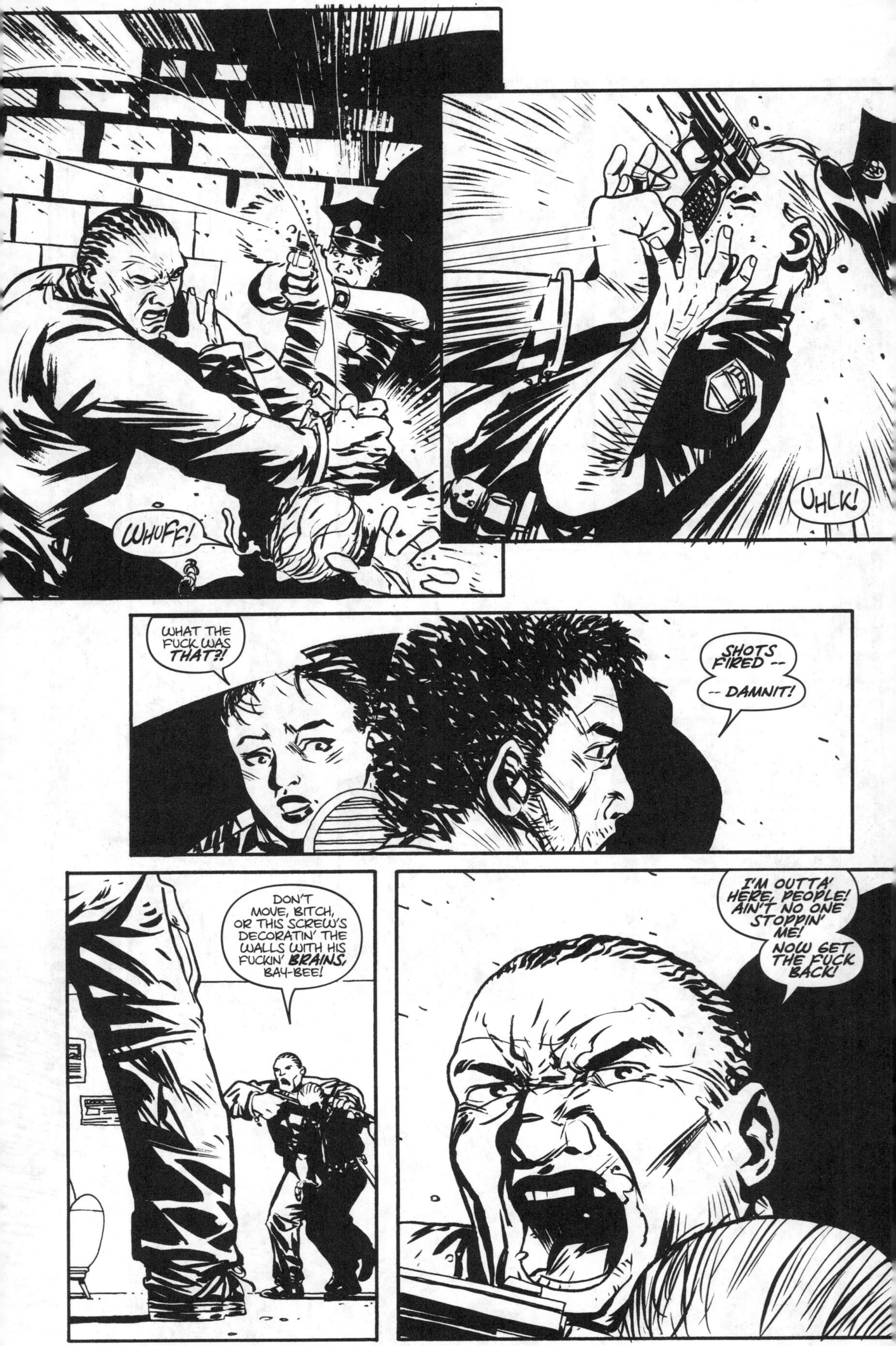
WHUFF!
UHLK!
WHAT THE FUCK WAS THAT?!
SHOTS FIRED --
-- DAMNIT!
DON'T MOVE, BITCH, OR THIS SCREW'S DECORATIN' THE WALLS WITH HIS FUCKIN' BRAINS, BAY-BEE!
I'M OUTTA' HERE, PEOPLE! AIN'T NO ONE STOPPIN' ME! NOW GET THE FUCK BACK!

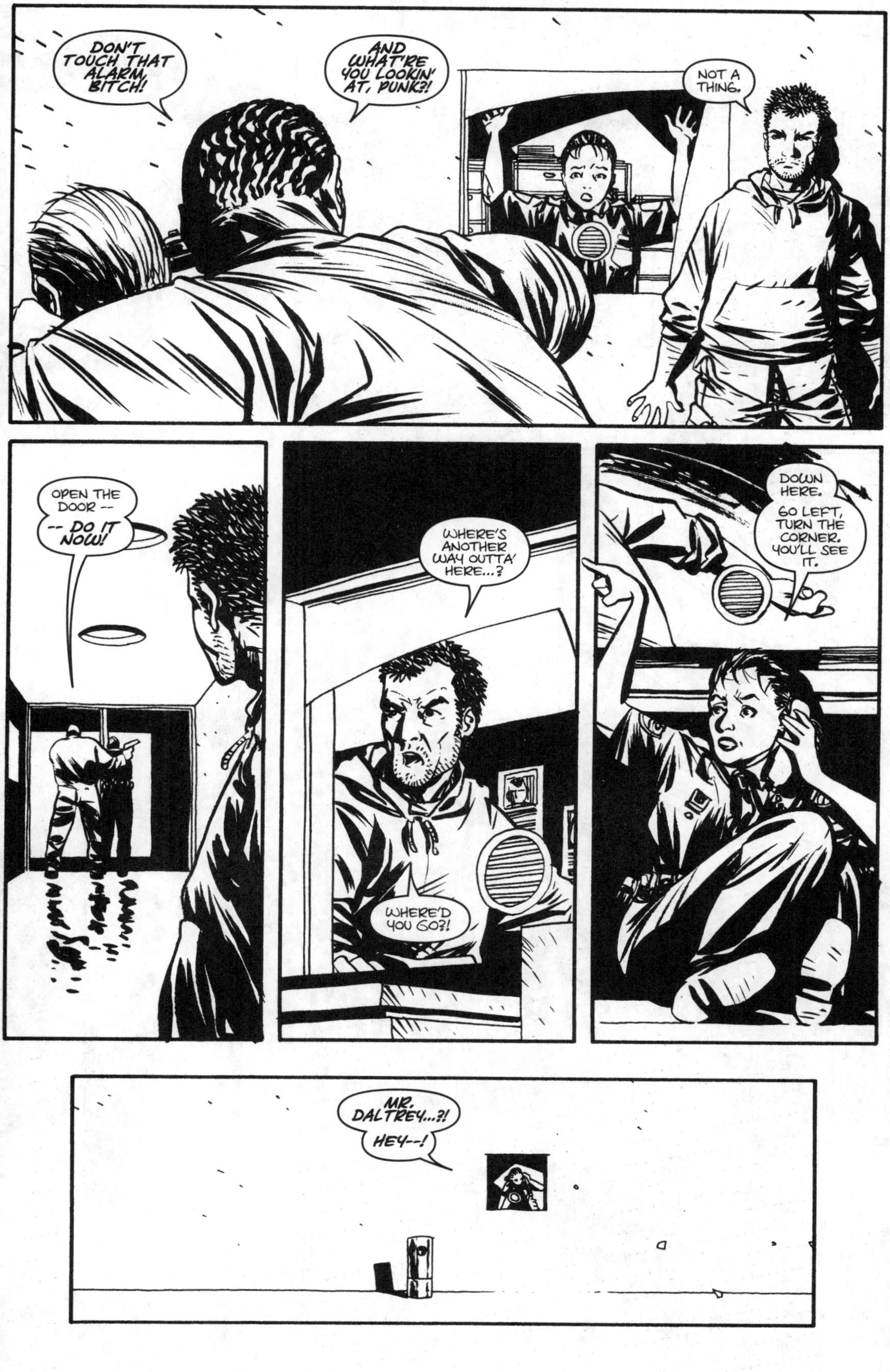
DON'T TOUCH THAT ALARM, BITCH!
AND WHAT'RE YOU LOOKIN' AT, PUNK?!
NOT A THING.
OPEN THE DOOR --
-- DO IT NOW!
WHERE'S ANOTHER WAY OUTTA' HERE...?
WHERE'D YOU GO?!
DOWN HERE.
GO LEFT, TURN THE CORNER. YOU'LL SEE IT.
MR. DALTREY...?!
HEY--!

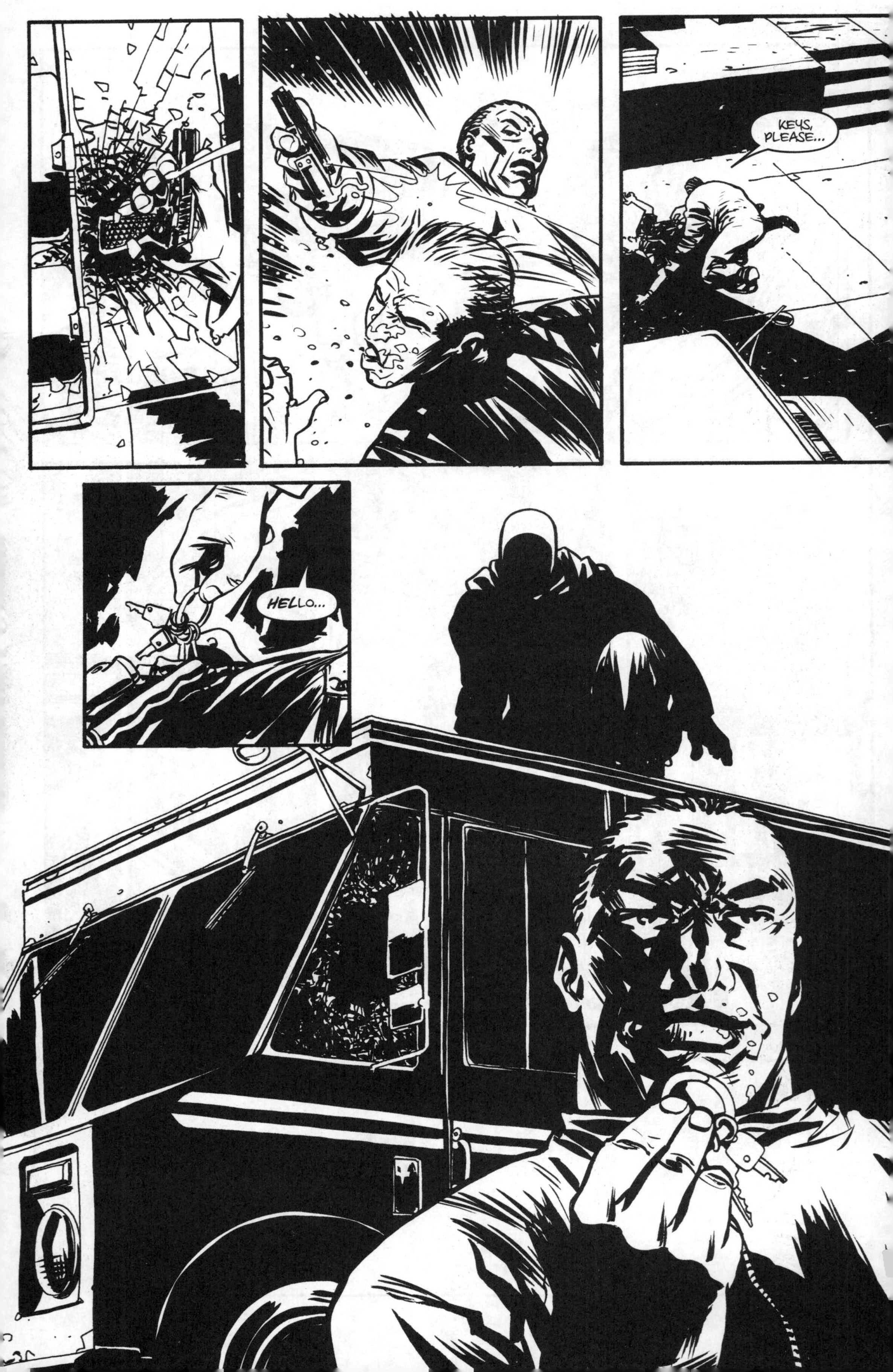
KEYS, PLEASE...
HELLO...

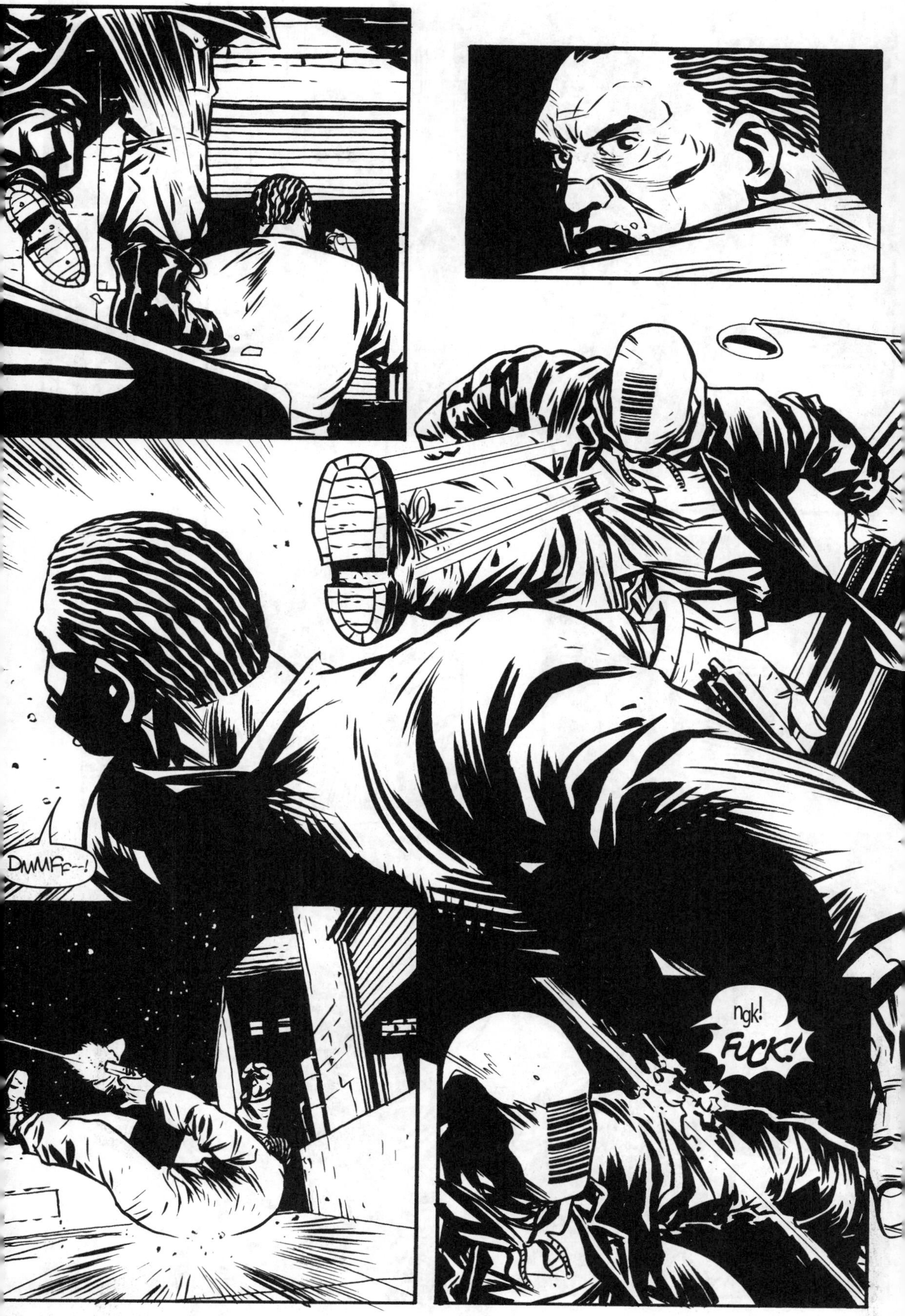
DMMFF--!
ngk!
FUCK!

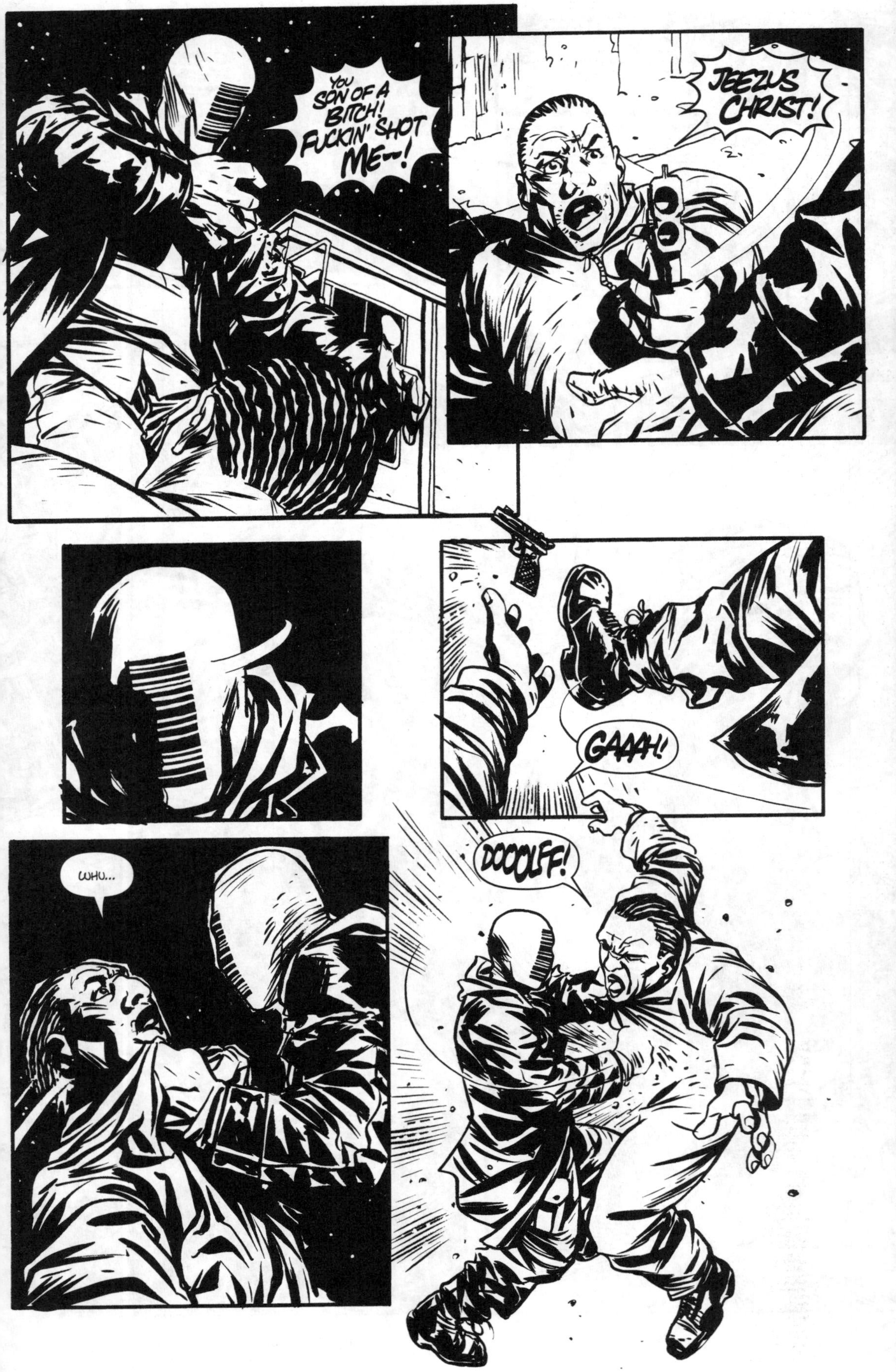
YOU SON OF A BITCH! FUCKIN' SHOT ME--!
JEEZUS CHRIST!
GAAAH!
WHU...
DOOOOFF!

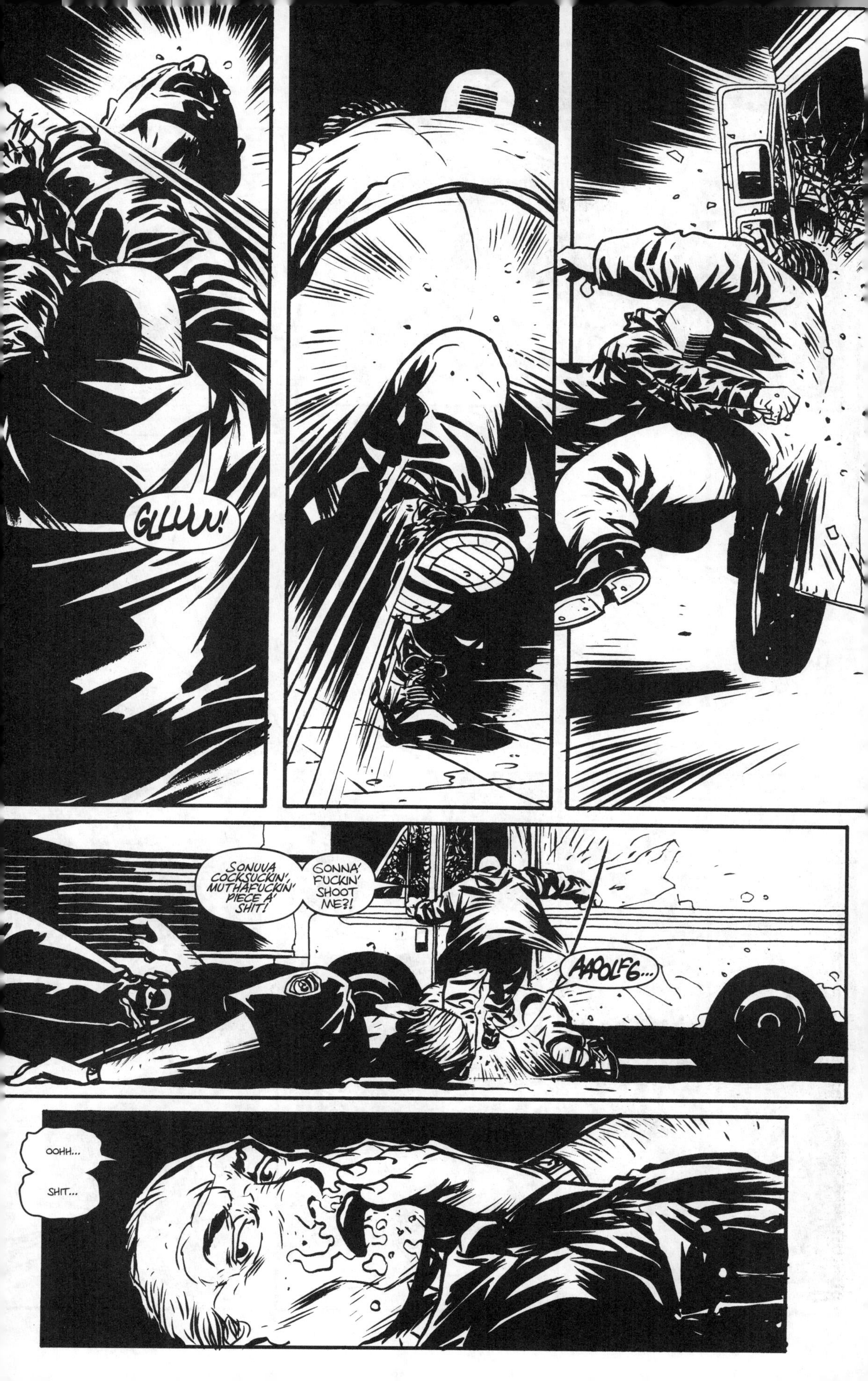
GLUUU!
SONUVA COCKSUCKIN', MUTHAFUCKIN' PIECE A' SHIT!
GONNA' FUCKIN' SHOOT ME?!
AAAOLF6...
OOHH...
SHIT...

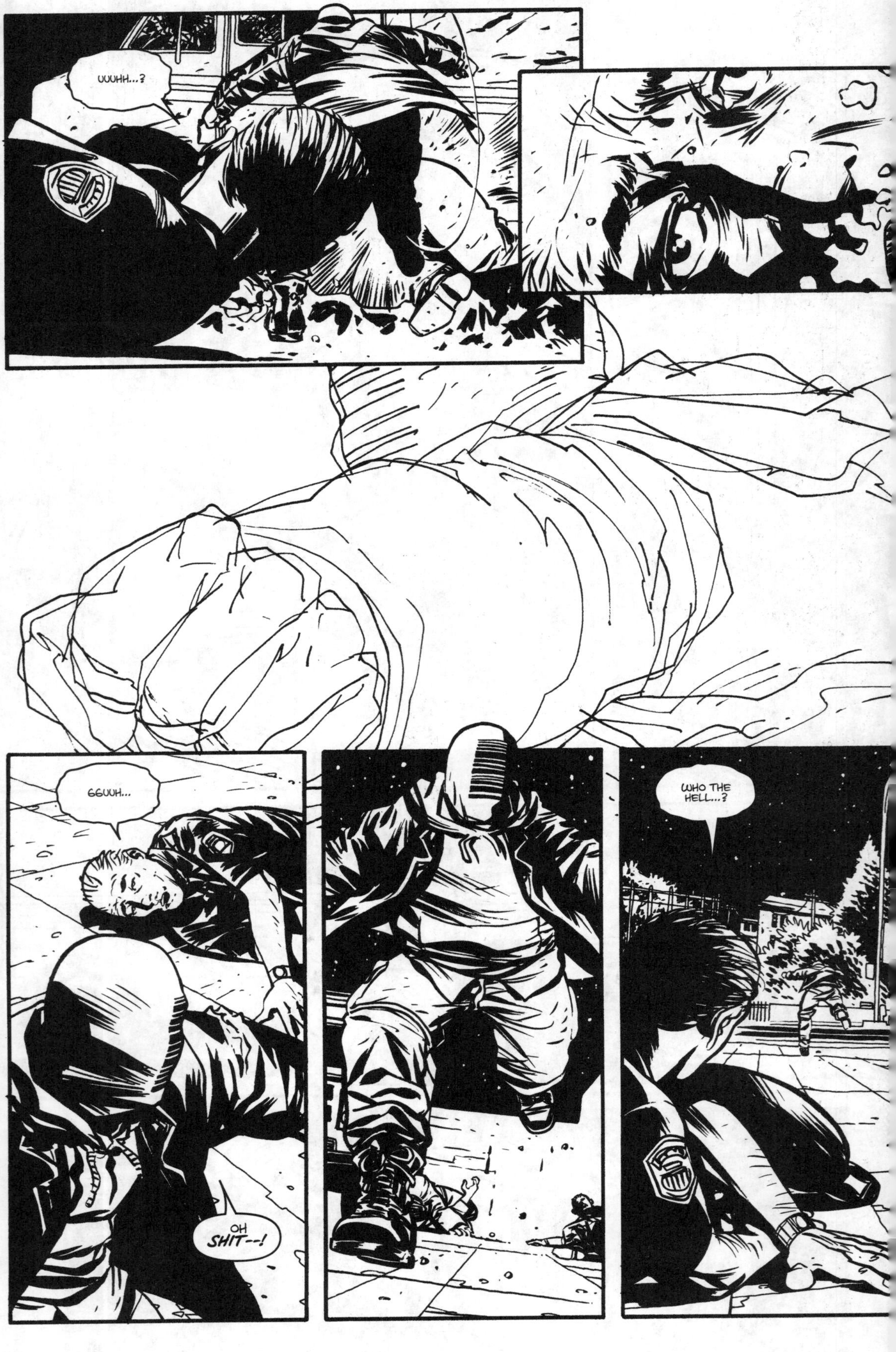
UUUHH...?
GGUUH...
OH SHIT--!
WHO THE HELL...?

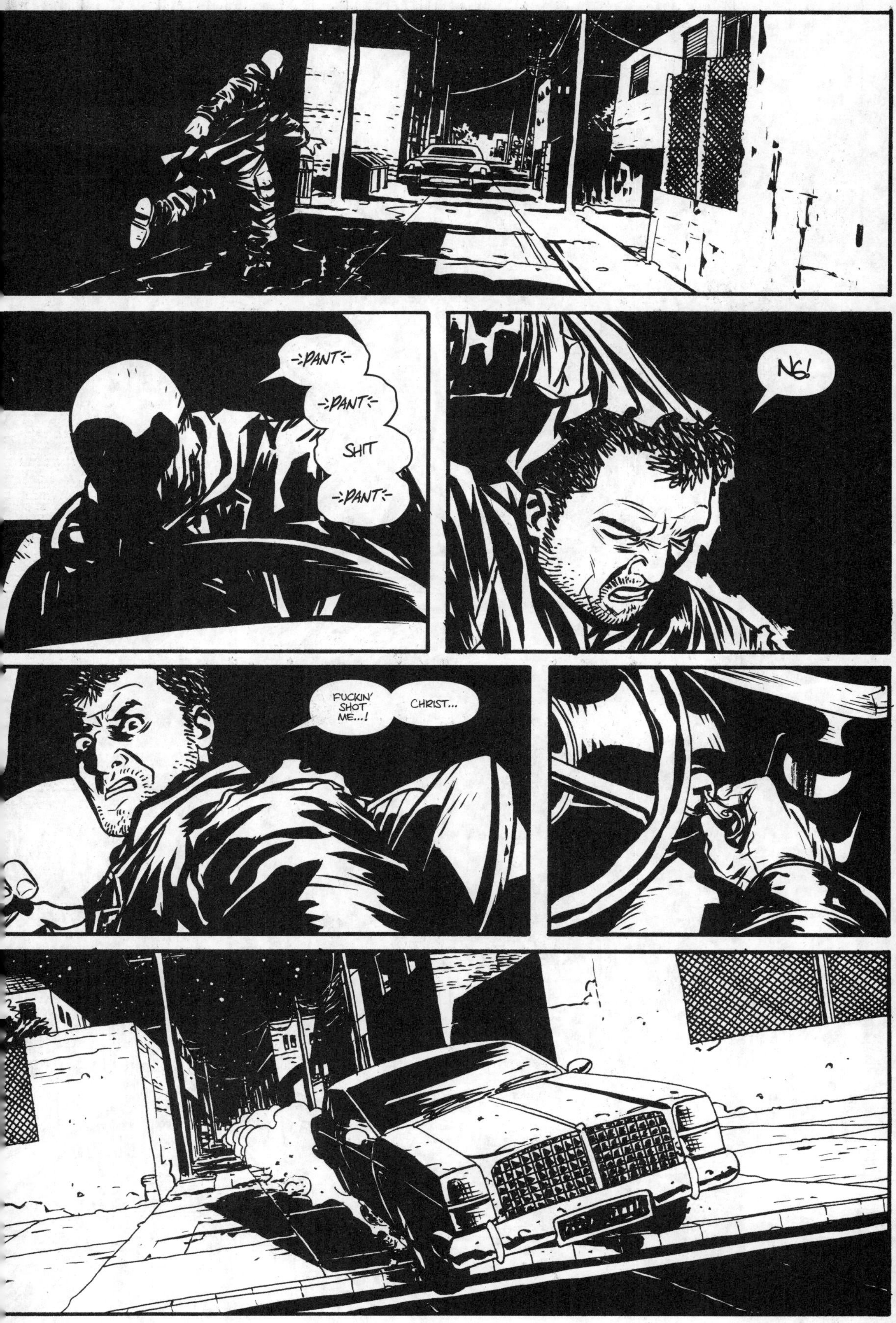
-PANT-
-PANT-
SHIT
-PANT-
NO!
FUCKIN' SHOT ME...!
CHRIST...

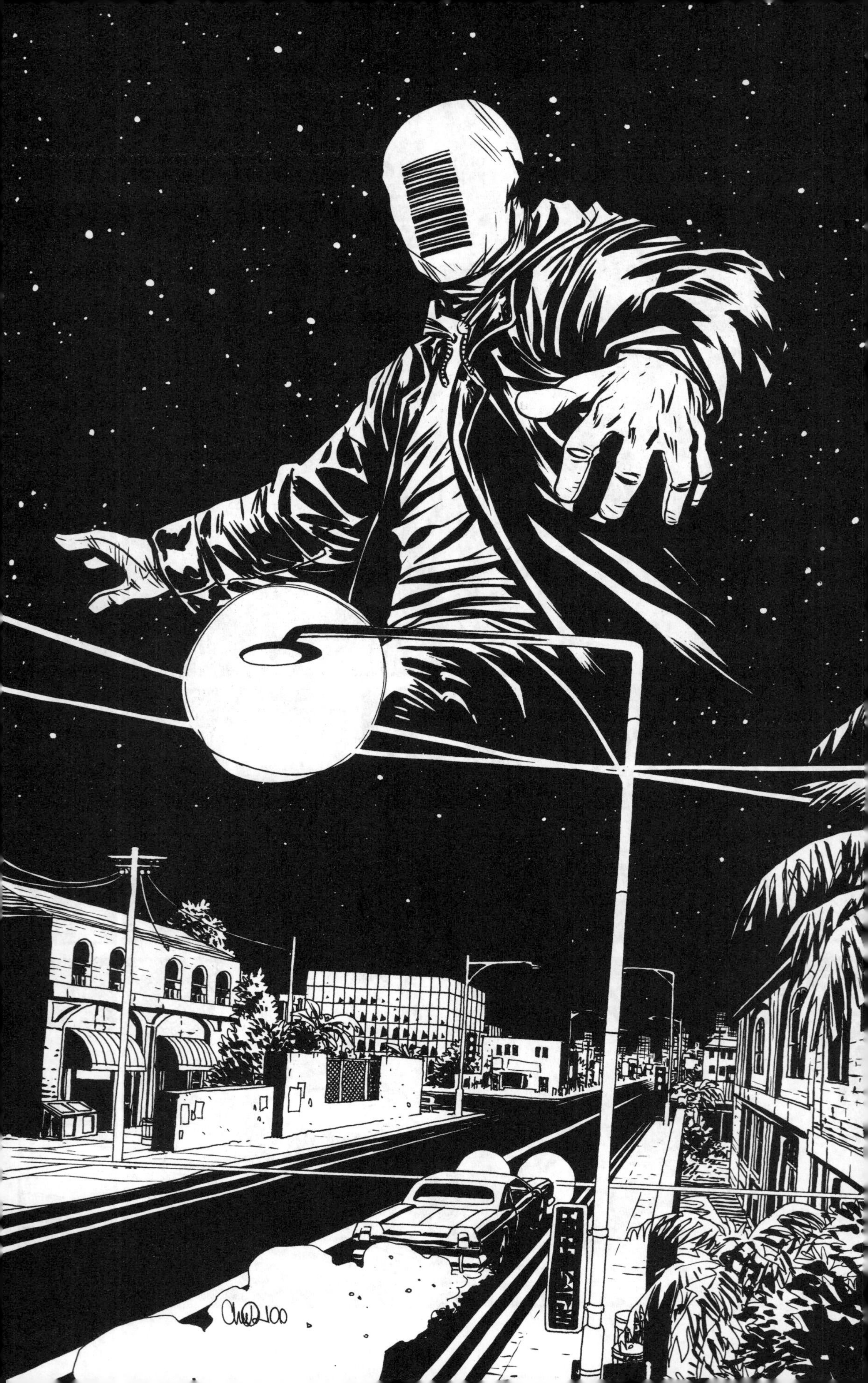

Voices echoed across the sanitized surfaces.
Even the sound of a pen on paper reverberated
through the corridor. And from a distance,
the methodical footsteps of what had to be a
permanent resident. The dull chimes of heavy
chains. The foul stench of confinement.

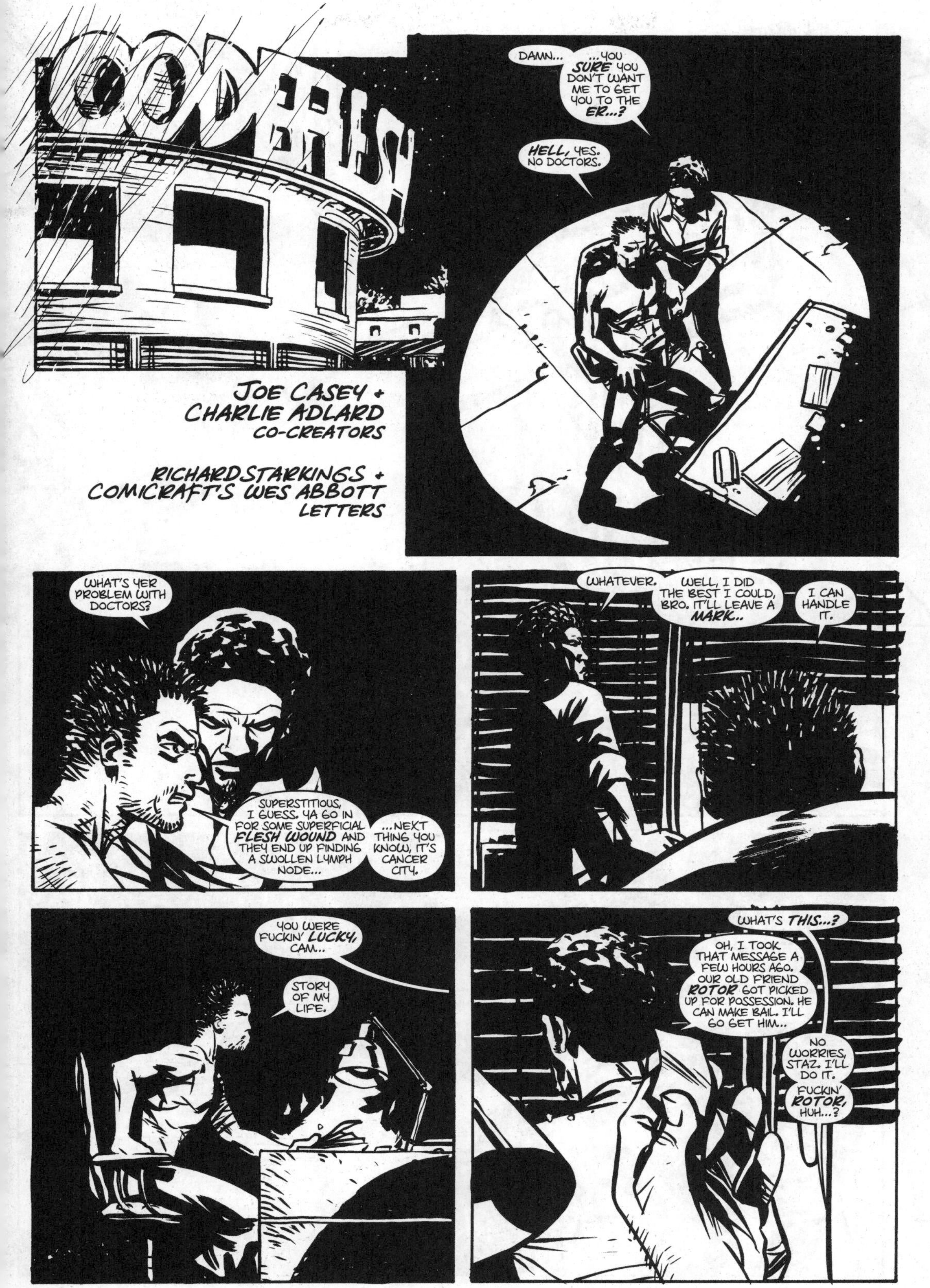

JOE CASEY + CHARLIE ADLARD
CO-CREATORS
RICHARDSTARKINGS + COMICRAFT'S WES ABBOTT
LETTERS
DAMN...
...YOU SURE YOU DON'T WANT ME TO GET YOU TO THE ER...?
HELL, YES. NO DOCTORS.
WHAT'S YER PROBLEM WITH DOCTORS?
SUPERSTITIOUS, I GUESS. YA GO IN FOR SOME SUPERFICIAL FLESH WOUND AND THEY END UP FINDING A SWOLLEN LYMPH NODE...
...NEXT THING YOU KNOW, IT'S CANCER CITY.
WHATEVER.
WELL, I DID THE BEST I COULD, BRO. IT'LL LEAVE A MARK..
I CAN HANDLE IT.
YOU WERE FUCKIN' LUCKY, CAM...
STORY OF MY LIFE.
WHAT'S THIS...?
OH, I TOOK THAT MESSAGE A FEW HOURS AGO. OUR OLD FRIEND ROTOR GOT PICKED UP FOR POSSESSION. HE CAN MAKE BAIL. I'LL GO GET HIM..
NO WORRIES, STAZ. I'LL DO IT.
FUCKIN' ROTOR, HUH...?

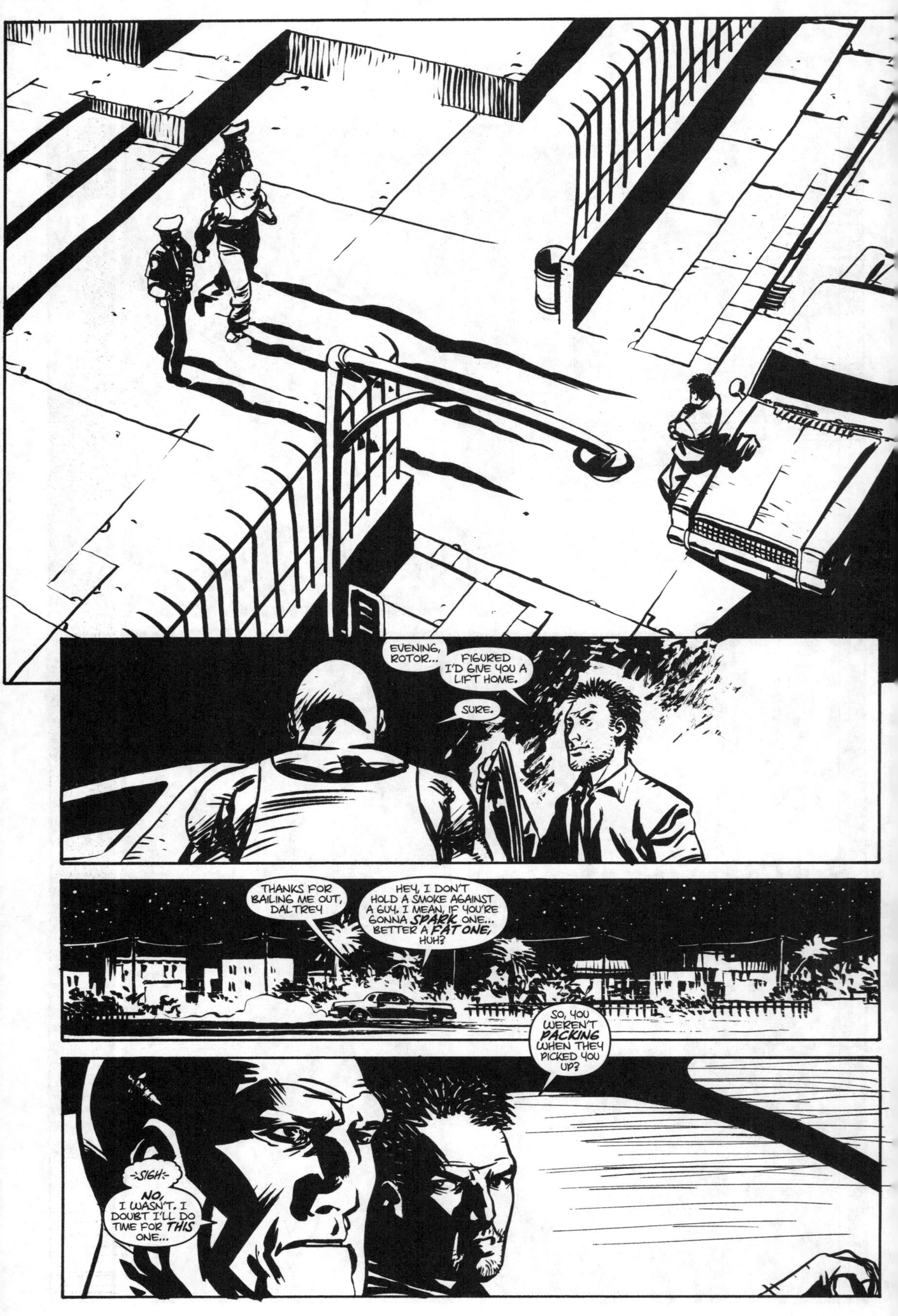
EVENING, ROTOR...
FIGURED I'D GIVE YOU A LIFT HOME.
SURE.
THANKS FOR BAILING ME OUT, DALTREY
HEY, I DON'T HOLD A SMOKE AGAINST A GUY. I MEAN, IF YOU'RE GONNA SPARK ONE... BETTER A FAT ONE, HUH?
SO, YOU WEREN'T PACKING WHEN THEY PICKED YOU UP?
-SIGH-
NO, I WASN'T. I DOUBT I'LL DO TIME FOR THIS ONE...

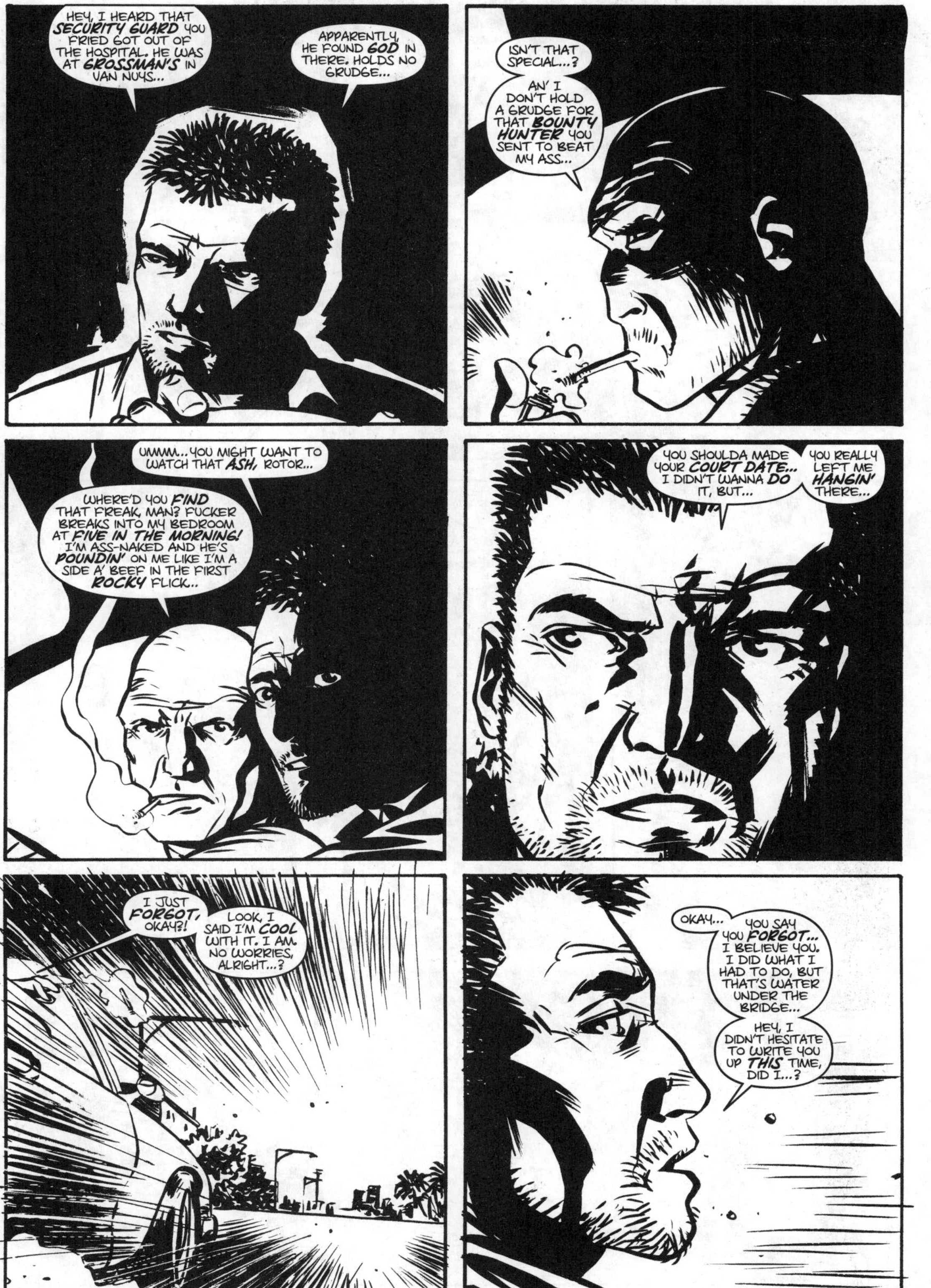
HEY, I HEARD THAT SECURITY GUARD YOU FRIED GOT OUT OF THE HOSPITAL. HE WAS AT GROSSMAN'S IN VAN NUYS...
APPARENTLY, HE FOUND GOD IN THERE. HOLDS NO GRUDGE...
ISN'T THAT SPECIAL...?
AN' I DON'T HOLD A GRUDGE FOR THAT BOUNTY HUNTER YOU SENT TO BEAT MY ASS...
UMMM... YOU MIGHT WANT TO WATCH THAT ASH, ROTOR...
WHERE'D YOU FIND THAT FREAK, MAN? FUCKER BREAKS INTO MY BEDROOM AT FIVE IN THE MORNING! I'M ASS-NAKED AND HE'S POUNDIN' ON ME LIKE I'M A SIDE A' BEEF IN THE FIRST ROCKY FLICK...
YOU SHOULDA MADE YOUR COURT DATE... I DIDN'T WANNA DO IT, BUT...
YOU REALLY LEFT ME HANGIN' THERE...
I JUST FORGOT, OKAY?!
LOOK, I SAID I'M COOL WITH IT. I AM. NO WORRIES, ALRIGHT...?
OKAY...
YOU SAY YOU FORGOT... I BELIEVE YOU. I DID WHAT I HAD TO DO, BUT THAT'S WATER UNDER THE BRIDGE...
HEY, I DIDN'T HESITATE TO WRITE YOU UP THIS TIME, DID I...?

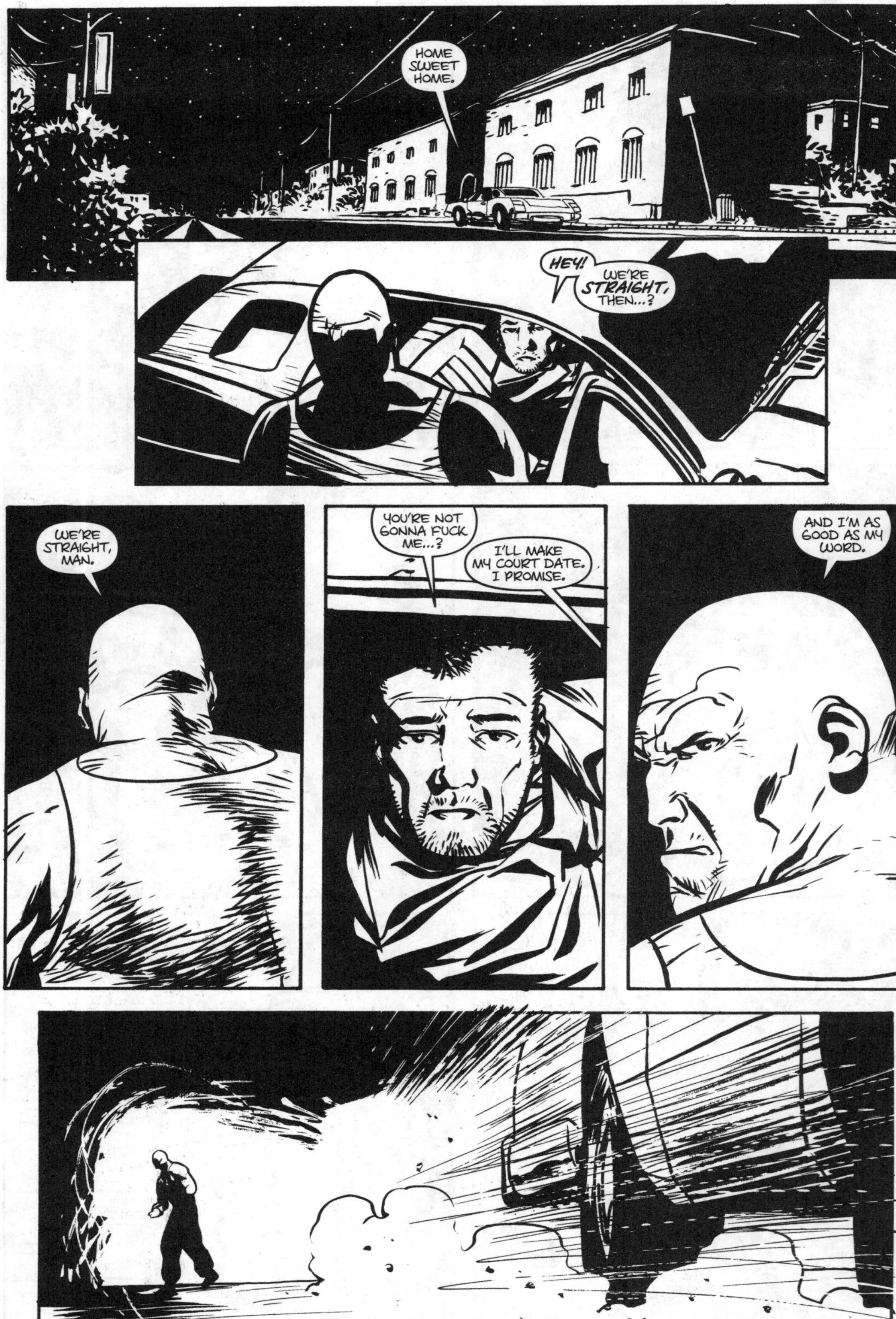
HOME SWEET HOME.
HEY! WE'RE STRAIGHT, THEN...?
WE'RE STRAIGHT, MAN.
YOU'RE NOT GONNA FUCK ME...?
I'LL MAKE MY COURT DATE. I PROMISE.
AND I'M AS GOOD AS MY WORD.

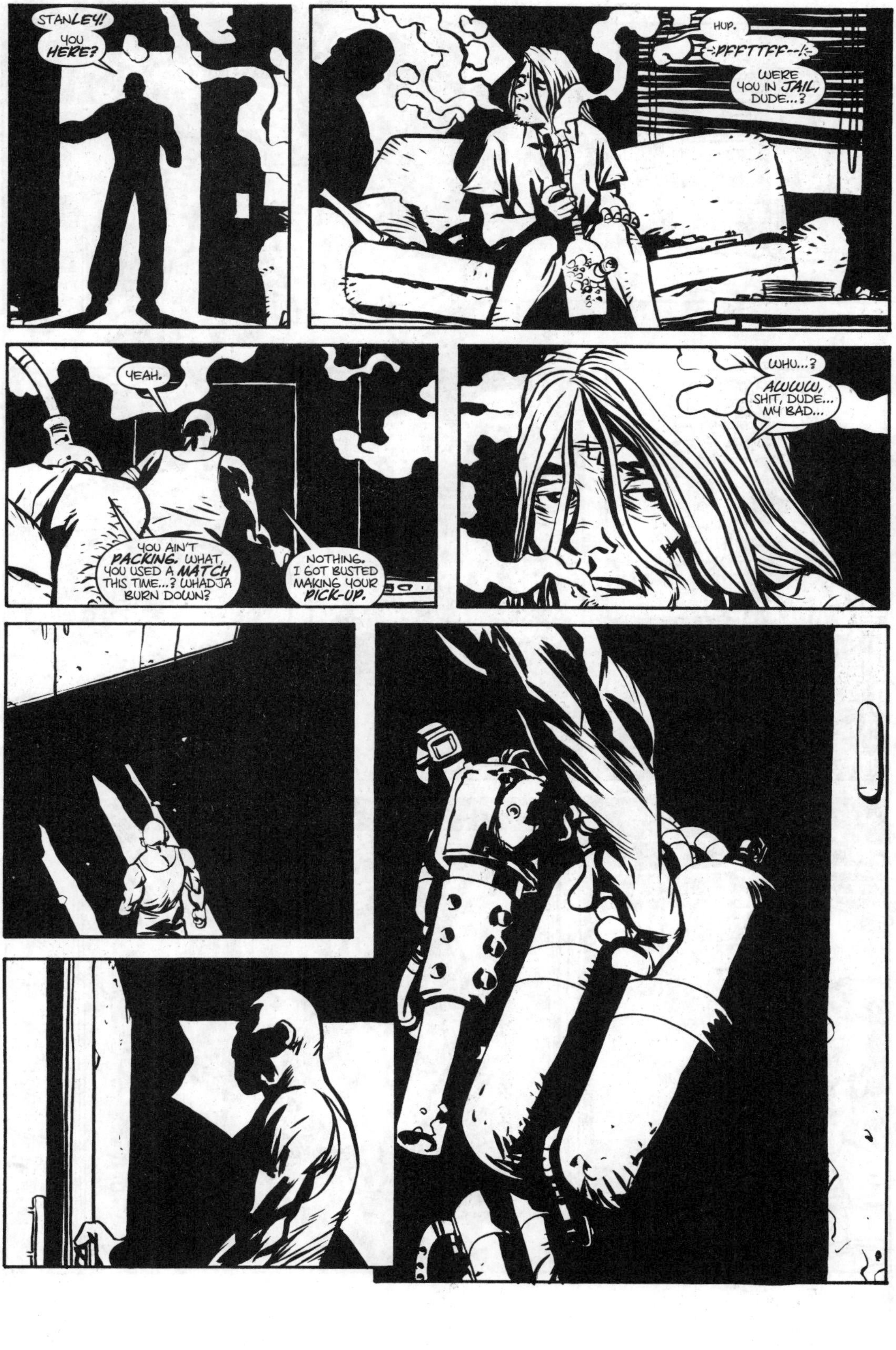

STANLEY!
YOU HERE?
HUP.
PFFTTFF--!
WERE YOU IN JAIL, DUDE...?
YEAH.
YOU AIN'T PACKING. WHAT, YOU USED A MATCH THIS TIME...? WHADJA BURN DOWN?
NOTHING. I GOT BUSTED MAKING YOUR PICK-UP.
WHU...?
AWWW, SHIT, DUDE... MY BAD...

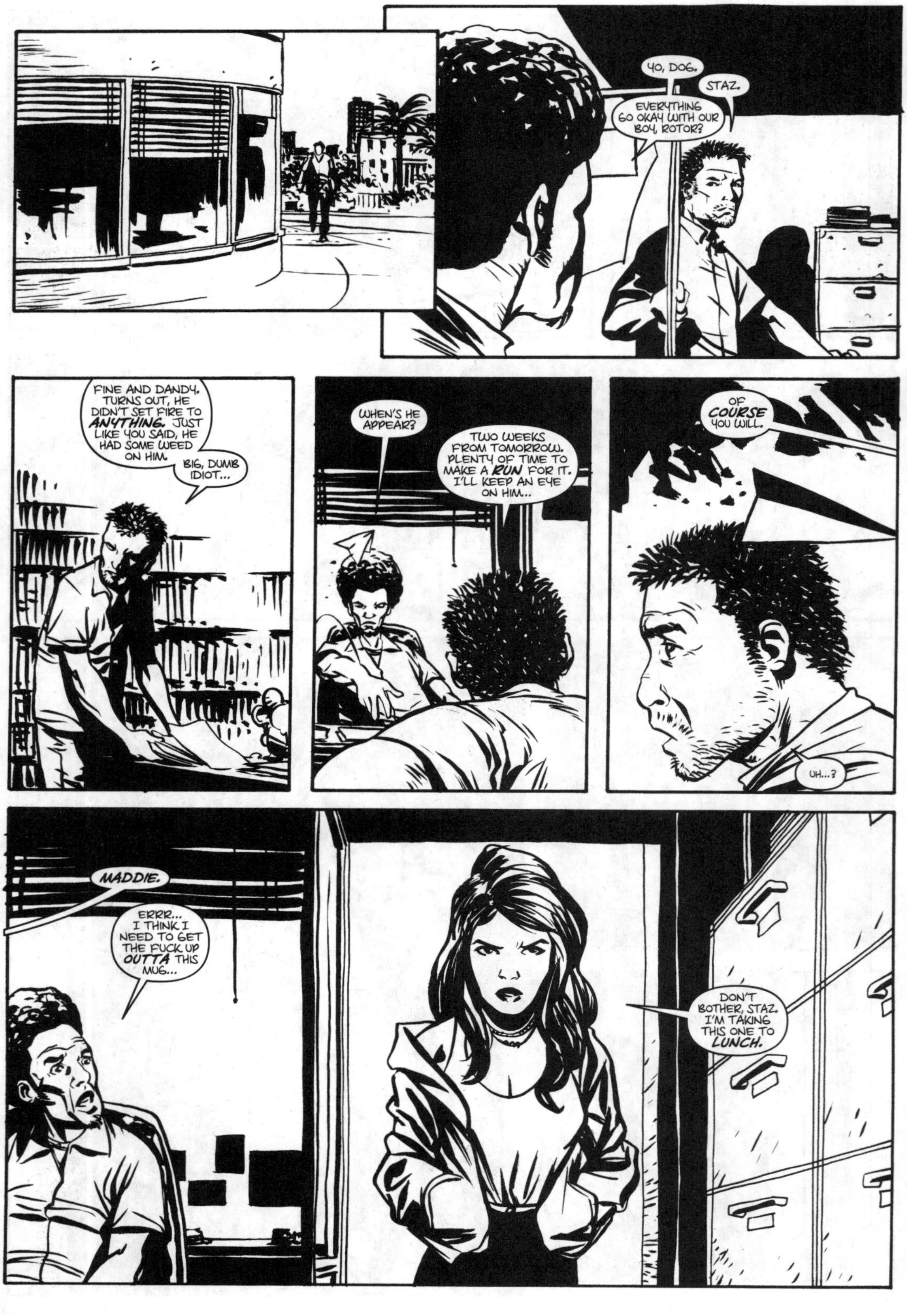
YO, DOG.
STAZ.
EVERYTHING GO OKAY WITH OUR BOY, ROTOR?
FINE AND DANDY. TURNS OUT, HE DIDN'T SET FIRE TO ANYTHING. JUST LIKE YOU SAID, HE HAD SOME WEED ON HIM.
BIG, DUMB IDIOT...
WHEN'S HE APPEAR?
TWO WEEKS FROM TOMORROW. PLENTY OF TIME TO MAKE A RUN FOR IT. I'LL KEEP AN EYE ON HIM...
OF COURSE YOU WILL.
UH...?
MADDIE.
ERRR... I THINK I NEED TO GET THE FUCK UP OUTTA THIS MUG...
DON'T BOTHER, STAZ. I'M TAKING THIS ONE TO LUNCH.

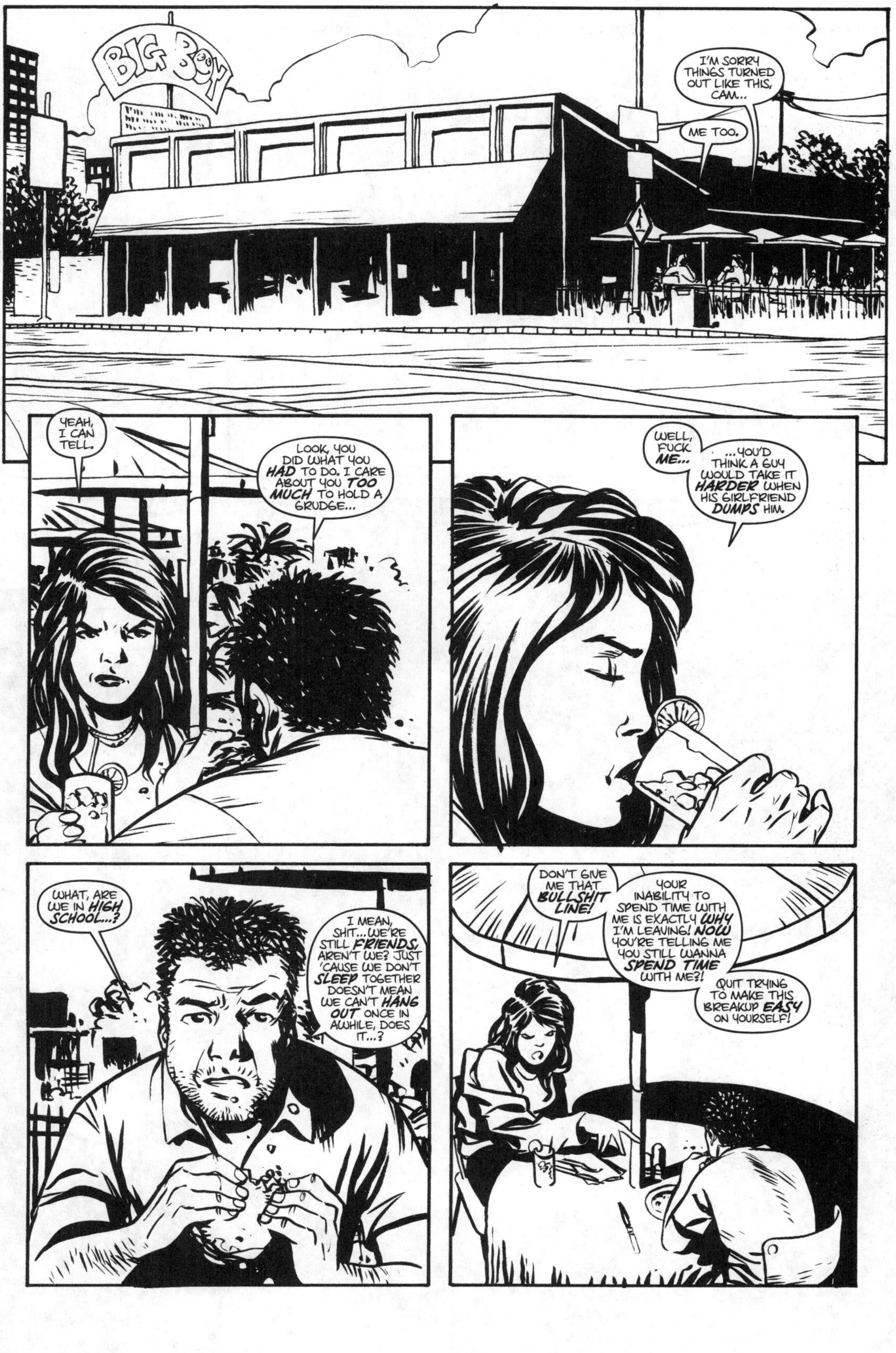

BIG BOY
I'M SORRY THINGS TURNED OUT LIKE THIS, CAM...
ME TOO.
YEAH, I CAN TELL.
LOOK, YOU DID WHAT YOU HAD TO DO. I CARE ABOUT YOU TOO MUCH TO HOLD A GRUDGE...
WELL, FUCK ME...
...YOU'D THINK A GUY WOULD TAKE IT HARDER WHEN HIS GIRLFRIEND DUMPS HIM.
WHAT, ARE WE IN HIGH SCHOOL...?
I MEAN, SHIT... WE'RE STILL FRIENDS, AREN'T WE? JUST 'CAUSE WE DON'T SLEEP TOGETHER DOESN'T MEAN WE CAN'T HANG OUT ONCE IN AWHILE, DOES IT...?
DON'T GIVE ME THAT BULLSHIT LINE!
YOUR INABILITY TO SPEND TIME WITH ME IS EXACTLY WHY I'M LEAVING! NOW YOU'RE TELLING ME YOU STILL WANNA SPEND TIME WITH ME?!
QUIT TRYING TO MAKE THIS BREAKUP EASY ON YOURSELF!

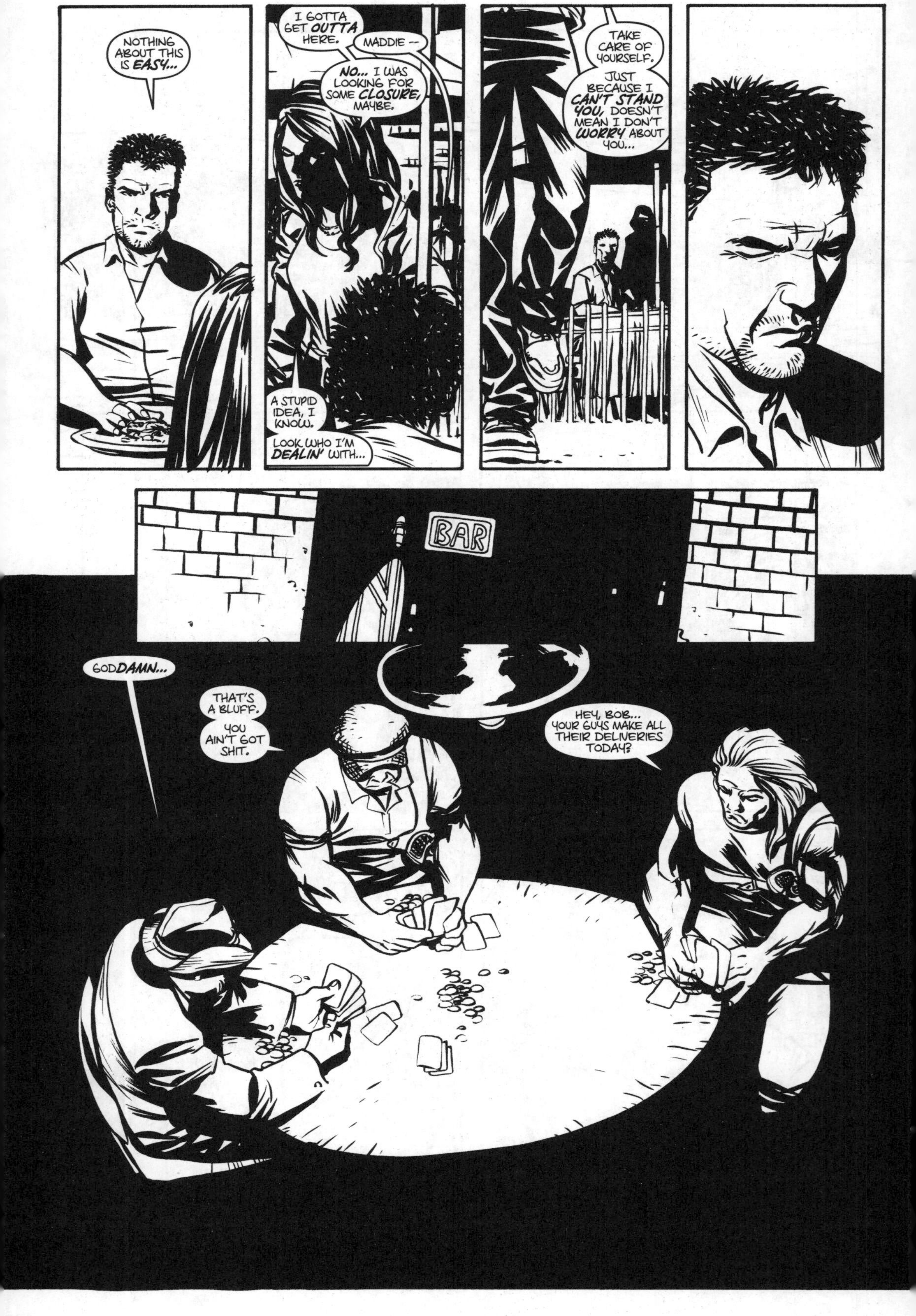
NOTHING ABOUT THIS IS EASY...
I GOTTA GET OUTTA HERE.
MADDIE --
NO... I WAS LOOKING FOR SOME CLOSURE, MAYBE.
A STUPID IDEA, I KNOW.
LOOK WHO I'M DEALIN' WITH...
TAKE CARE OF YOURSELF.
JUST BECAUSE I CAN'T STAND YOU, DOESN'T MEAN I DON'T WORRY ABOUT YOU...
BAR
GODDAMN...
THAT'S A BLUFF.
YOU AIN'T GOT SHIT.
HEY, BOB... YOUR GUYS MAKE ALL THEIR DELIVERIES TODAY?

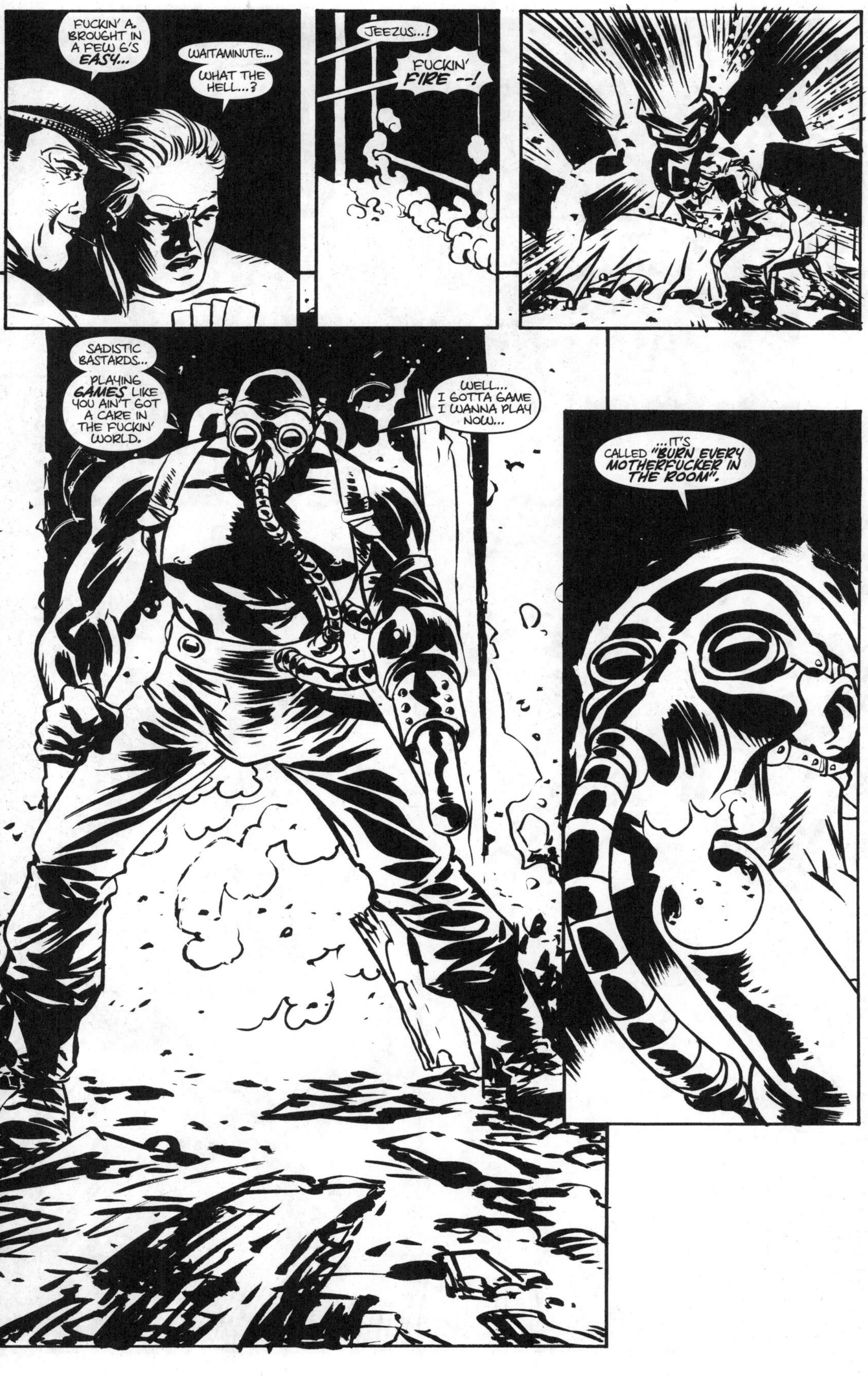
FUCKIN' A. BROUGHT IN A FEW G'S EASY...
WAITAMINUTE...
WHAT THE HELL...?
JEEZUS...!
FUCKIN' FIRE --!
SADISTIC BASTARDS...
PLAYING GAMES LIKE YOU AIN'T GOT A CARE IN THE FUCKIN' WORLD.
WELL... I GOTTA GAME I WANNA PLAY NOW...
...IT'S CALLED "BURN EVERY MOTHERFUCKER IN THE ROOM".

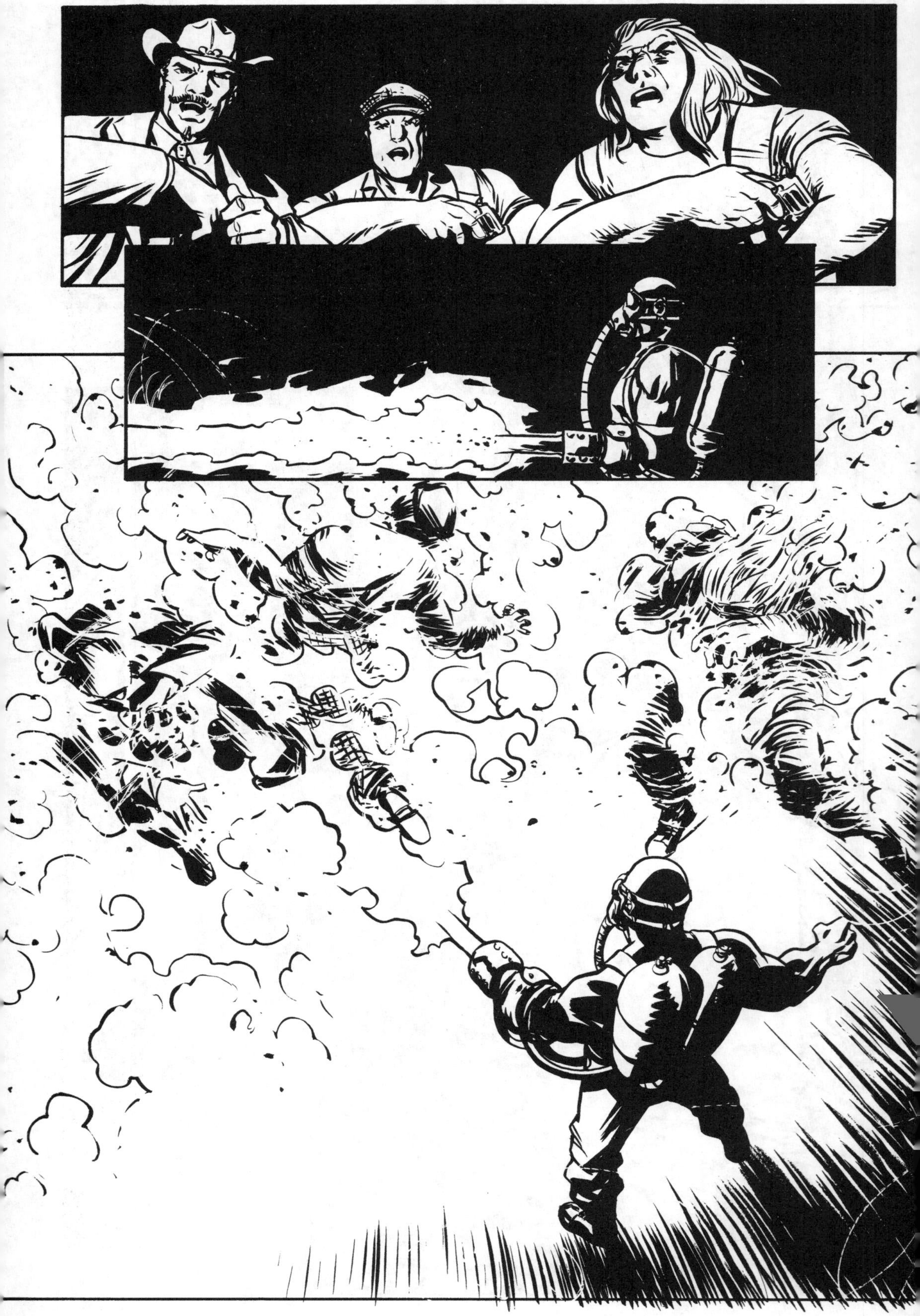

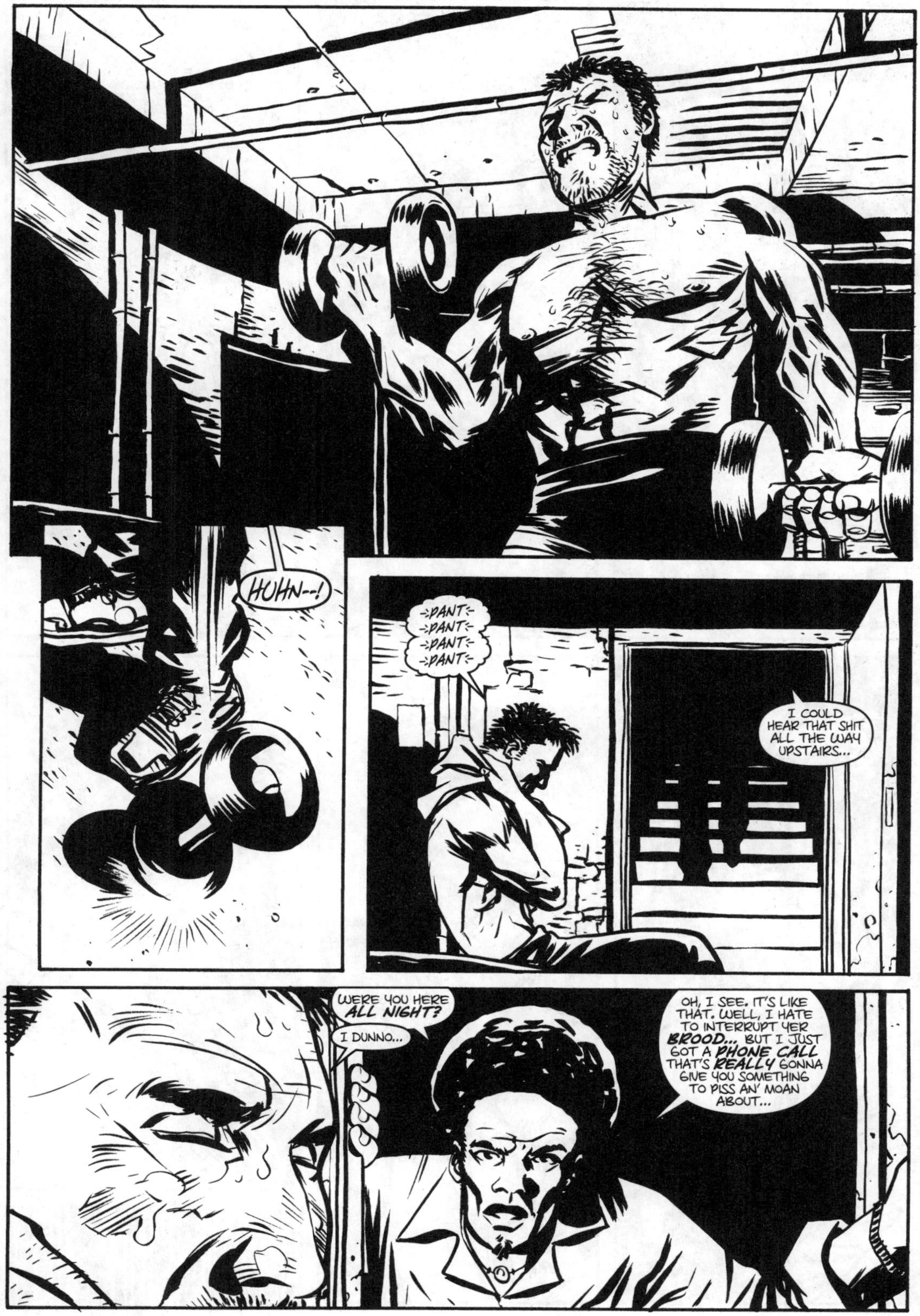
HUHN--!
-PANT -PANT -PANT -PANT
I COULD HEAR THAT SHIT ALL THE WAY UPSTAIRS...
WERE YOU HERE ALL NIGHT?
I DUNNO...
OH, I SEE. IT'S LIKE THAT. WELL, I HATE TO INTERRUPT YER BROOD... BUT I JUST GOT A PHONE CALL THAT'S REALLY GONNA GIVE YOU SOMETHING TO PISS AN' MOAN ABOUT...

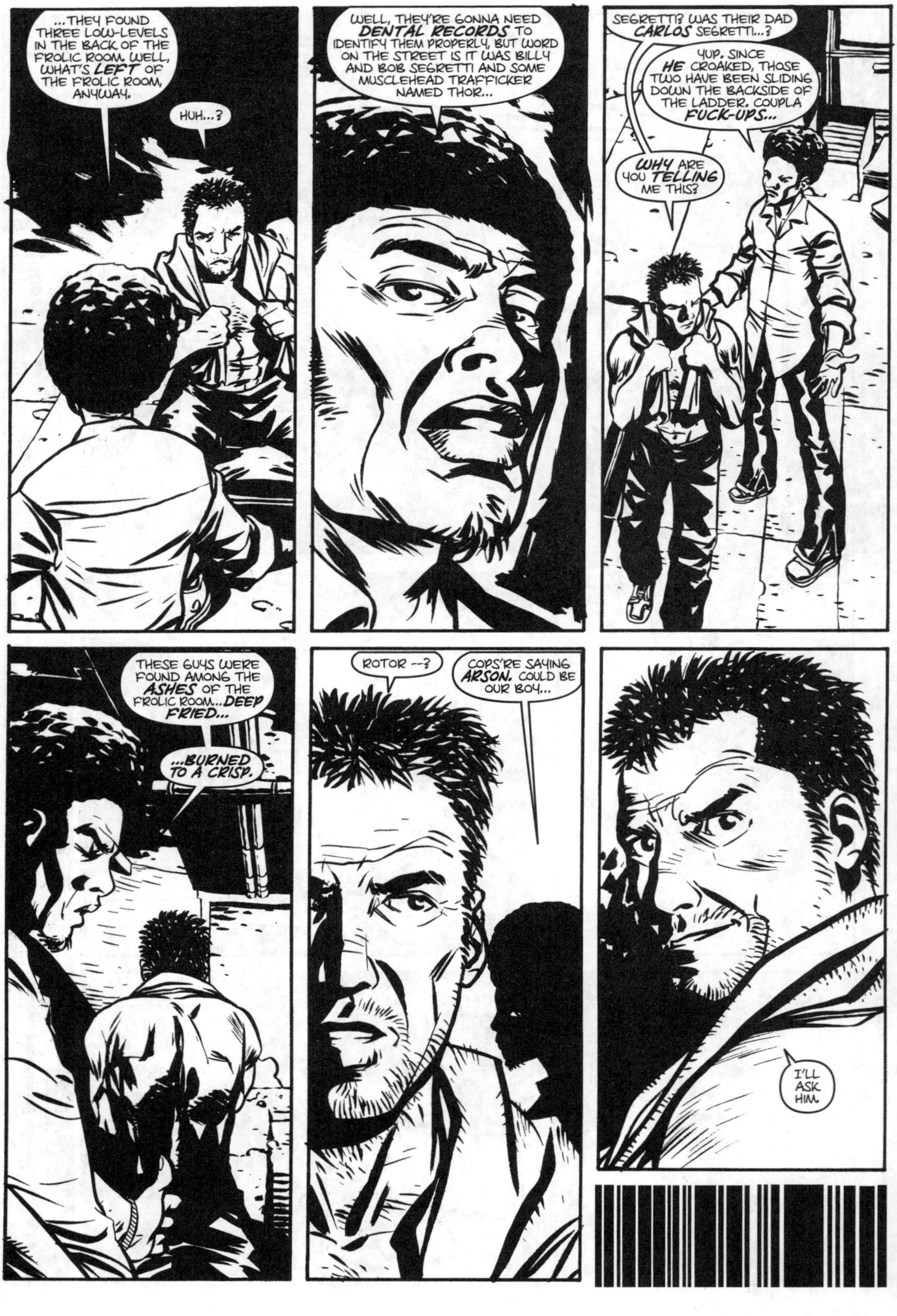
...THEY FOUND THREE LOW-LEVELS IN THE BACK OF THE FROLIC ROOM. WELL, WHAT'S LEFT OF THE FROLIC ROOM, ANYWAY.
HUH...?
WELL, THEY'RE GONNA NEED DENTAL RECORDS TO IDENTIFY THEM PROPERLY, BUT WORD ON THE STREET IS IT WAS BILLY AND BOB SEGRETTI AND SOME MUSCLEHEAD TRAFFICKER NAMED THOR...
SEGRETTI? WAS THEIR DAD CARLOS SEGRETTI...?
YUP. SINCE HE CROAKED, THOSE TWO HAVE BEEN SLIDING DOWN THE BACKSIDE OF THE LADDER. COUPLA FUCK-UPS...
WHY ARE YOU TELLING ME THIS?
THESE GUYS WERE FOUND AMONG THE ASHES OF THE FROLIC ROOM...DEEP FRIED...
...BURNED TO A CRISP.
ROTOR --?
COPS'RE SAYING ARSON. COULD BE OUR BOY...
I'LL ASK HIM.

There was something about the way the
metal rubbed his flesh. There would always
be a   rawness. Like a scratch on his soul,
never allowed to heal. A constant reminder
   of the road he'd taken. Terrifying and
unforgiving, a life descending into chaos...

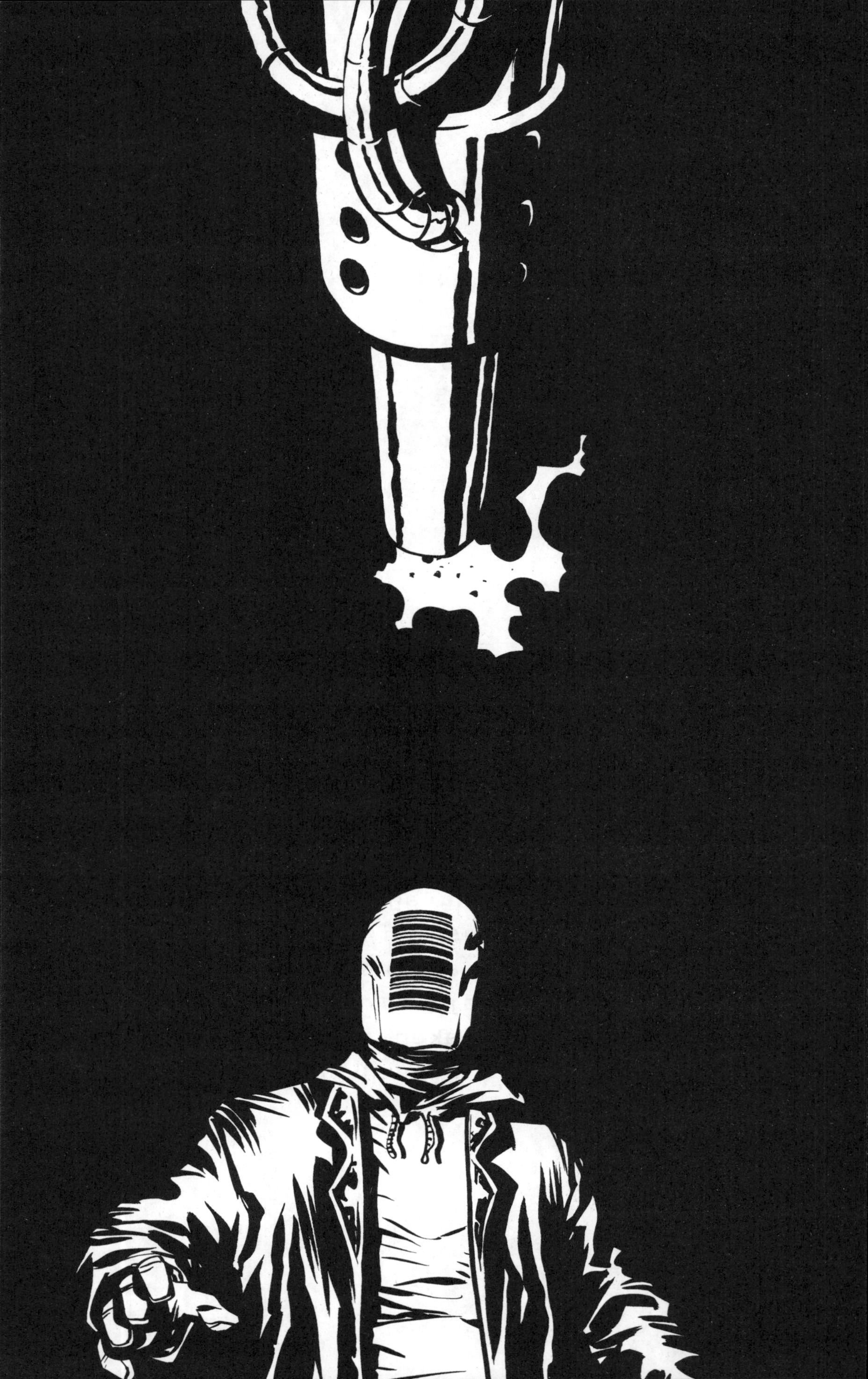

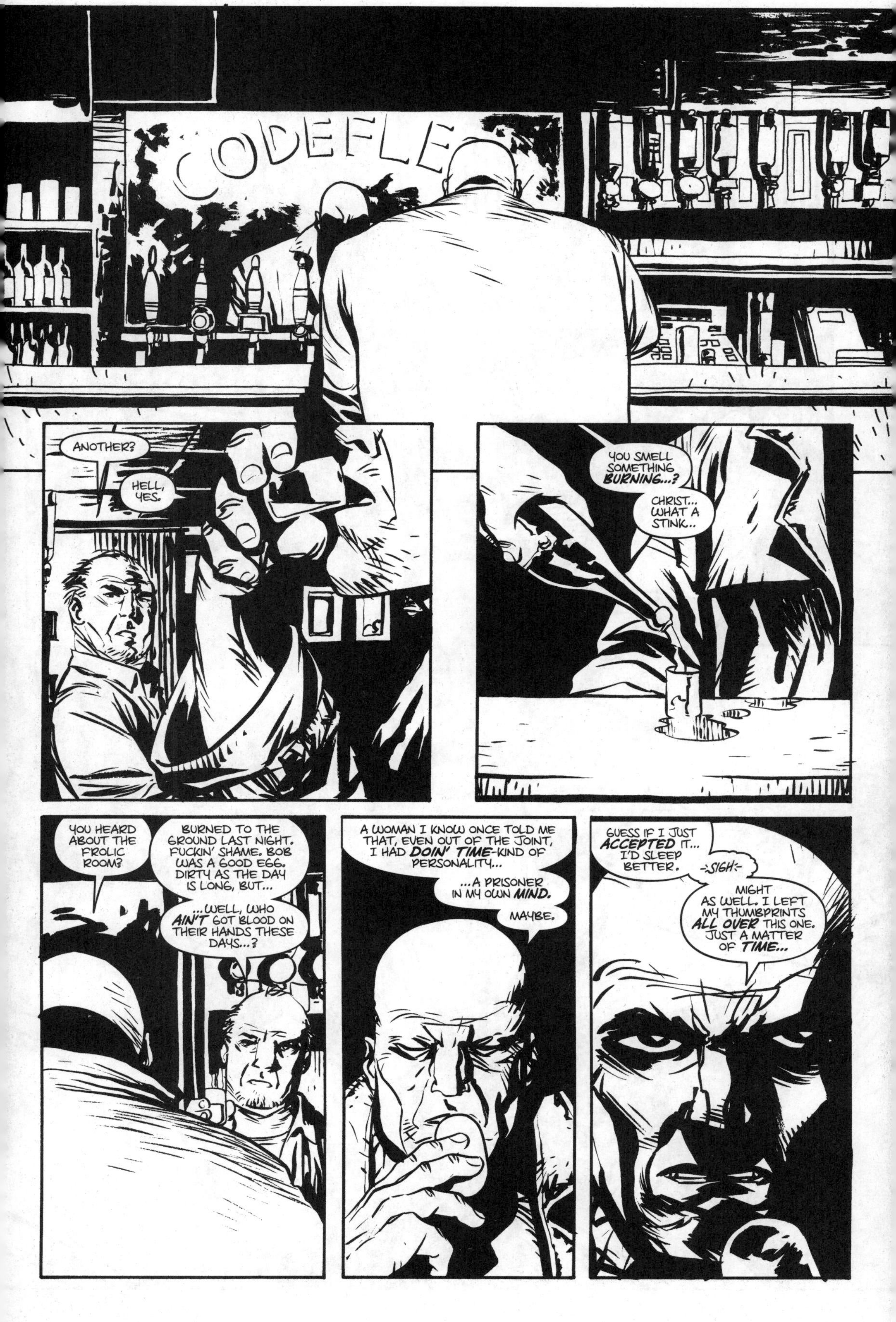
CODEFLE
ANOTHER?
HELL, YES.
YOU SMELL SOMETHING BURNING...?
CHRIST... WHAT A STINK...
YOU HEARD ABOUT THE FROLIC ROOM?
BURNED TO THE GROUND LAST NIGHT. FUCKIN' SHAME. BOB WAS A GOOD EGG. DIRTY AS THE DAY IS LONG, BUT...
...WELL, WHO AIN'T GOT BLOOD ON THEIR HANDS THESE DAYS...?
A WOMAN I KNOW ONCE TOLD ME THAT, EVEN OUT OF THE JOINT, I HAD DOIN' TIME-KIND OF PERSONALITY...
...A PRISONER IN MY OWN MIND.
MAYBE.
GUESS IF I JUST ACCEPTED IT... I'D SLEEP BETTER.
-SIGH-
MIGHT AS WELL. I LEFT MY THUMBPRINTS ALL OVER THIS ONE. JUST A MATTER OF TIME...

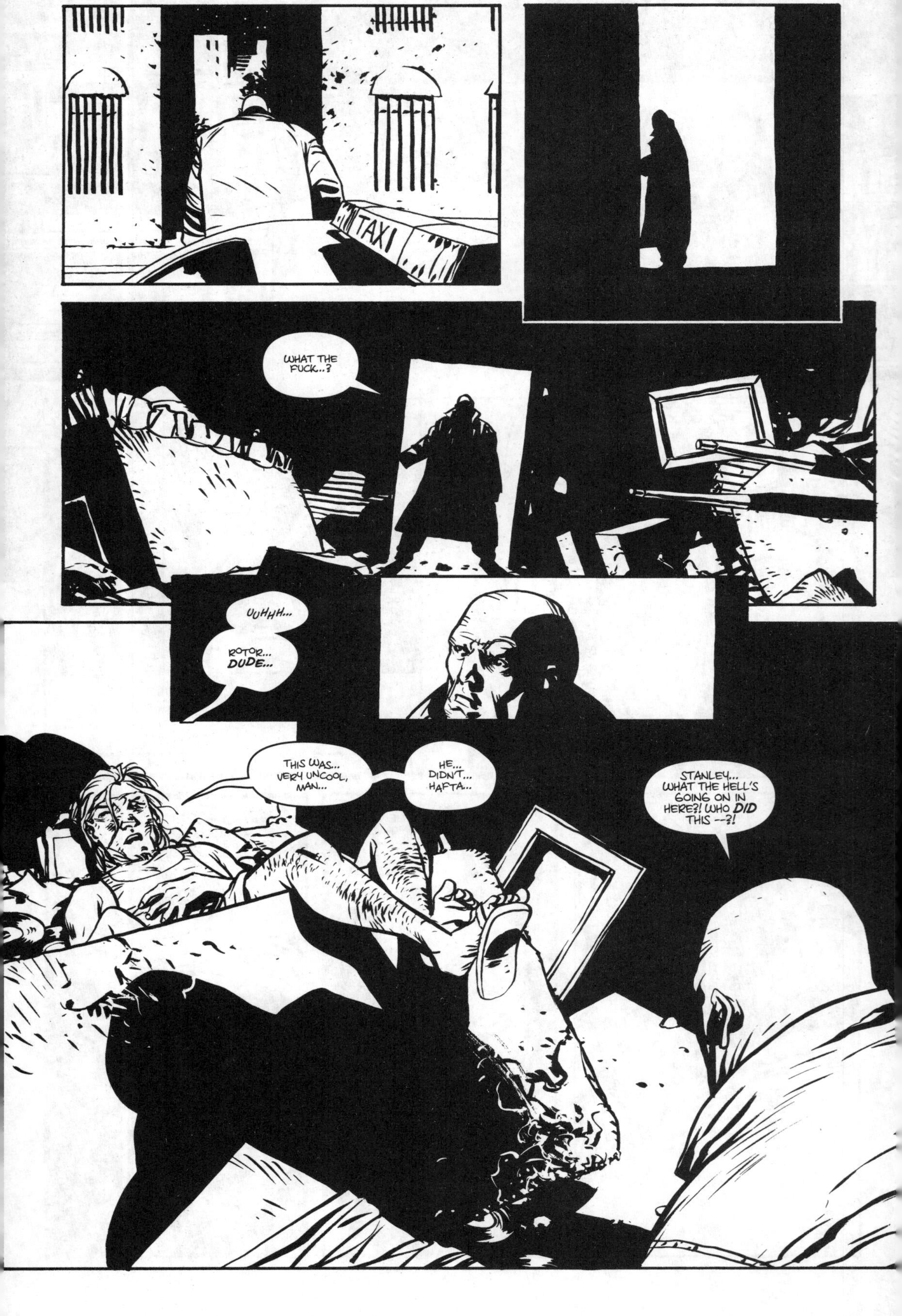

TAXI
WHAT THE FUCK...?
UUHHH...
ROTOR... DUDE...
THIS WAS... VERY UNCOOL, MAN...
HE... DIDN'T... HAFTA...
STANLEY... WHAT THE HELL'S GOING ON IN HERE?! WHO DID THIS --?!

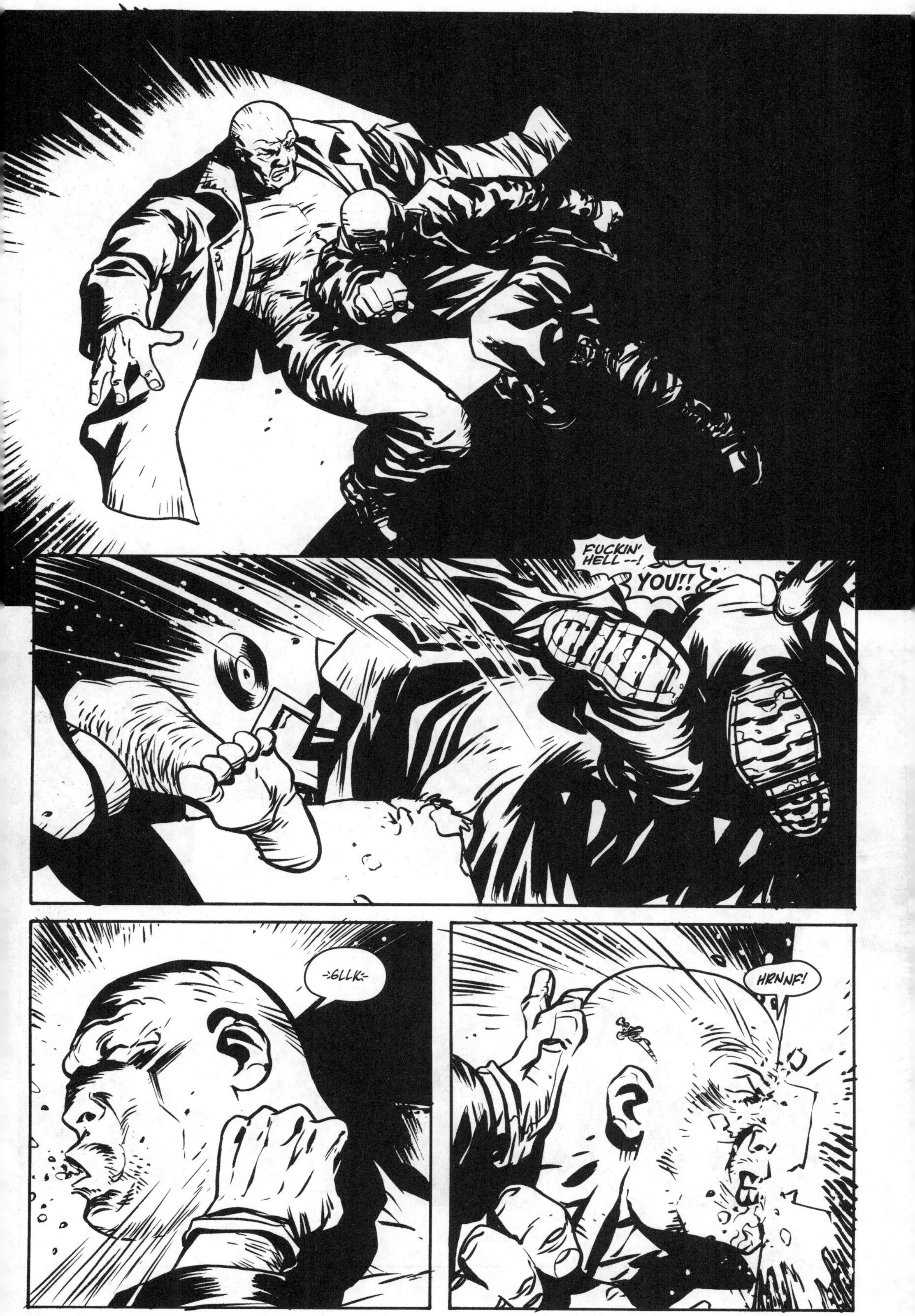
FUCKIN' HELL --!
YOU!!
-GLLK-
HRNNF!

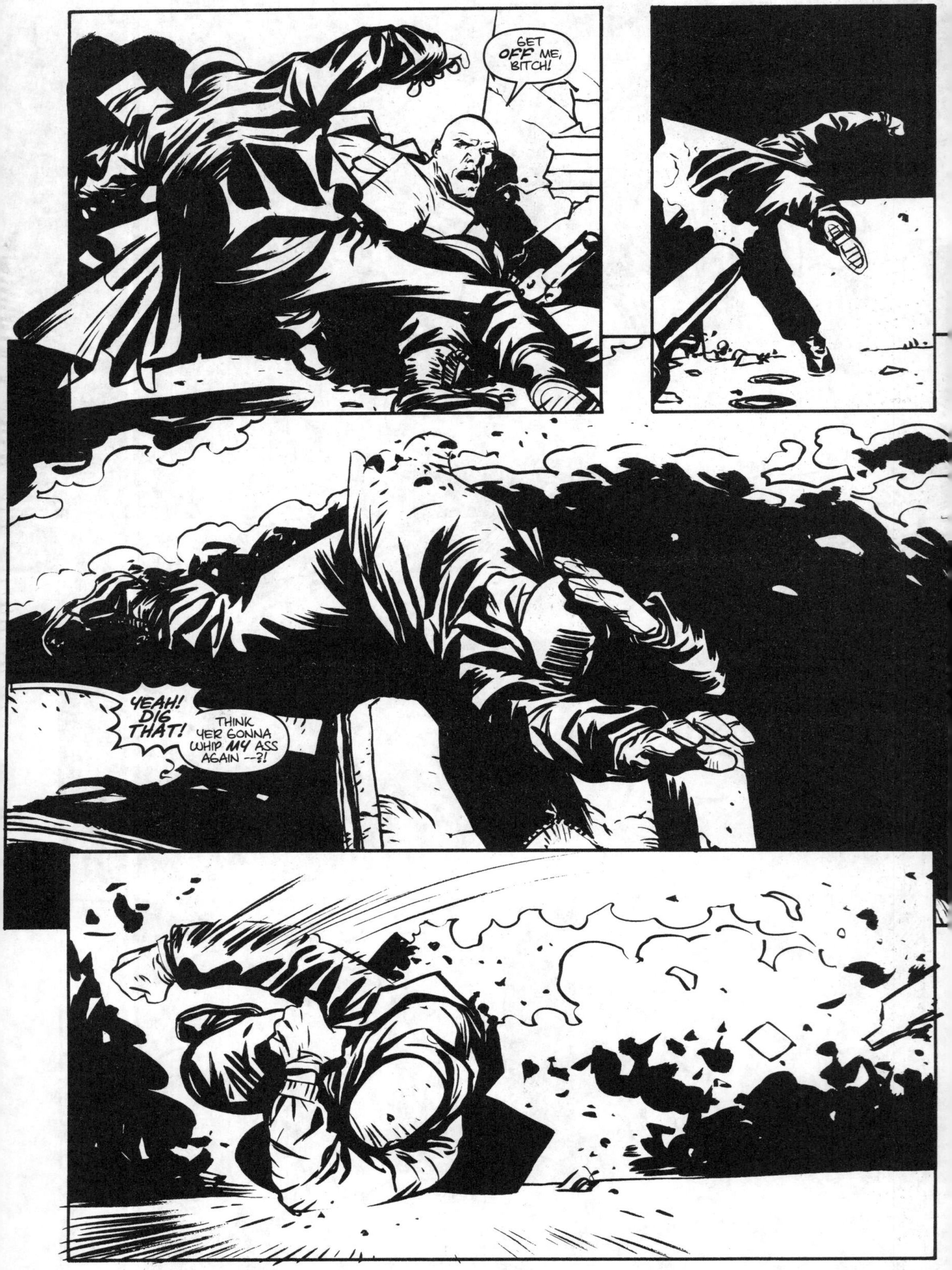
GET OFF ME, BITCH!
YEAH! DIG THAT!
THINK YER GONNA WHIP MY ASS AGAIN --?!

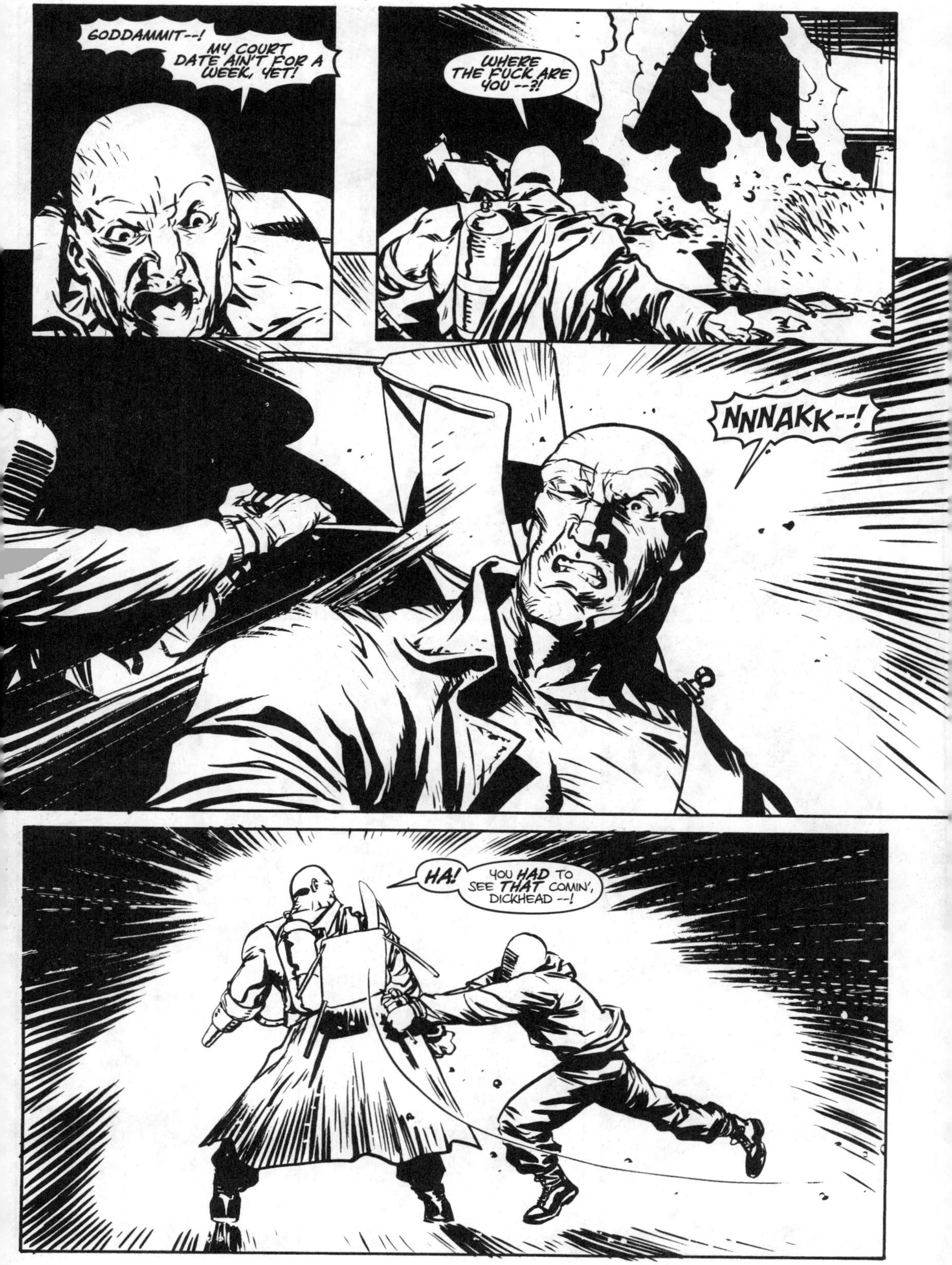
GODDAMMIT--! MY COURT DATE AIN'T FOR A WEEK, YET!
WHERE THE FUCK ARE YOU --?!
NNNAKK--!
HA!
YOU HAD TO SEE THAT COMIN', DICKHEAD --!

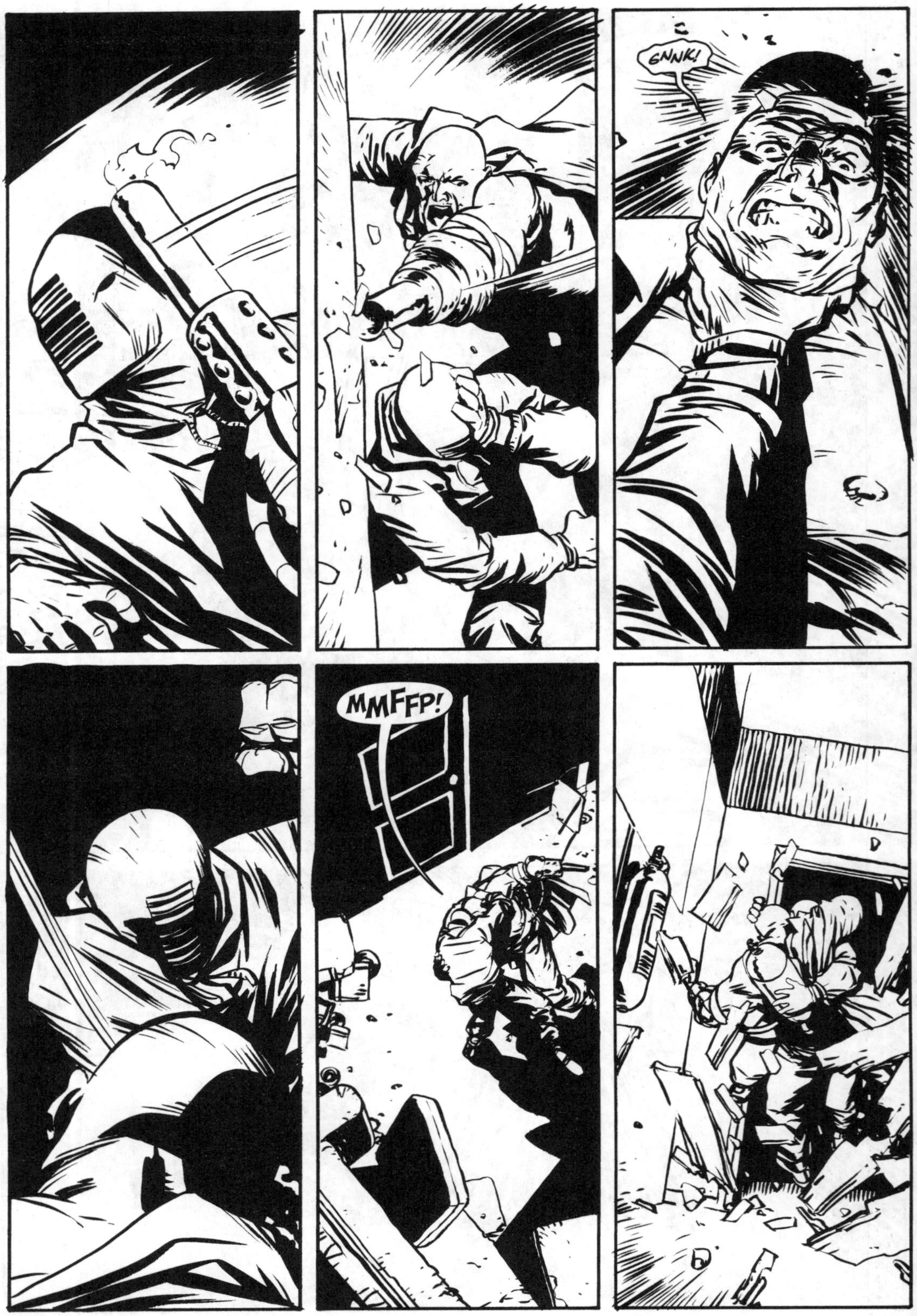
GNNK!
MMFFP!

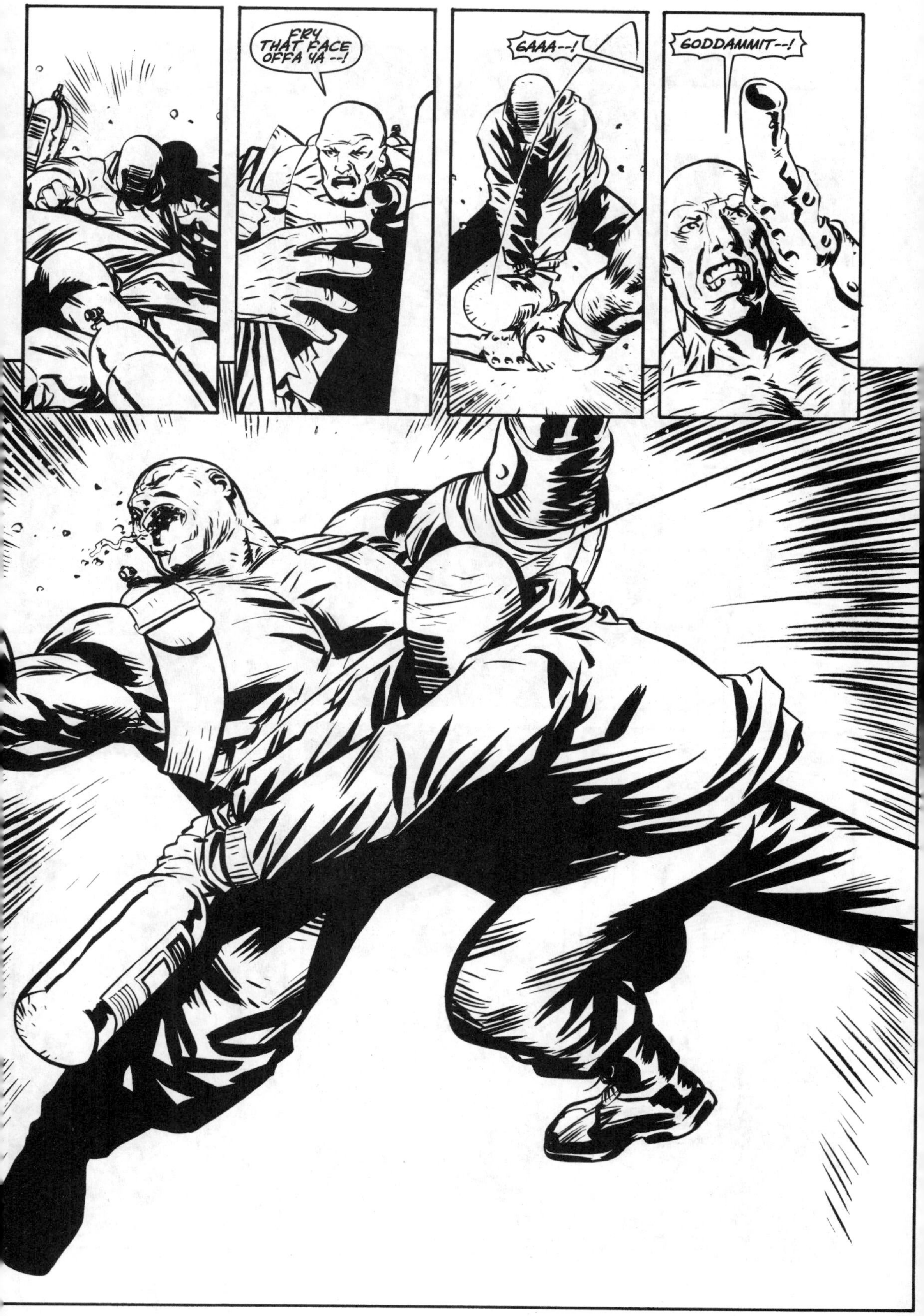
FRY THAT FACE OFFA YA --!
GAAA--!
GODDAMMIT--!

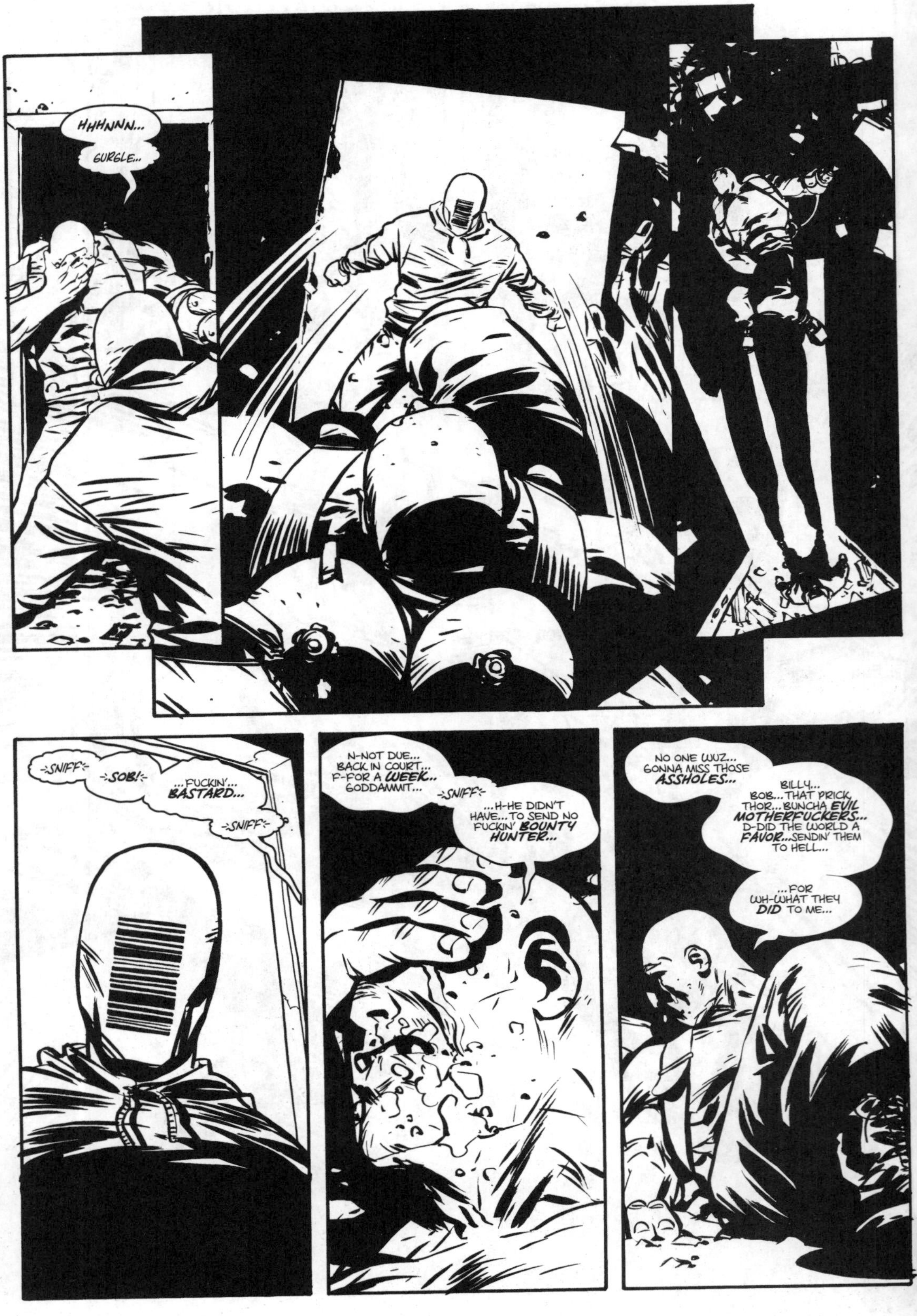
HHHNNN...
GURGLE...
-SNIFF-
-SOB!-
...FUCKIN' BASTARD...
-SNIFF-
N-NOT DUE... BACK IN COURT... F-FOR A WEEK... GODDAMMIT...
-SNIFF-
...H-HE DIDN'T HAVE... TO SEND NO FUCKIN' BOUNTY HUNTER...
NO ONE WUZ... GONNA MISS THOSE ASSHOLES...
BILLY... BOB... THAT PRICK THOR... BUNCHA EVIL MOTHERFUCKERS... D-DID THE WORLD A FAVOR... SENDIN' THEM TO HELL...
...FOR WH-WHAT THEY DID TO ME...

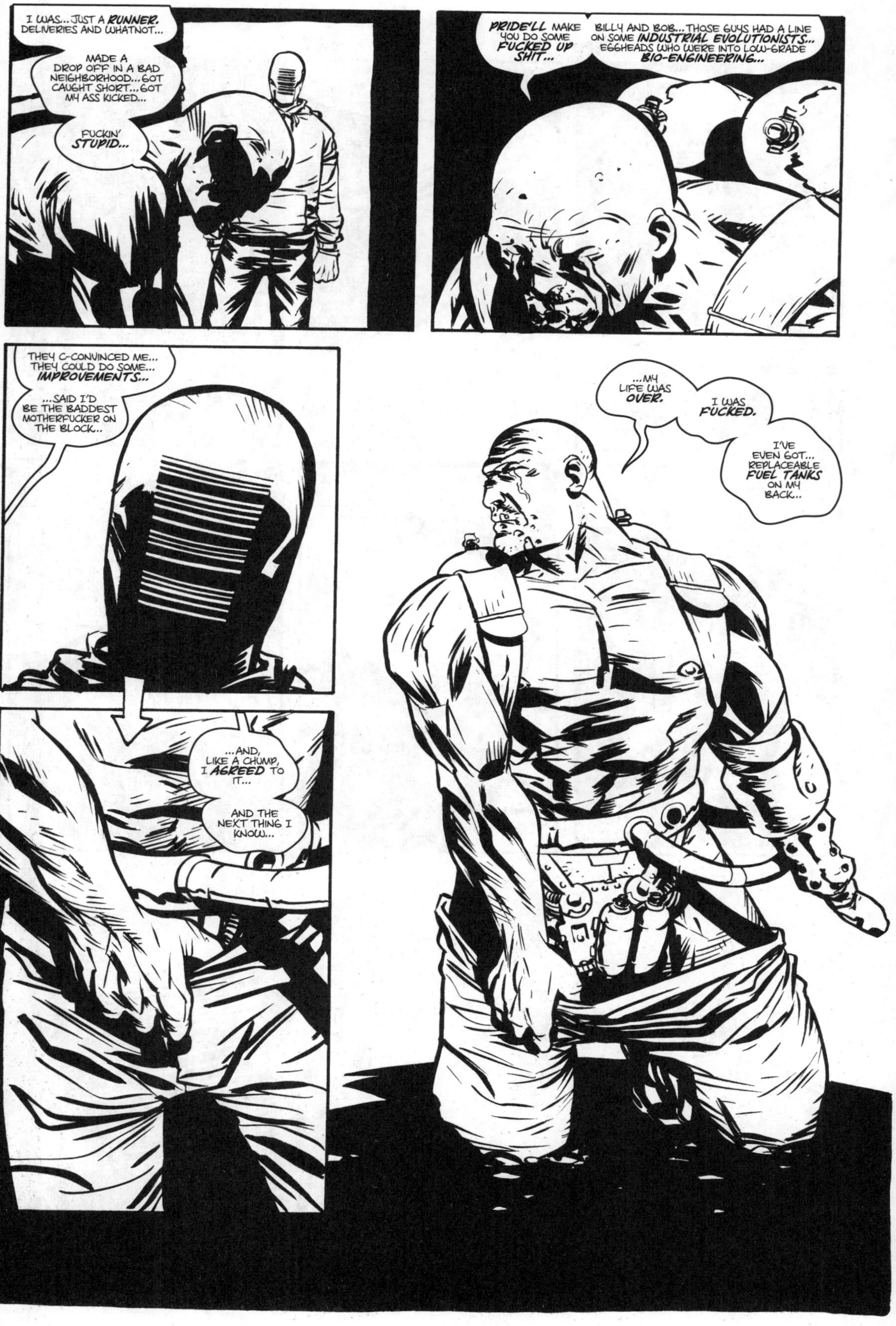
I WAS... JUST A RUNNER. DELIVERIES AND WHATNOT...
MADE A DROP OFF IN A BAD NEIGHBORHOOD... GOT CAUGHT SHORT... GOT MY ASS KICKED...
FUCKIN' STUPID...
PRIDE'LL MAKE YOU DO SOME FUCKED UP SHIT...
BILLY AND BOB... THOSE GUYS HAD A LINE ON SOME INDUSTRIAL EVOLUTIONISTS... EGGHEADS WHO WERE INTO LOW-GRADE BIO-ENGINEERING...
THEY C-CONVINCED ME... THEY COULD DO SOME... IMPROVEMENTS...
...SAID I'D BE THE BADDEST MOTHERFUCKER ON THE BLOCK...
...AND, LIKE A CHUMP, I AGREED TO IT...
AND THE NEXT THING I KNOW...
...MY LIFE WAS OVER.
I WAS FUCKED.
I'VE EVEN GOT... REPLACEABLE FUEL TANKS ON MY BACK...

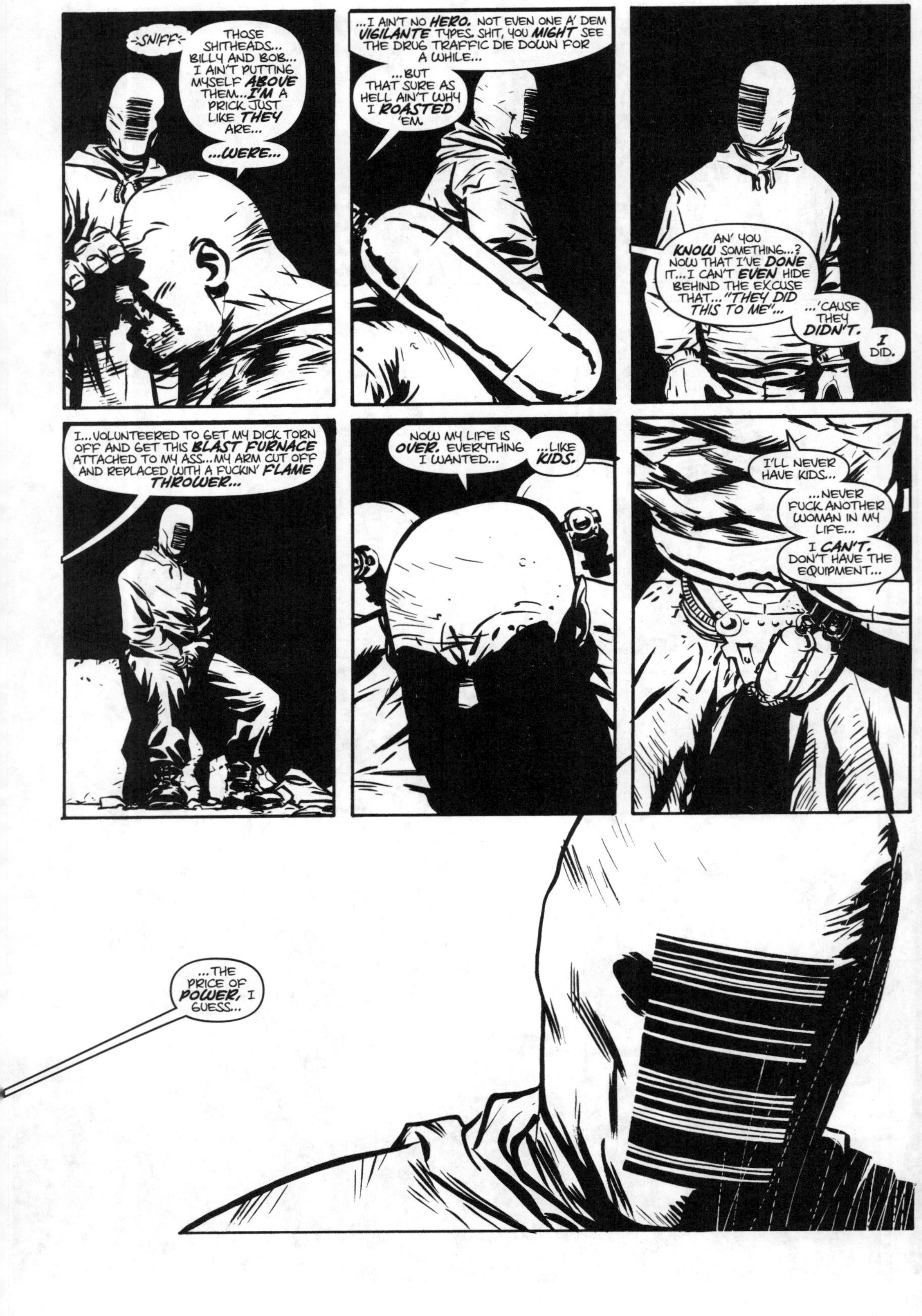
-SNIFF-
THOSE SHITHEADS... BILLY AND BOB... I AIN'T PUTTING MYSELF ABOVE THEM...I'M A PRICK JUST LIKE THEY ARE...
...WERE...
...I AIN'T NO HERO. NOT EVEN ONE A' DEM VIGILANTE TYPES. SHIT, YOU MIGHT SEE THE DRUG TRAFFIC DIE DOWN FOR A WHILE...
...BUT THAT SURE AS HELL AIN'T WHY I ROASTED 'EM.
AN' YOU KNOW SOMETHING...? NOW THAT I'VE DONE IT...I CAN'T EVEN HIDE BEHIND THE EXCUSE THAT..."THEY DID THIS TO ME"...
...'CAUSE THEY DIDN'T.
I DID.
I...VOLUNTEERED TO GET MY DICK TORN OFF AND GET THIS BLAST FURNACE ATTACHED TO MY ASS...MY ARM CUT OFF AND REPLACED WITH A FUCKIN' FLAME THROWER...
NOW MY LIFE IS OVER. EVERYTHING I WANTED...
...LIKE KIDS.
I'LL NEVER HAVE KIDS...
...NEVER FUCK ANOTHER WOMAN IN MY LIFE...
I CAN'T. DON'T HAVE THE EQUIPMENT...
...THE PRICE OF POWER, I GUESS...

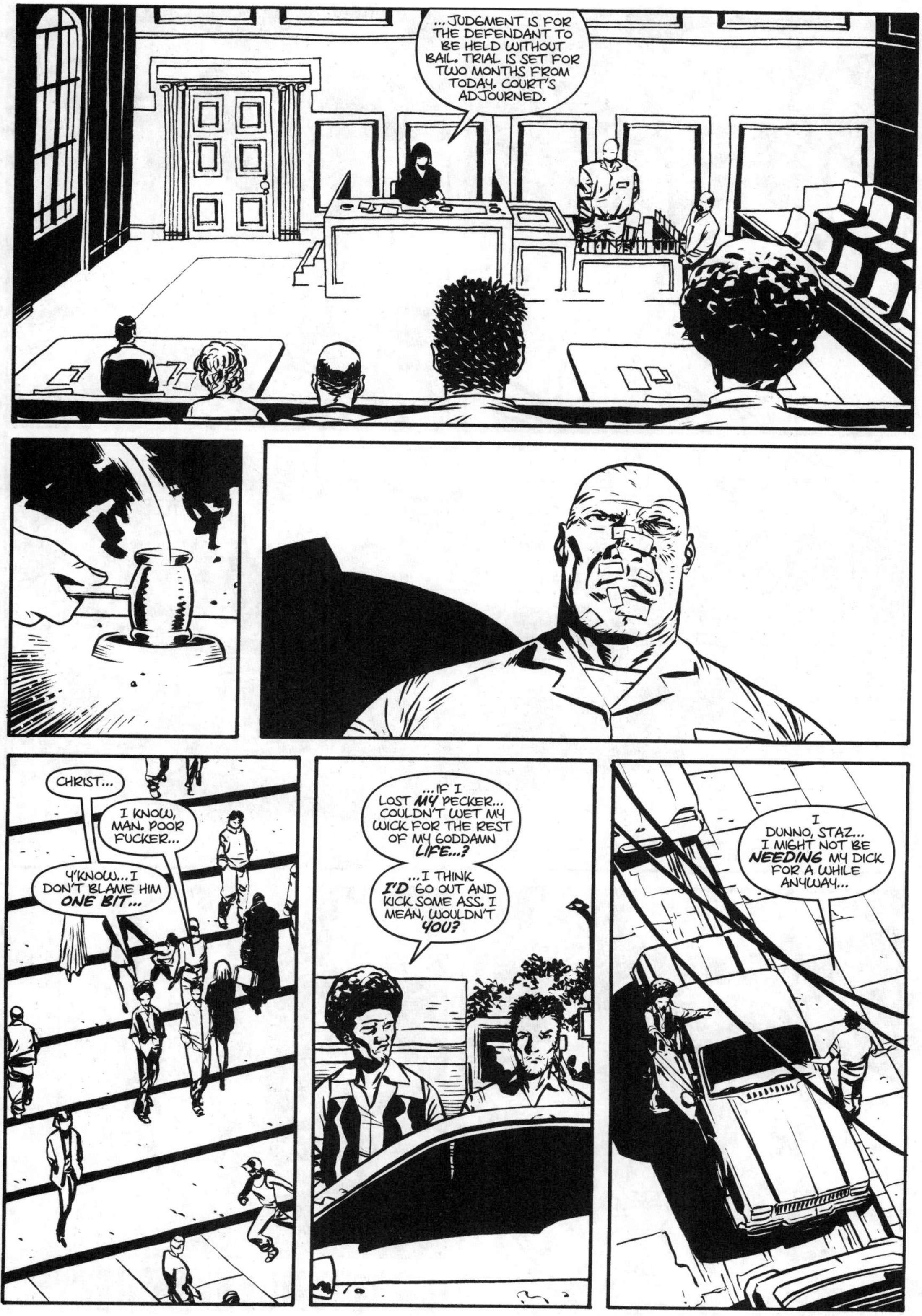
...JUDGMENT IS FOR THE DEFENDANT TO BE HELD WITHOUT BAIL. TRIAL IS SET FOR TWO MONTHS FROM TODAY. COURT'S ADJOURNED.
CHRIST...
I KNOW, MAN. POOR FUCKER...
Y'KNOW...I DON'T BLAME HIM ONE BIT...
...IF I LOST MY PECKER... COULDN'T WET MY WICK FOR THE REST OF MY GODDAMN LIFE...?
...I THINK I'D GO OUT AND KICK SOME ASS. I MEAN, WOULDN'T YOU?
I DUNNO, STAZ... I MIGHT NOT BE NEEDING MY DICK FOR A WHILE ANYWAY...

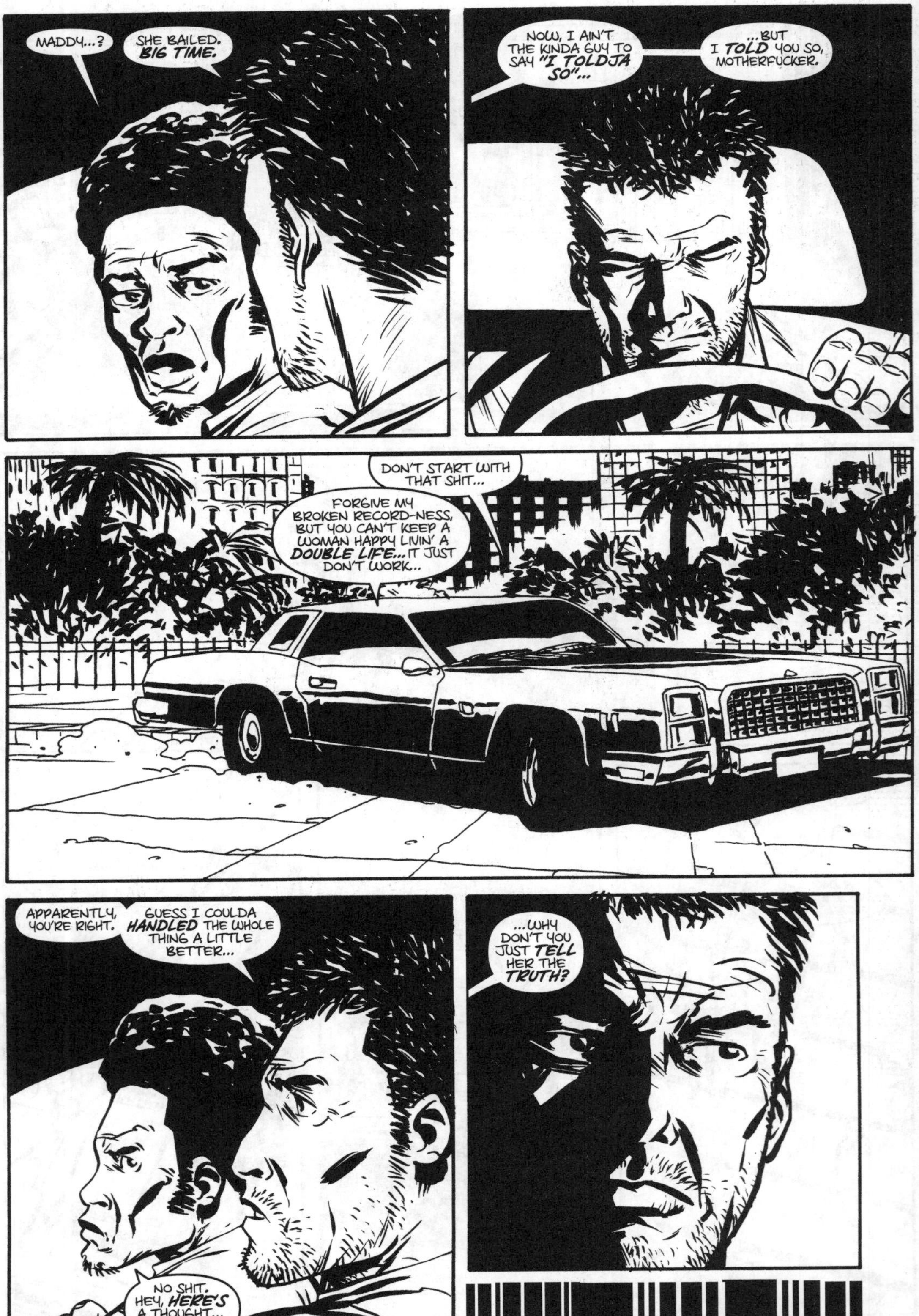
MADDY...?
SHE BAILED. BIG TIME.
NOW, I AIN'T THE KINDA GUY TO SAY "I TOLDJA SO"...
...BUT I TOLD YOU SO, MOTHERFUCKER.
FORGIVE MY BROKEN RECORD-NESS, BUT YOU CAN'T KEEP A WOMAN HAPPY LIVIN' A DOUBLE LIFE... IT JUST DON'T WORK...
DON'T START WITH THAT SHIT...
APPARENTLY, YOU'RE RIGHT.
GUESS I COULDA HANDLED THE WHOLE THING A LITTLE BETTER...
NO SHIT. HEY, HERE'S A THOUGHT...
...WHY DON'T YOU JUST TELL HER THE TRUTH?

He knew the smell of burning flesh. He knew it was the smell of death, all too familiar. At this point, it was kill or be killed. Survival of the fittest. This one had just moved beyond bonding some asshole out of County. He felt a steel-toed boot crushing against his sternum...

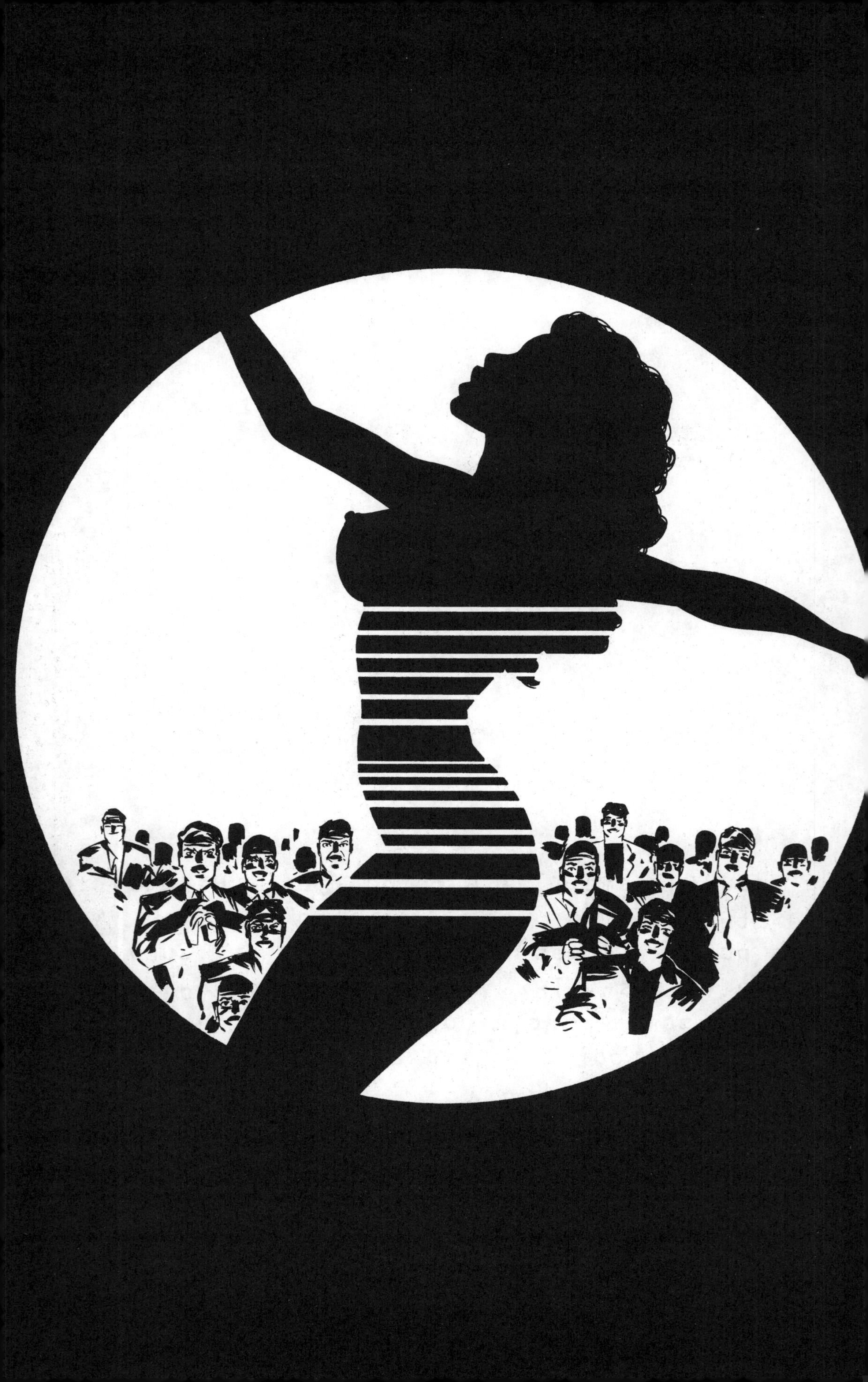

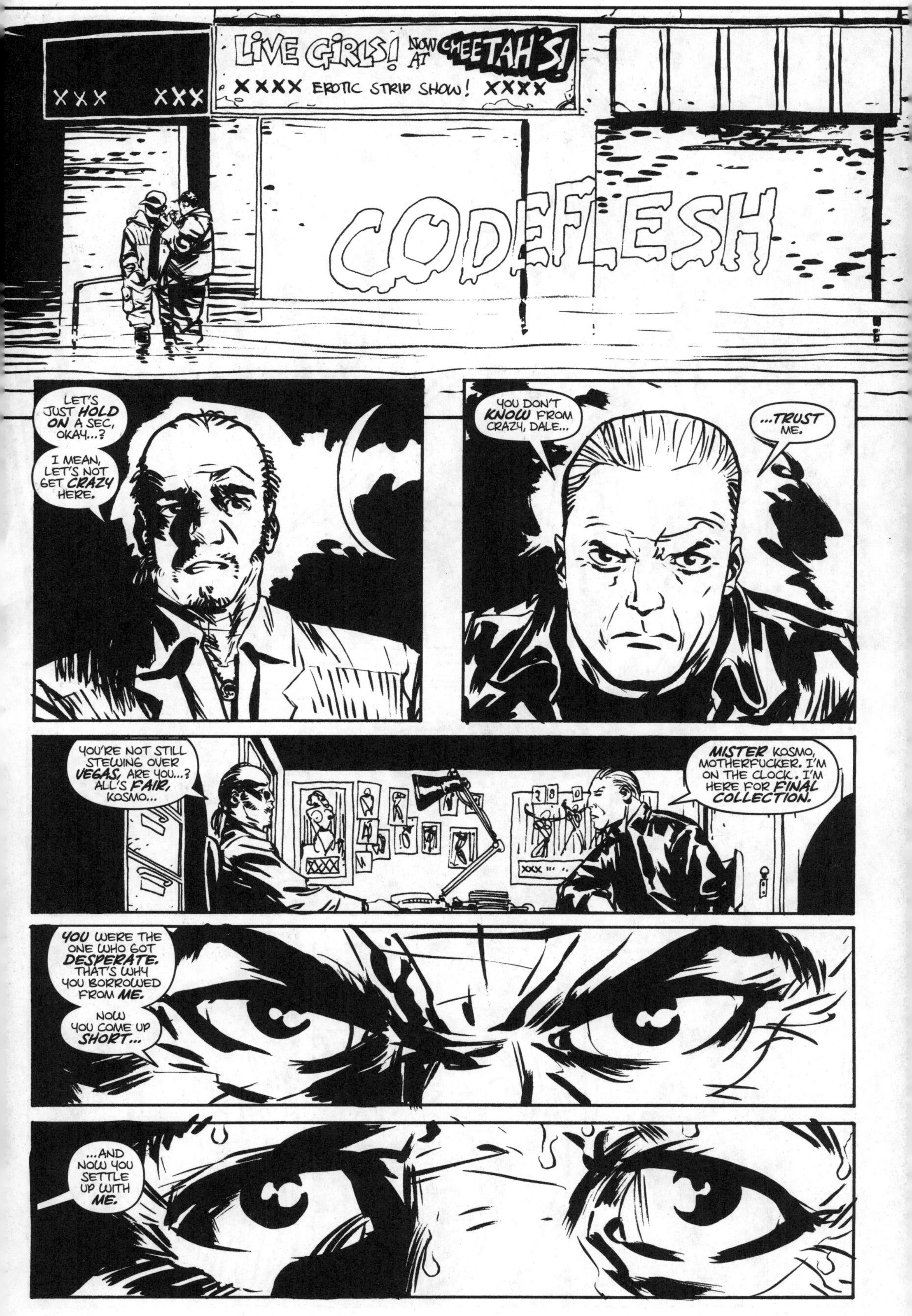

LIVE GIRLS! NOW AT CHEETAH'S!
XXXX EROTIC STRIP SHOW! XXXX
XXX XXX
CODEFLESH
LET'S JUST HOLD ON A SEC, OKAY...?
I MEAN, LET'S NOT GET CRAZY HERE.
YOU DON'T KNOW FROM CRAZY, DALE...
...TRUST ME.
YOU'RE NOT STILL STEWING OVER VEGAS, ARE YOU...? ALL'S FAIR, KOSMO...
MISTER KOSMO, MOTHERFUCKER. I'M ON THE CLOCK. I'M HERE FOR FINAL COLLECTION.
YOU WERE THE ONE WHO GOT DESPERATE. THAT'S WHY YOU BORROWED FROM ME.
NOW YOU COME UP SHORT...
...AND NOW YOU SETTLE UP WITH ME.

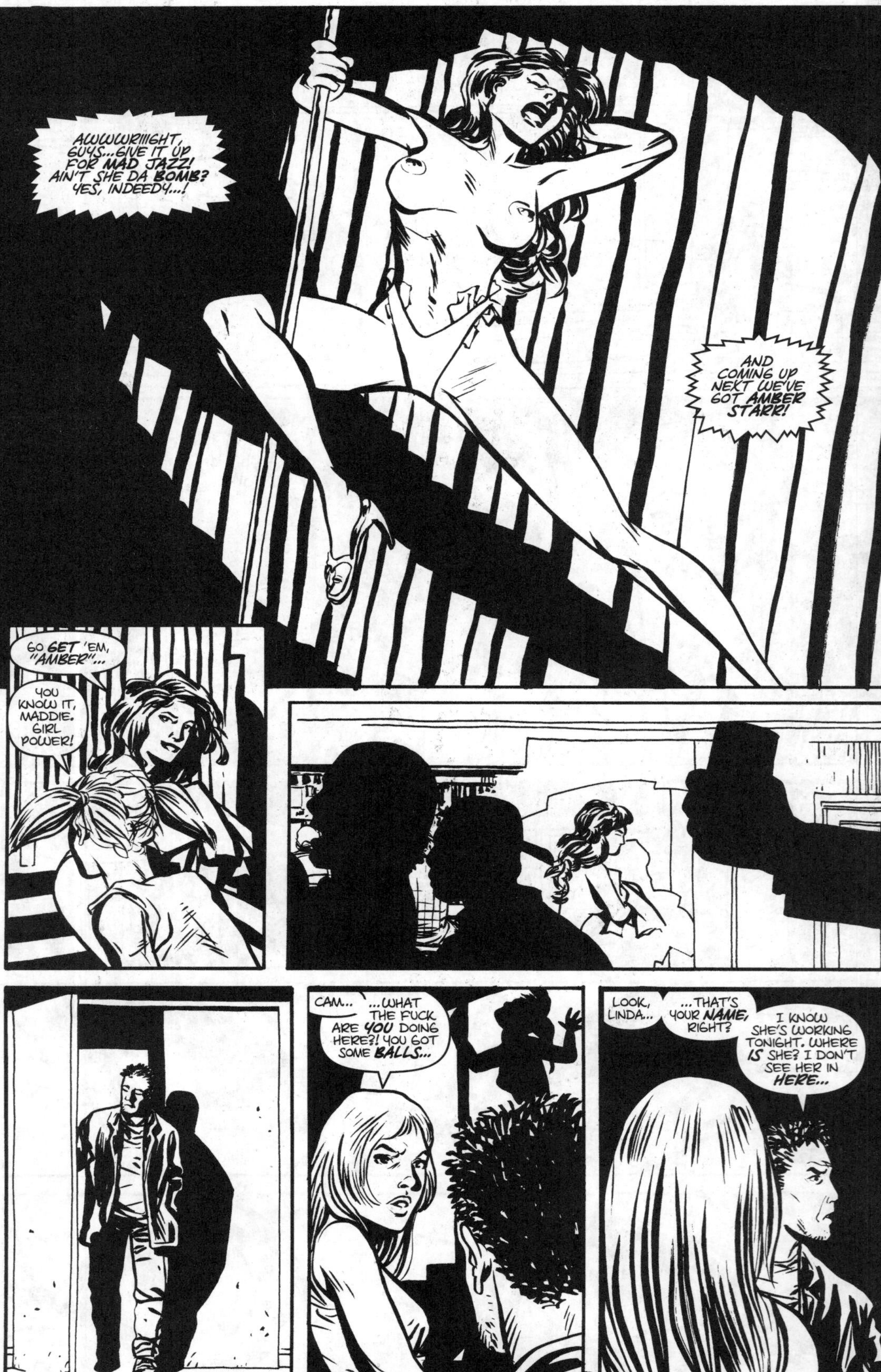
AWWWRIIIGHT, GUYS...GIVE IT UP FOR MAD JAZZ! AIN'T SHE DA BOMB? YES, INDEEDY...!
AND COMING UP NEXT WE'VE GOT AMBER STARR!
GO GET 'EM, "AMBER"...
YOU KNOW IT, MADDIE. GIRL POWER!
CAM...
...WHAT THE FUCK ARE YOU DOING HERE?! YOU GOT SOME BALLS...
LOOK, LINDA...
...THAT'S YOUR NAME, RIGHT?
I KNOW SHE'S WORKING TONIGHT. WHERE IS SHE? I DON'T SEE HER IN HERE...

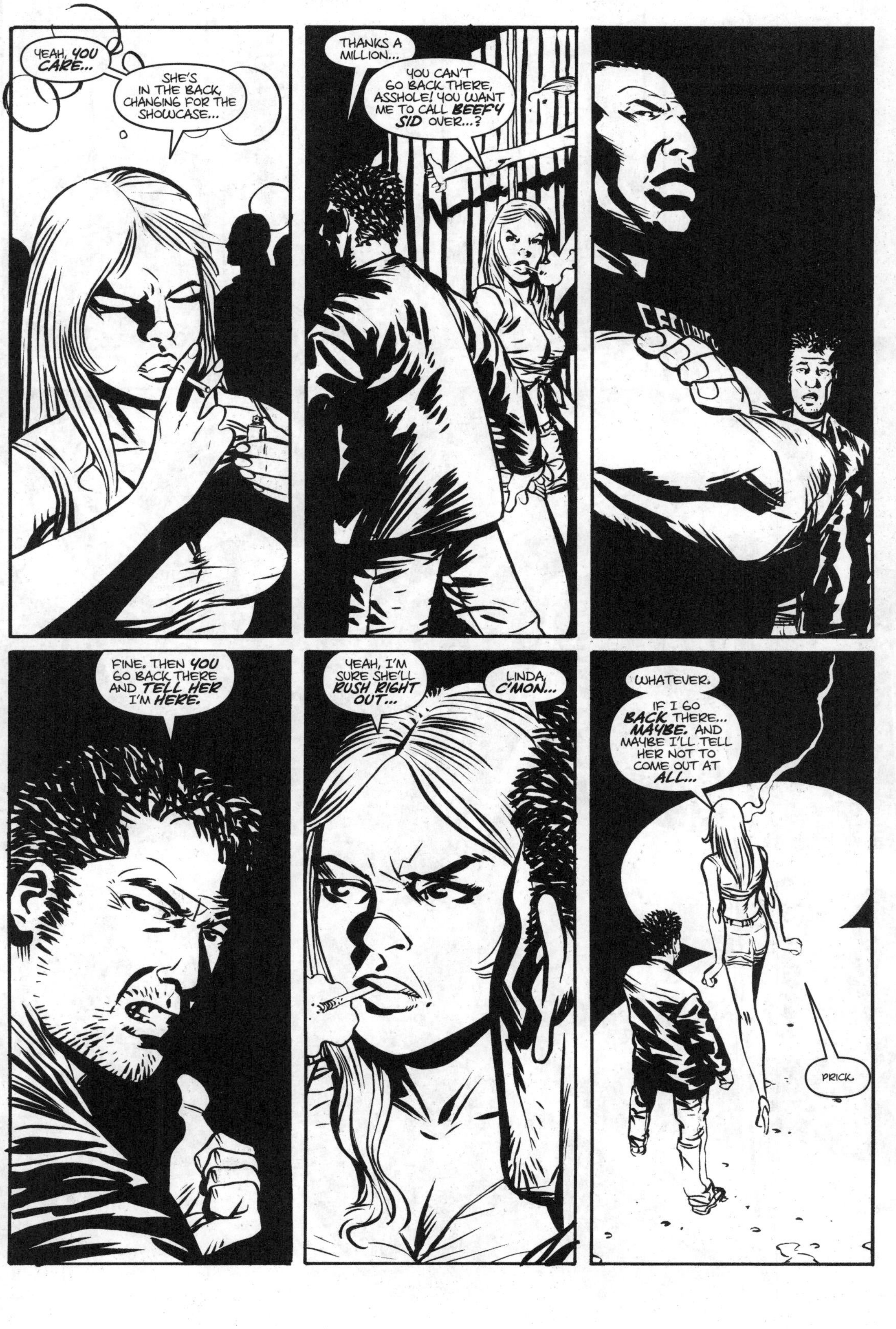
YEAH, YOU CARE...
SHE'S IN THE BACK, CHANGING FOR THE SHOWCASE...
THANKS A MILLION...
YOU CAN'T GO BACK THERE, ASSHOLE! YOU WANT ME TO CALL BEEFY SID OVER...?
FINE. THEN YOU GO BACK THERE AND TELL HER I'M HERE.
YEAH, I'M SURE SHE'LL RUSH RIGHT OUT...
LINDA, C'MON...
WHATEVER.
IF I GO BACK THERE... MAYBE. AND MAYBE I'LL TELL HER NOT TO COME OUT AT ALL...
PRICK.

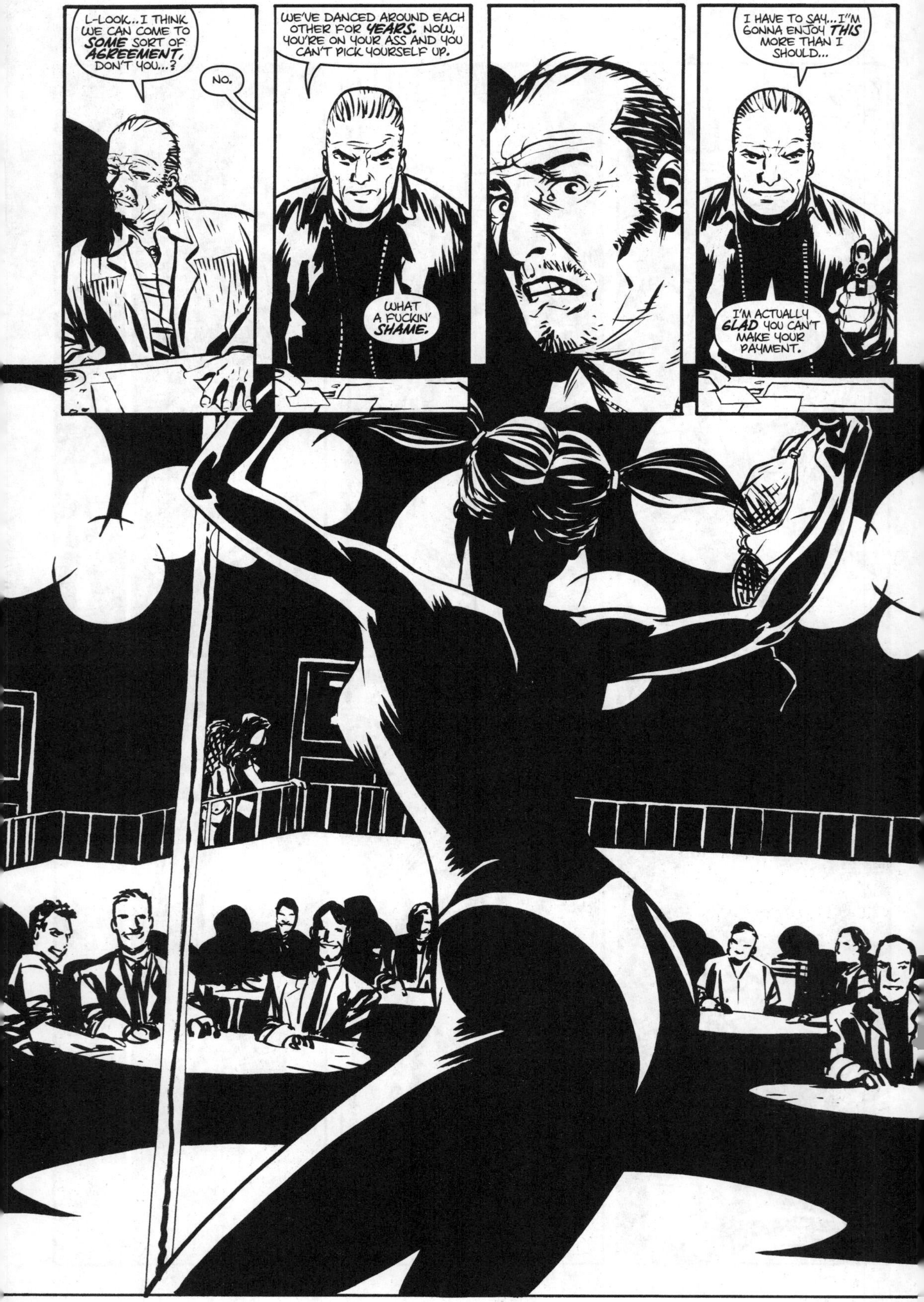

L-LOOK...I THINK WE CAN COME TO SOME SORT OF AGREEMENT, DON'T YOU...?
NO.
WE'VE DANCED AROUND EACH OTHER FOR YEARS. NOW, YOU'RE ON YOUR ASS AND YOU CAN'T PICK YOURSELF UP.
WHAT A FUCKIN' SHAME.
I HAVE TO SAY...I'M GONNA ENJOY THIS MORE THAN I SHOULD...
I'M ACTUALLY GLAD YOU CAN'T MAKE YOUR PAYMENT.

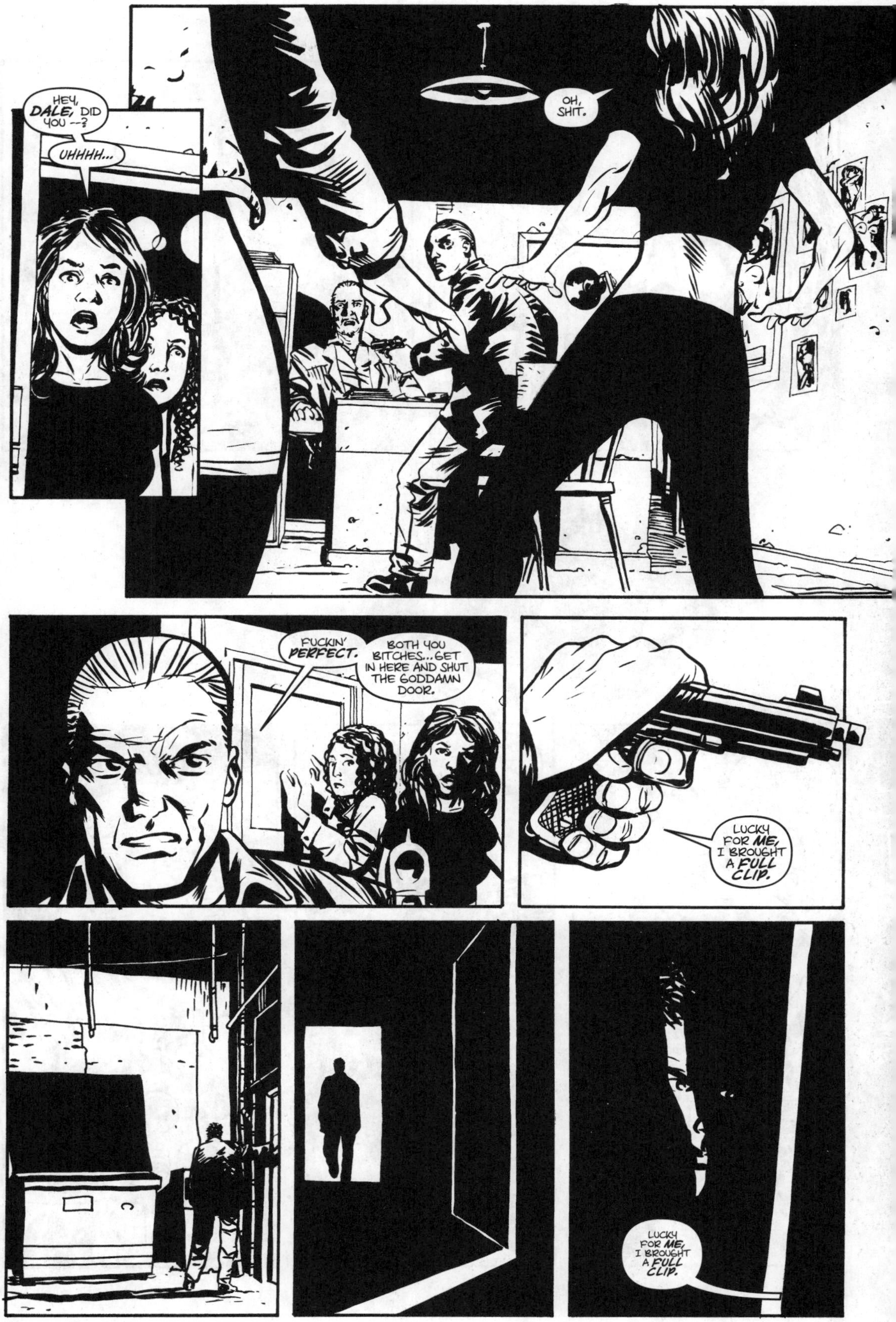
HEY, DALE, DID YOU --?
UHHHH...
OH, SHIT.
FUCKIN' PERFECT.
BOTH YOU BITCHES...GET IN HERE AND SHUT THE GODDAMN DOOR.
LUCKY FOR ME, I BROUGHT A FULL CLIP.
LUCKY FOR ME, I BROUGHT A FULL CLIP.

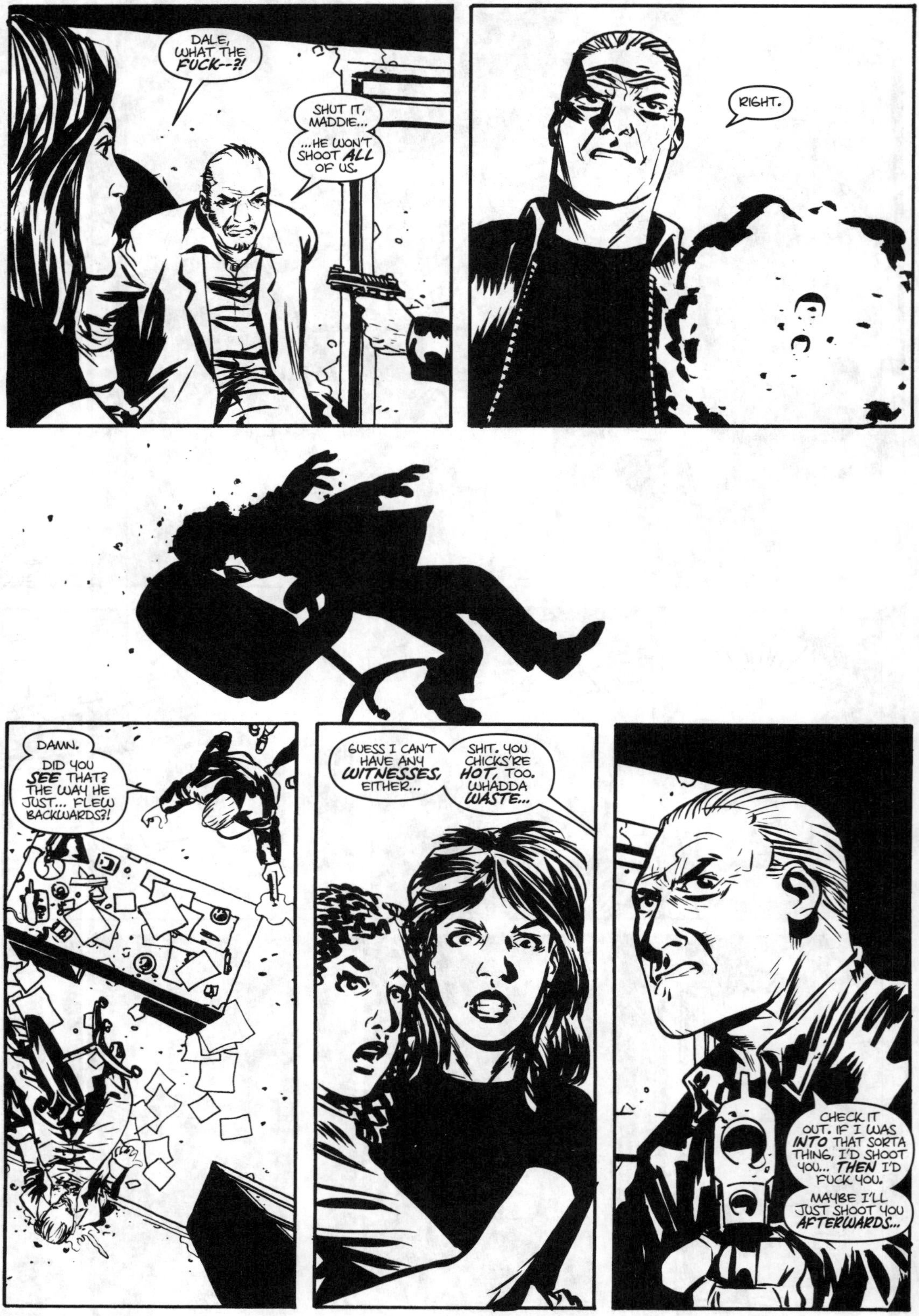
DALE, WHAT THE FUCK--?!
SHUT IT, MADDIE...
...HE WON'T SHOOT ALL OF US.
RIGHT.
DAMN.
DID YOU SEE THAT? THE WAY HE JUST... FLEW BACKWARDS?!
GUESS I CAN'T HAVE ANY WITNESSES, EITHER...
SHIT. YOU CHICKS'RE HOT, TOO. WHADDA WASTE...
CHECK IT OUT. IF I WAS INTO THAT SORTA THING, I'D SHOOT YOU... THEN I'D FUCK YOU.
MAYBE I'LL JUST SHOOT YOU AFTERWARDS...

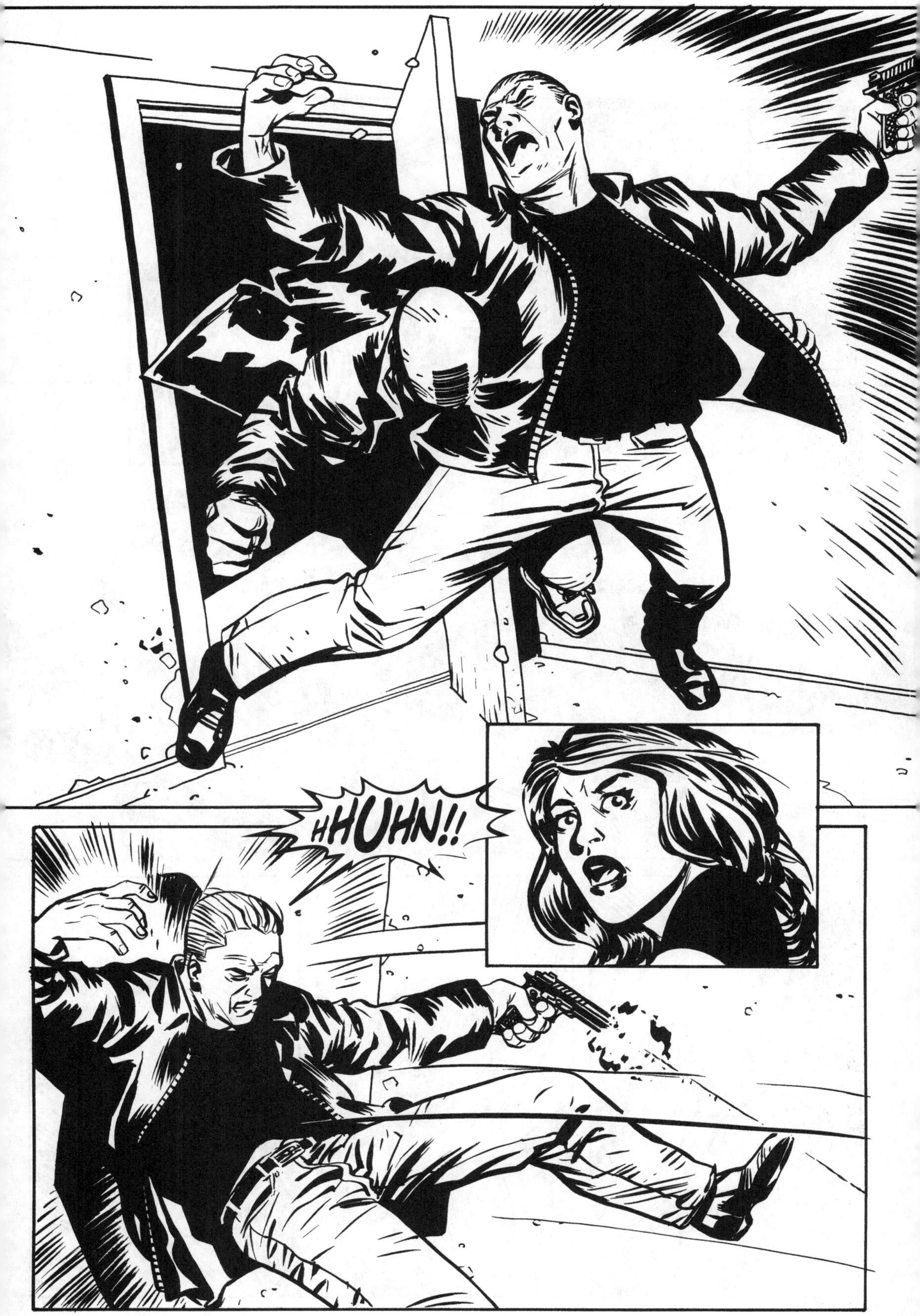
HHUHN!!

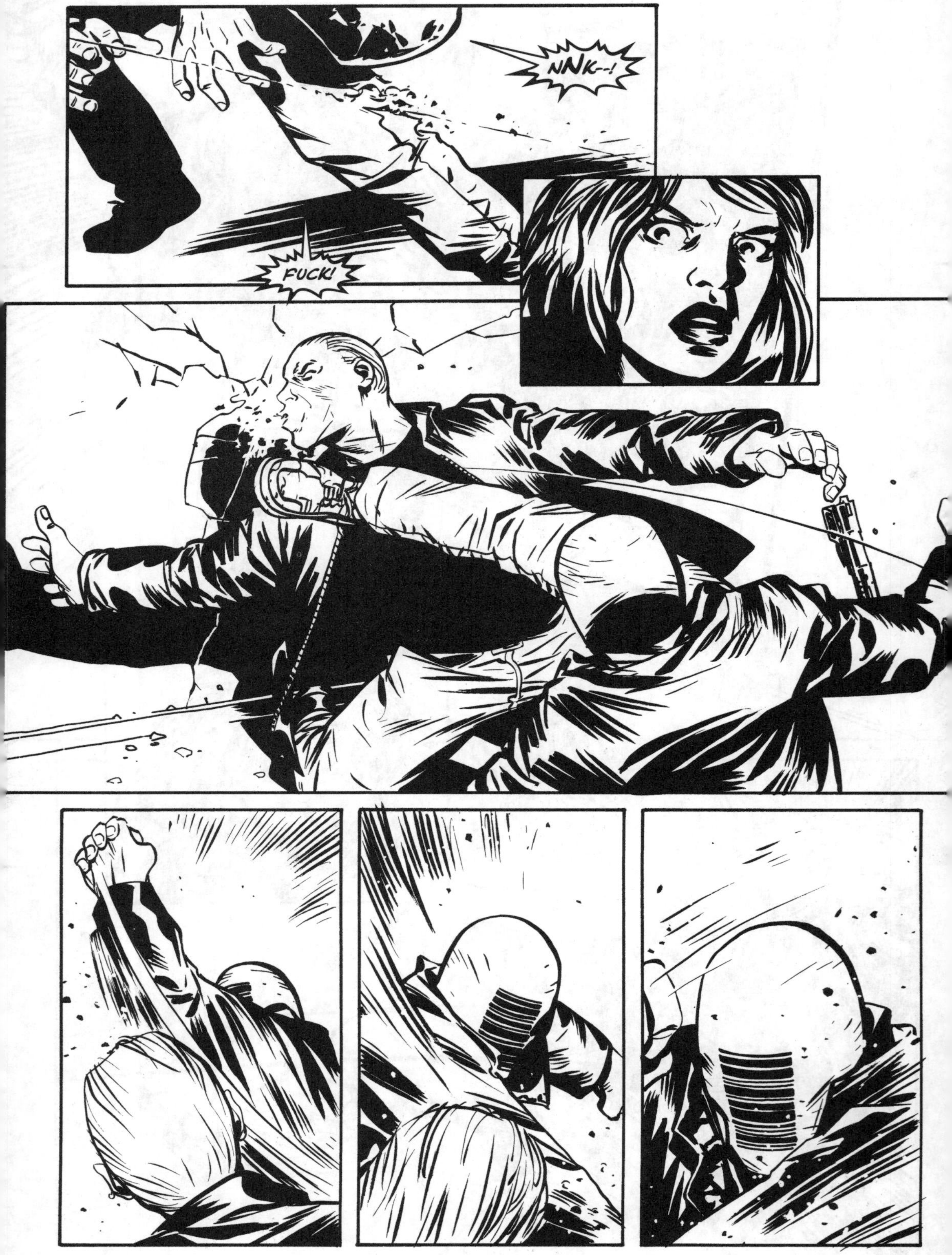
NNK--!
FUCK!

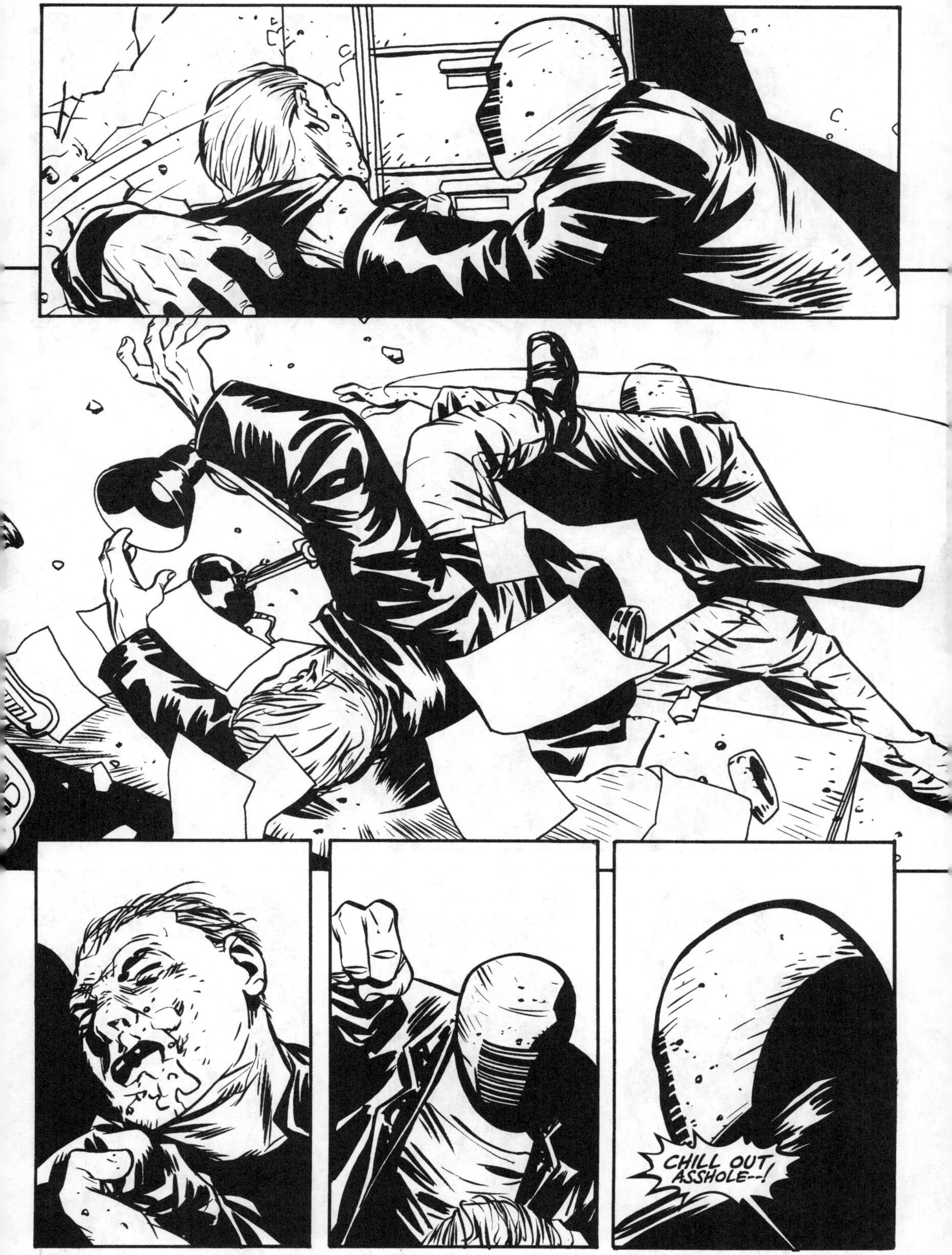
CHILL OUT ASSHOLE--!

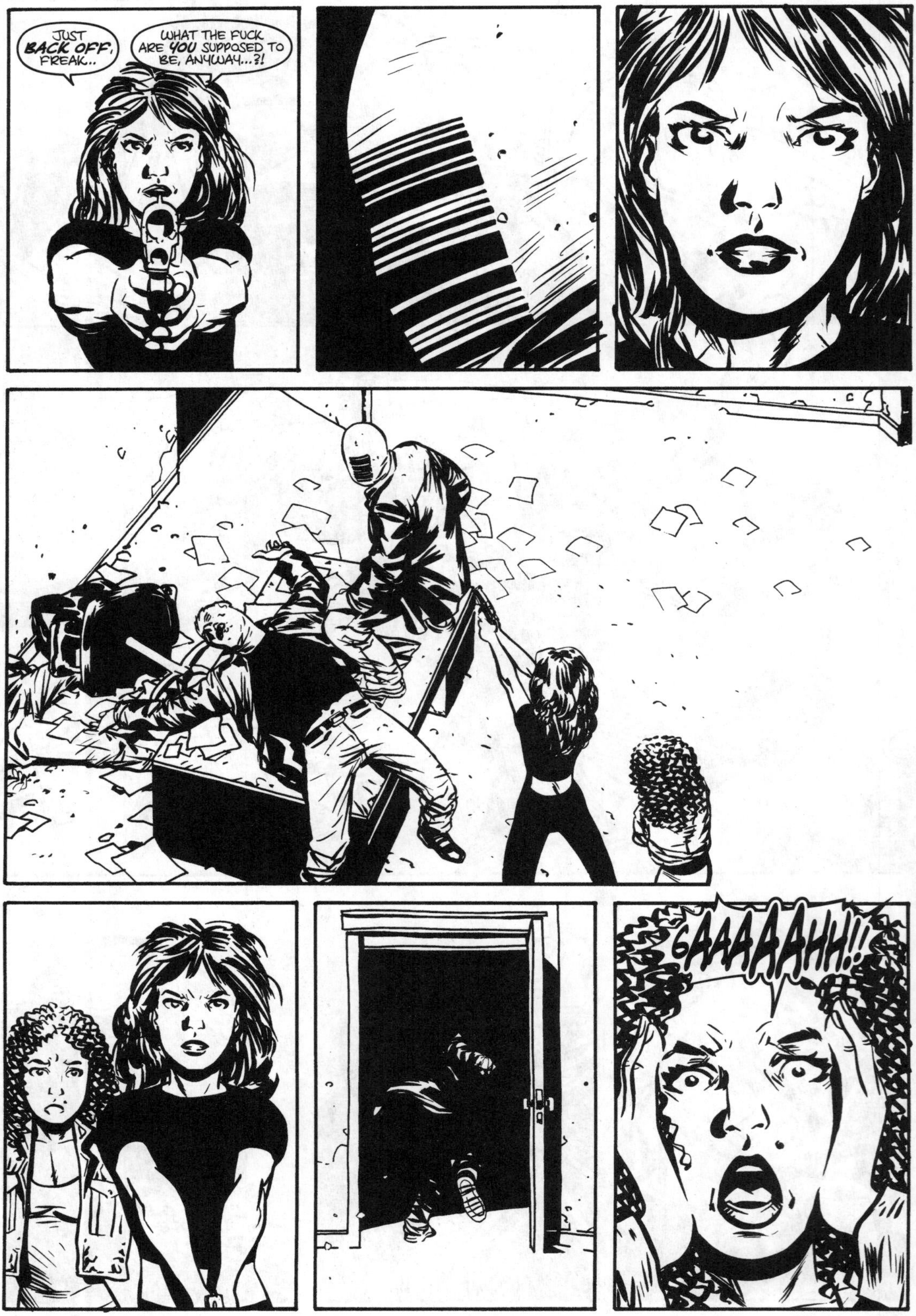
JUST BACK OFF, FREAK...
WHAT THE FUCK ARE YOU SUPPOSED TO BE, ANYWAY...?!
GAAAAAAHH!!

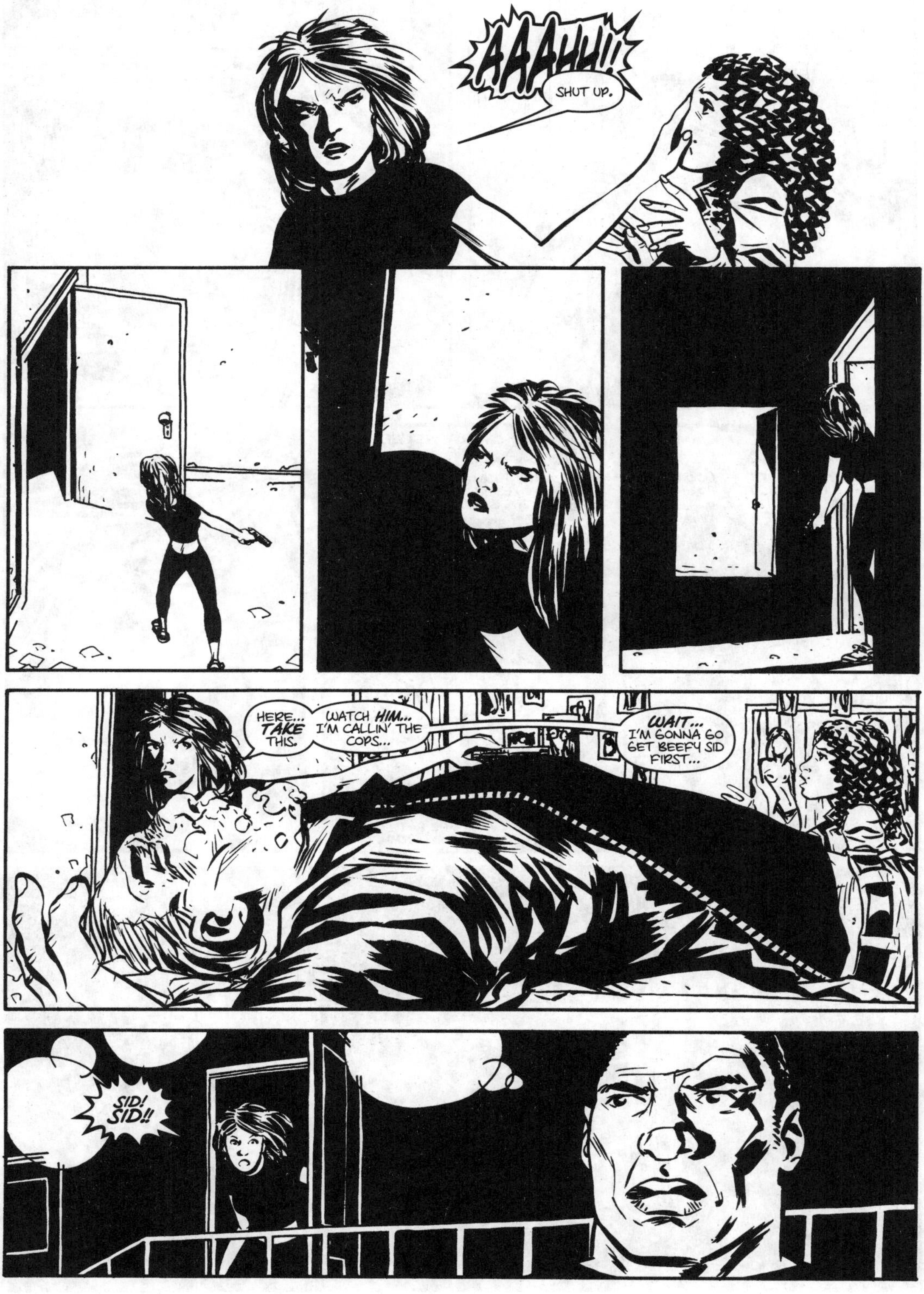
AAAHH!!
SHUT UP.
HERE... TAKE THIS.
WATCH HIM... I'M CALLIN' THE COPS...
WAIT... I'M GONNA GO GET BEEFY SID FIRST...
SID! SID!!

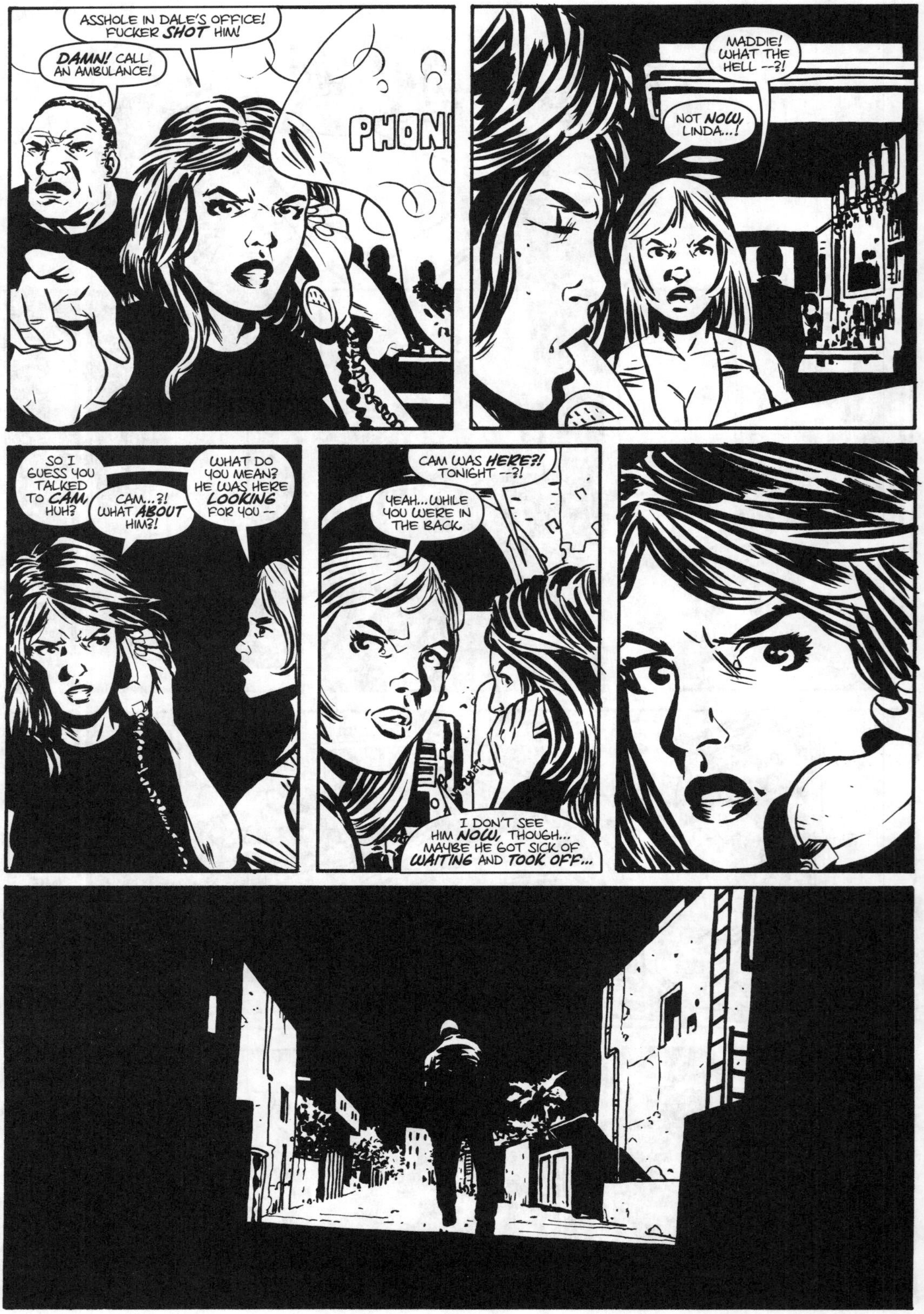

ASSHOLE IN DALE'S OFFICE! FUCKER SHOT HIM!
DAMN! CALL AN AMBULANCE!
PHON
MADDIE! WHAT THE HELL --?!
NOT NOW, LINDA...!
SO I GUESS YOU TALKED TO CAM, HUH?
CAM...?! WHAT ABOUT HIM?!
WHAT DO YOU MEAN? HE WAS HERE LOOKING FOR YOU --
CAM WAS HERE?! TONIGHT --?!
YEAH...WHILE YOU WERE IN THE BACK.
I DON'T SEE HIM NOW, THOUGH... MAYBE HE GOT SICK OF WAITING AND TOOK OFF...

She could see the fear in his eyes.
The beads of sweat forming on his upper lip.
His quivering chin. His eye twitching.
The sad bastard didn't even know he was
bleeding... that his life was spilling out
onto the shag carpeting...

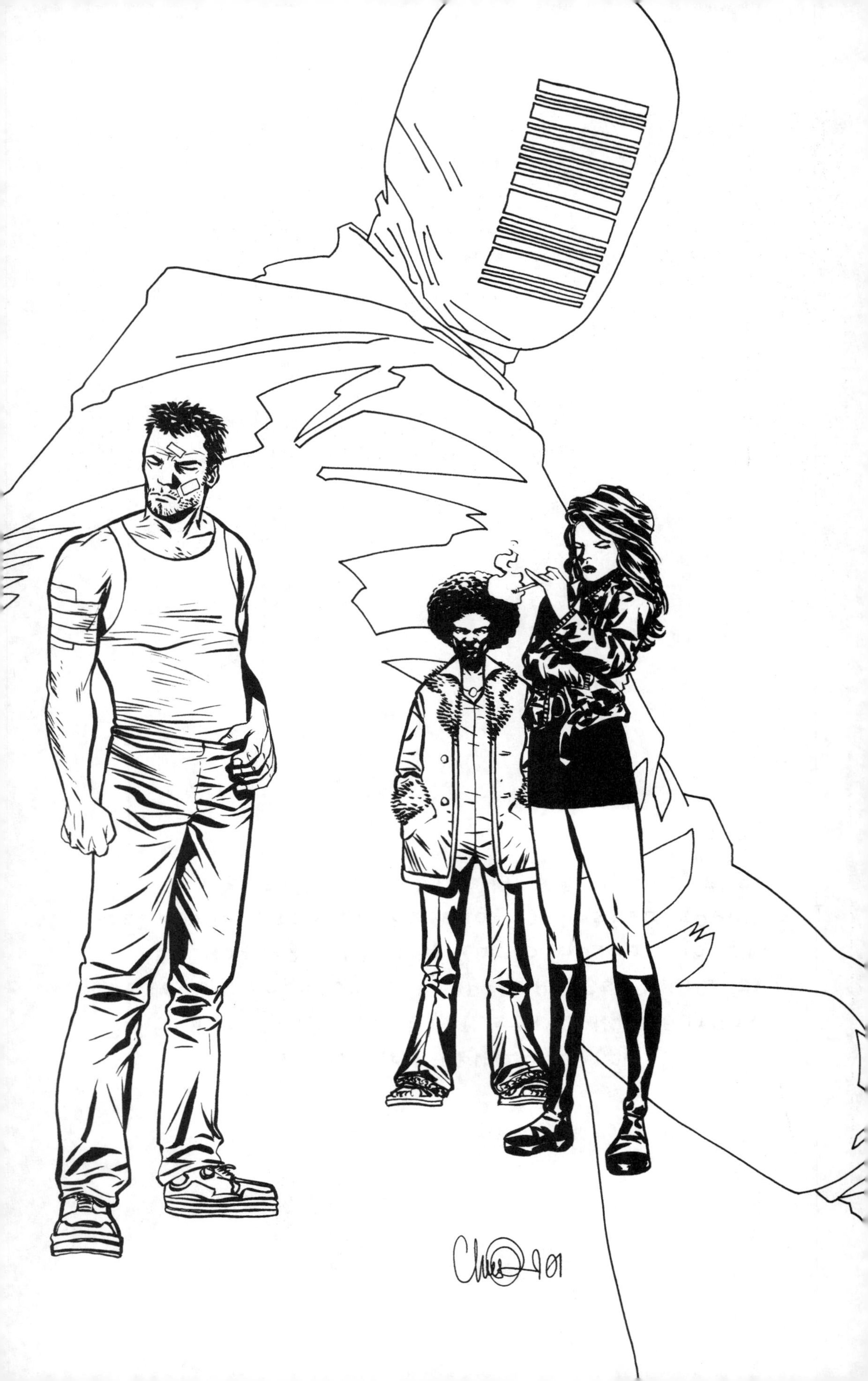

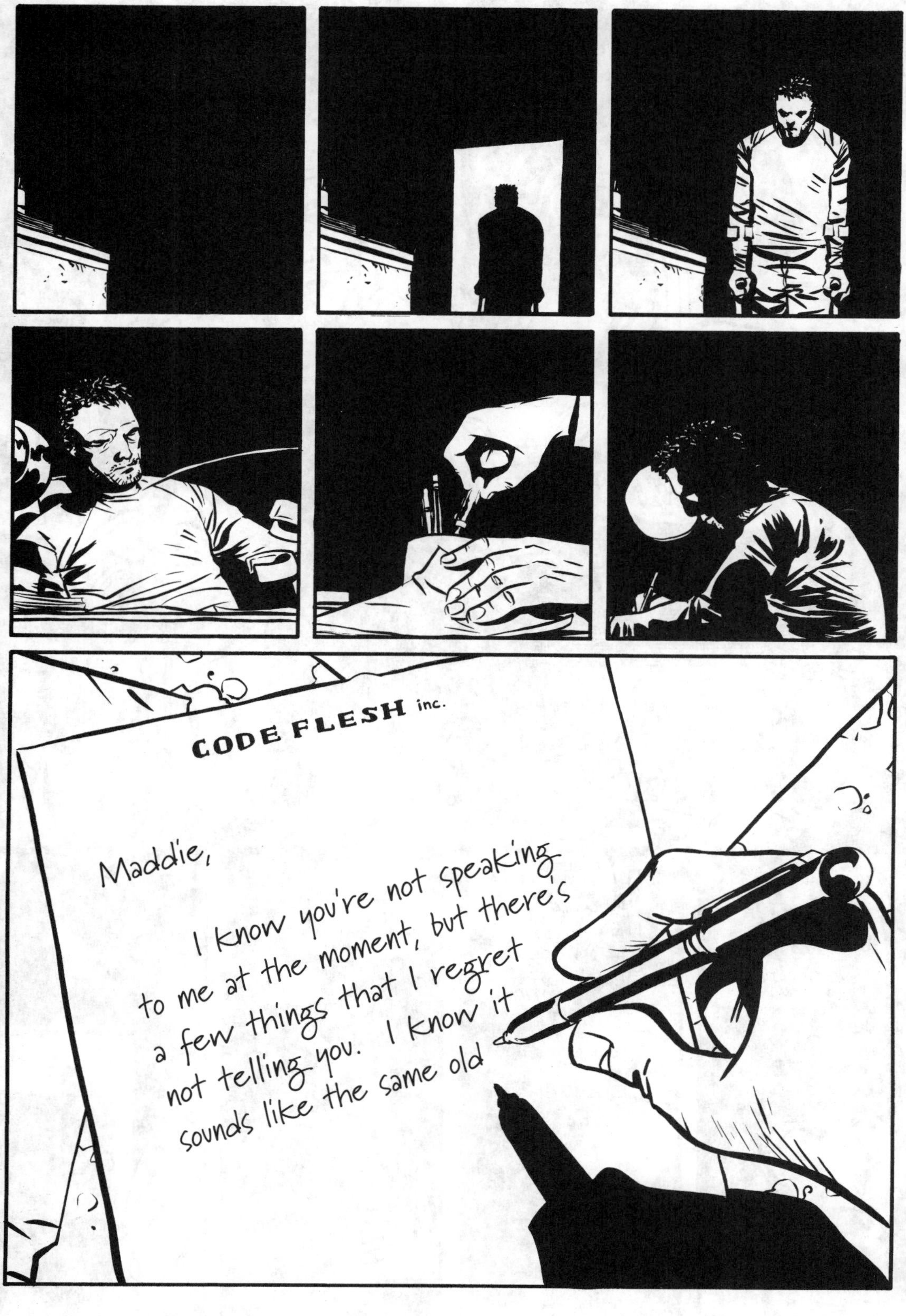
CODE FLESH inc.
Maddie,
I know you're not speaking to me at the moment, but there's a few things that I regret not telling you. I know it sounds like the same old

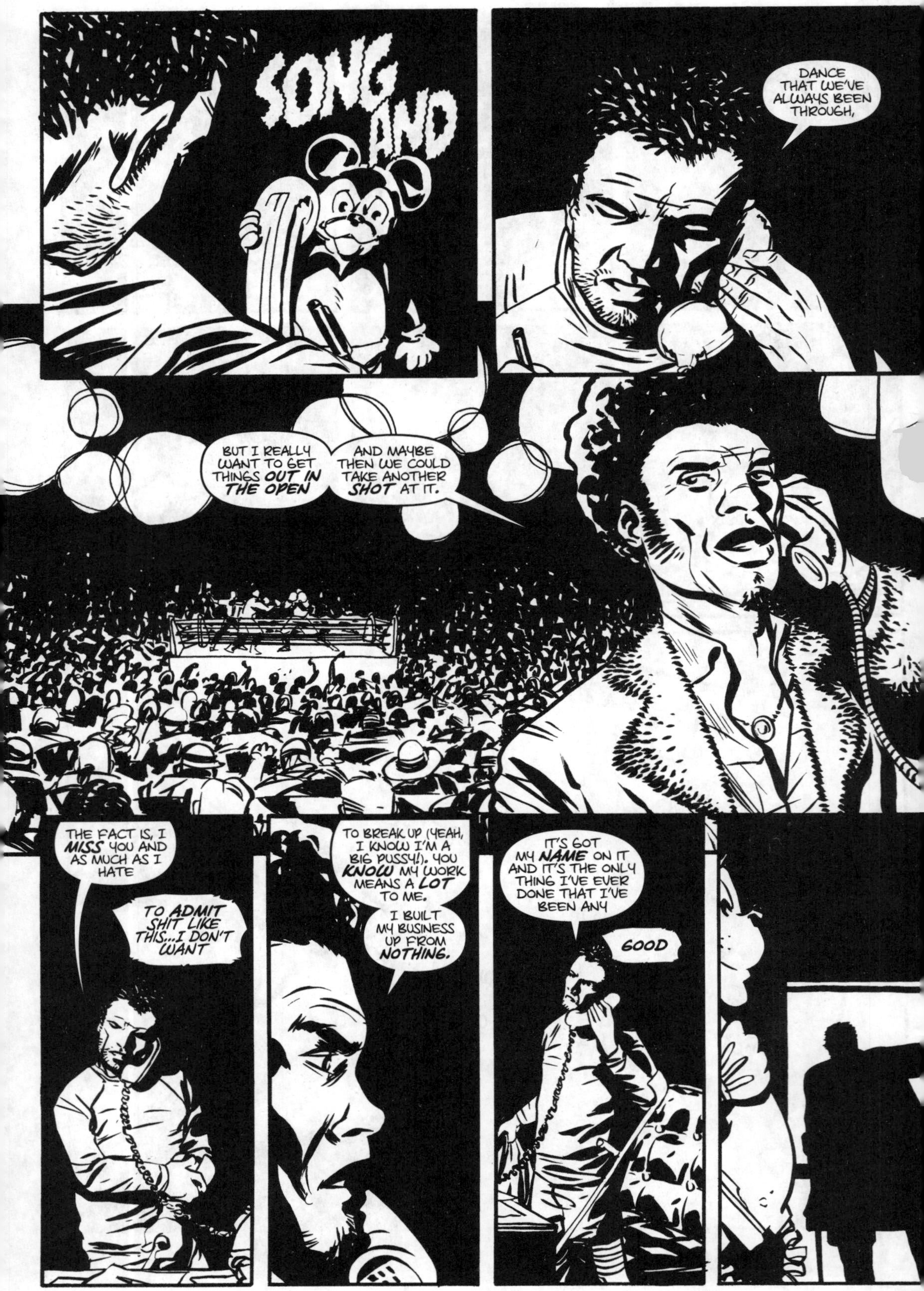
SONG AND
DANCE THAT WE'VE ALWAYS BEEN THROUGH,
BUT I REALLY WANT TO GET THINGS OUT IN THE OPEN
AND MAYBE THEN WE COULD TAKE ANOTHER SHOT AT IT.
THE FACT IS, I MISS YOU AND AS MUCH AS I HATE
TO ADMIT SHIT LIKE THIS...I DON'T WANT
TO BREAK UP (YEAH, I KNOW I'M A BIG PUSSY!). YOU KNOW MY WORK MEANS A LOT TO ME.
I BUILT MY BUSINESS UP FROM NOTHING.
IT'S GOT MY NAME ON IT AND IT'S THE ONLY THING I'VE EVER DONE THAT I'VE BEEN ANY
GOOD

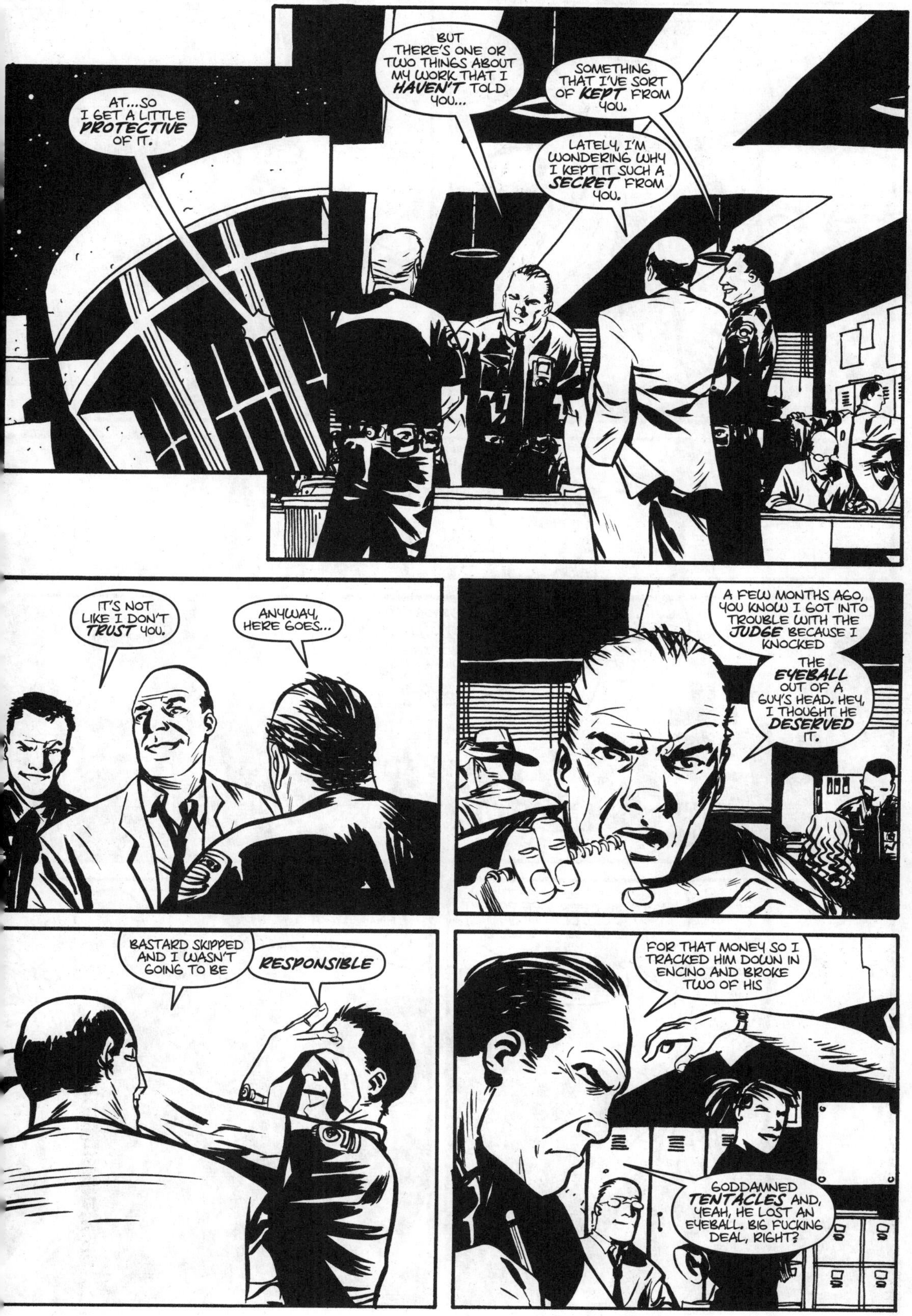

AT...SO I GET A LITTLE PROTECTIVE OF IT.
BUT THERE'S ONE OR TWO THINGS ABOUT MY WORK THAT I HAVEN'T TOLD YOU...
SOMETHING THAT I'VE SORT OF KEPT FROM YOU.
LATELY, I'M WONDERING WHY I KEPT IT SUCH A SECRET FROM YOU.
IT'S NOT LIKE I DON'T TRUST YOU.
ANYWAY, HERE GOES...
A FEW MONTHS AGO, YOU KNOW I GOT INTO TROUBLE WITH THE JUDGE BECAUSE I KNOCKED
THE EYEBALL OUT OF A GUY'S HEAD. HEY, I THOUGHT HE DESERVED IT.
BASTARD SKIPPED AND I WASN'T GOING TO BE
RESPONSIBLE
FOR THAT MONEY SO I TRACKED HIM DOWN IN ENCINO AND BROKE TWO OF HIS
GODDAMNED TENTACLES AND, YEAH, HE LOST AN EYEBALL. BIG FUCKING DEAL, RIGHT?

WELL, THE *JUDGE* DIDN'T SEE IT THAT WAY

AND HE CLIPPED MY WINGS, *BIG TIME.*

HE LET ME KEEP THE BUSINESS,

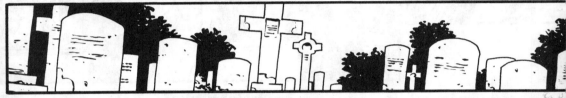

BUT I COULDN'T GO AFTER THE SKIPS ANYMORE. I HAD TO HIRE *BOUNTY HUNTERS.*

I ALSO HAD TO GET MYSELF INTO AN *ANGER MANAGEMENT PROGRAM.* STILL WORKING ON THAT ONE. OKAY, THIS IS ALL STUFF YOU ALREADY *KNOW...*

BUT GET READY FOR THE PART I'VE BEEN *KEEPING* FROM YOU. I DIDN'T WANT TO *GIVE UP* WHAT I *LOVE* ABOUT THIS JOB...

BRINGING IN THE *SKIPS.*

SO I FIGURED OUT A WAY TO KEEP *DOING* IT

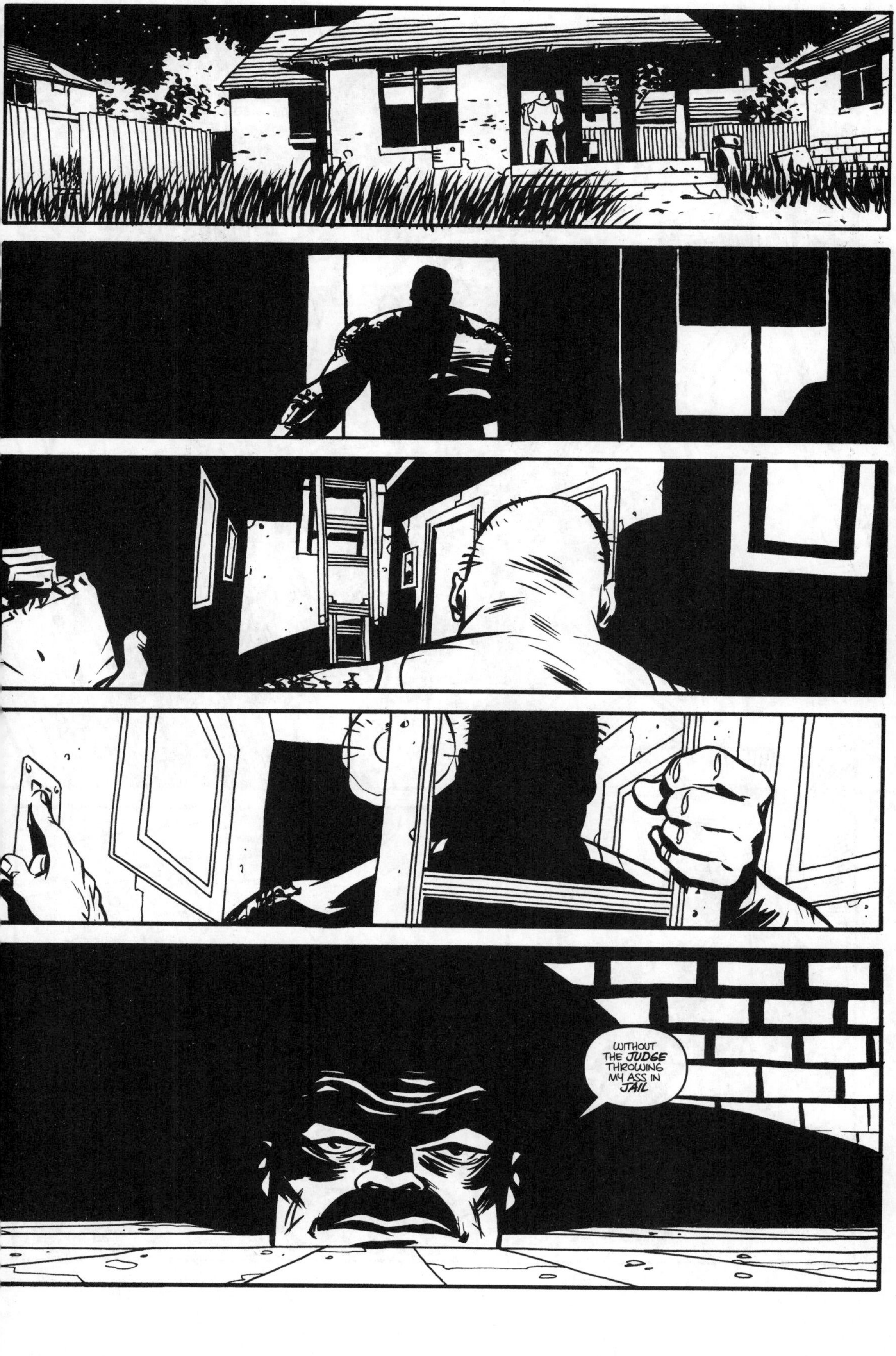
WITHOUT THE JUDGE THROWING MY ASS IN JAIL

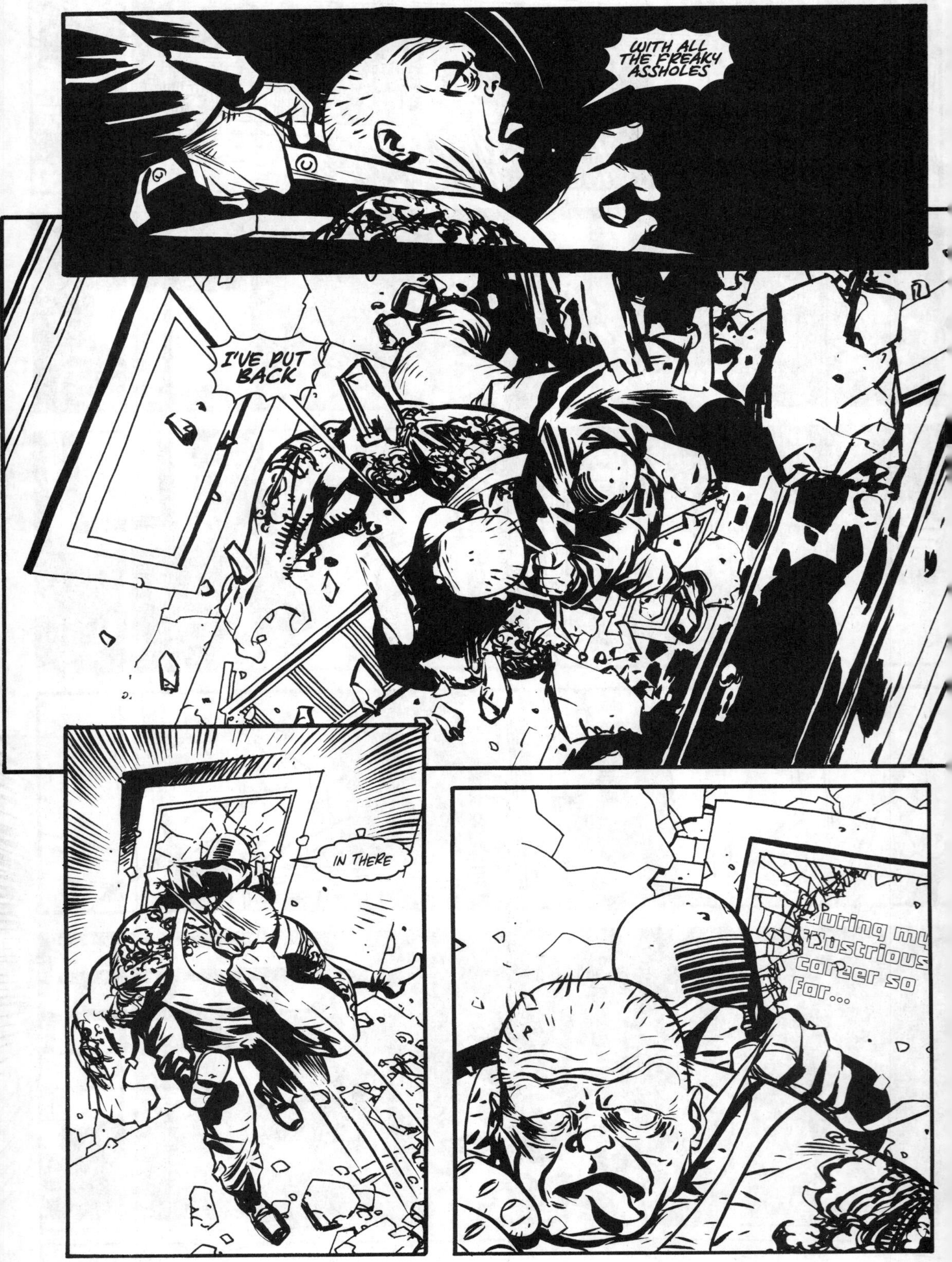
WITH ALL THE FREAKY ASSHOLES
I'VE PUT BACK
IN THERE
uring my
lustrious
career so
far...

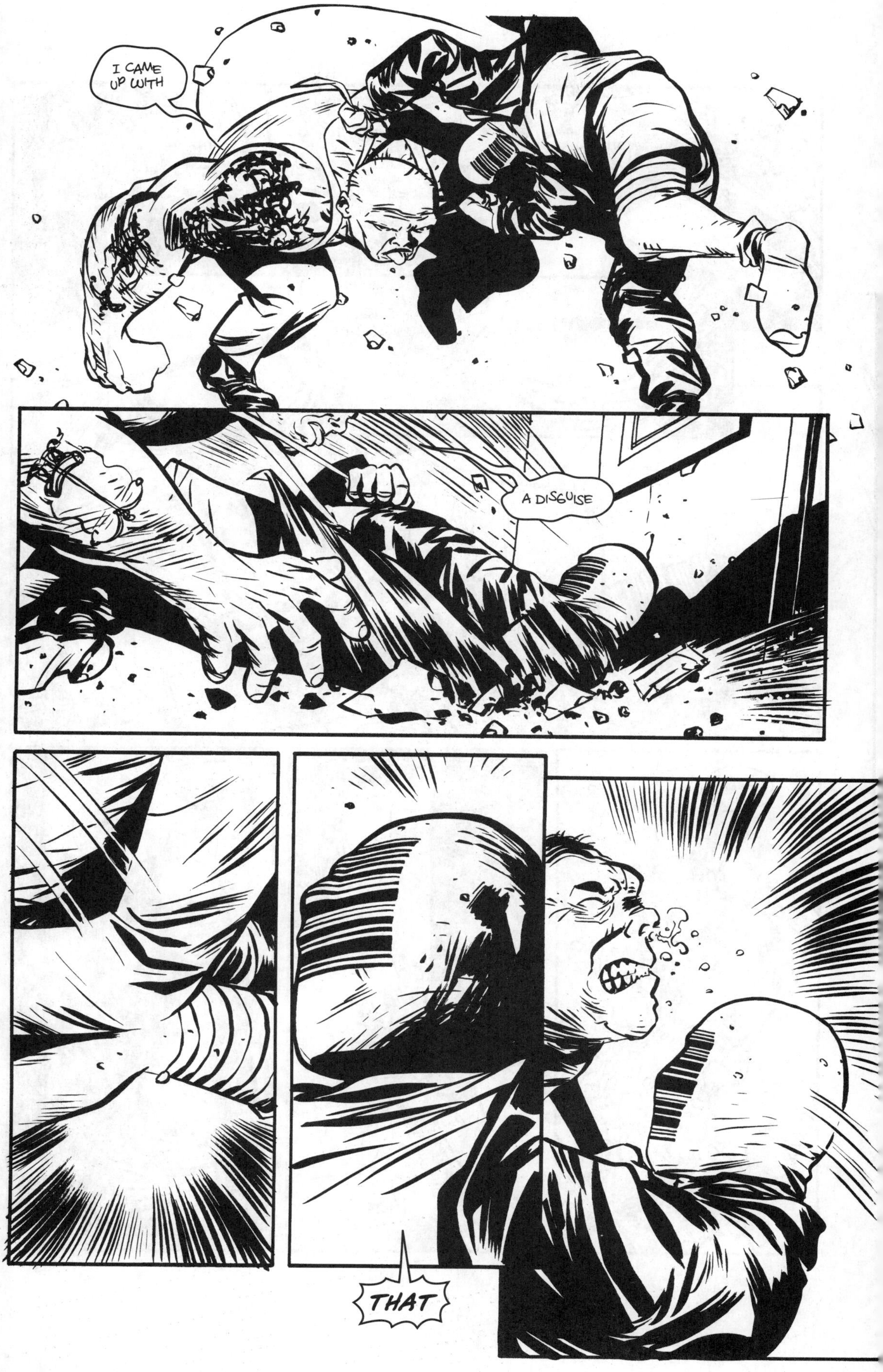
I CAME UP WITH
A DISGUISE
THAT

GUARANTEED ANONYMITY.
A FULL-FACE MASK
THAT
ALLOWED ME TO BASICALLY HIRE MYSELF AS A BOUNTY HUNTER!
PRETTY FUCKING BRILLIANT, RIGHT?

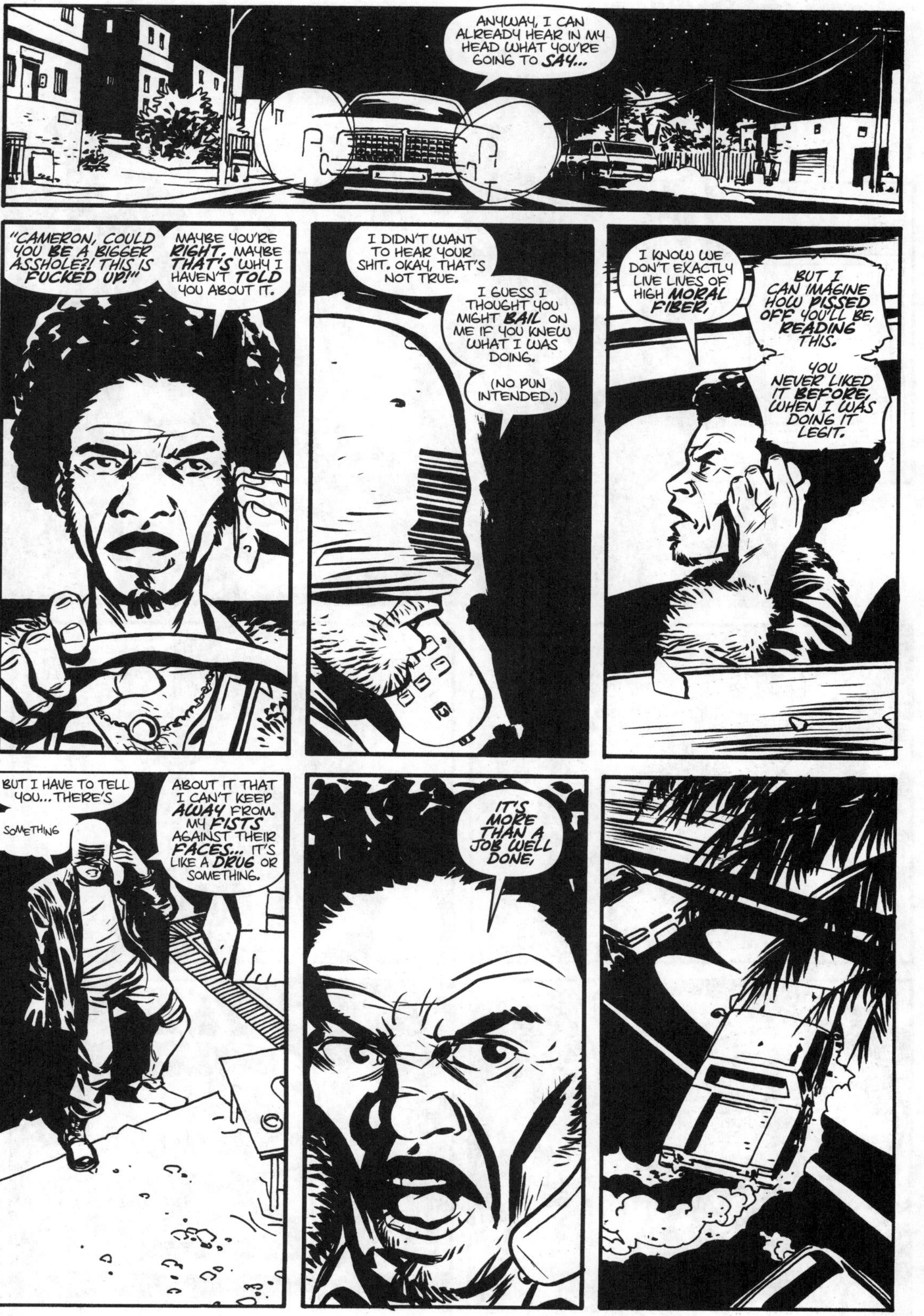

ANYWAY, I CAN ALREADY HEAR IN MY HEAD WHAT YOU'RE GOING TO SAY...
"CAMERON, COULD YOU BE A BIGGER ASSHOLE?! THIS IS FUCKED UP!"
MAYBE YOU'RE RIGHT. MAYBE THAT'S WHY I HAVEN'T TOLD YOU ABOUT IT.
I DIDN'T WANT TO HEAR YOUR SHIT. OKAY, THAT'S NOT TRUE.
I GUESS I THOUGHT YOU MIGHT BAIL ON ME IF YOU KNEW WHAT I WAS DOING.
(NO PUN INTENDED.)
I KNOW WE DON'T EXACTLY LIVE LIVES OF HIGH MORAL FIBER,
BUT I CAN IMAGINE HOW PISSED OFF YOU'LL BE, READING THIS.
YOU NEVER LIKED IT BEFORE, WHEN I WAS DOING IT LEGIT.
BUT I HAVE TO TELL YOU... THERE'S
SOMETHING
ABOUT IT THAT I CAN'T KEEP AWAY FROM. MY FISTS AGAINST THEIR FACES... IT'S LIKE A DRUG OR SOMETHING.
IT'S MORE THAN A JOB WELL DONE,

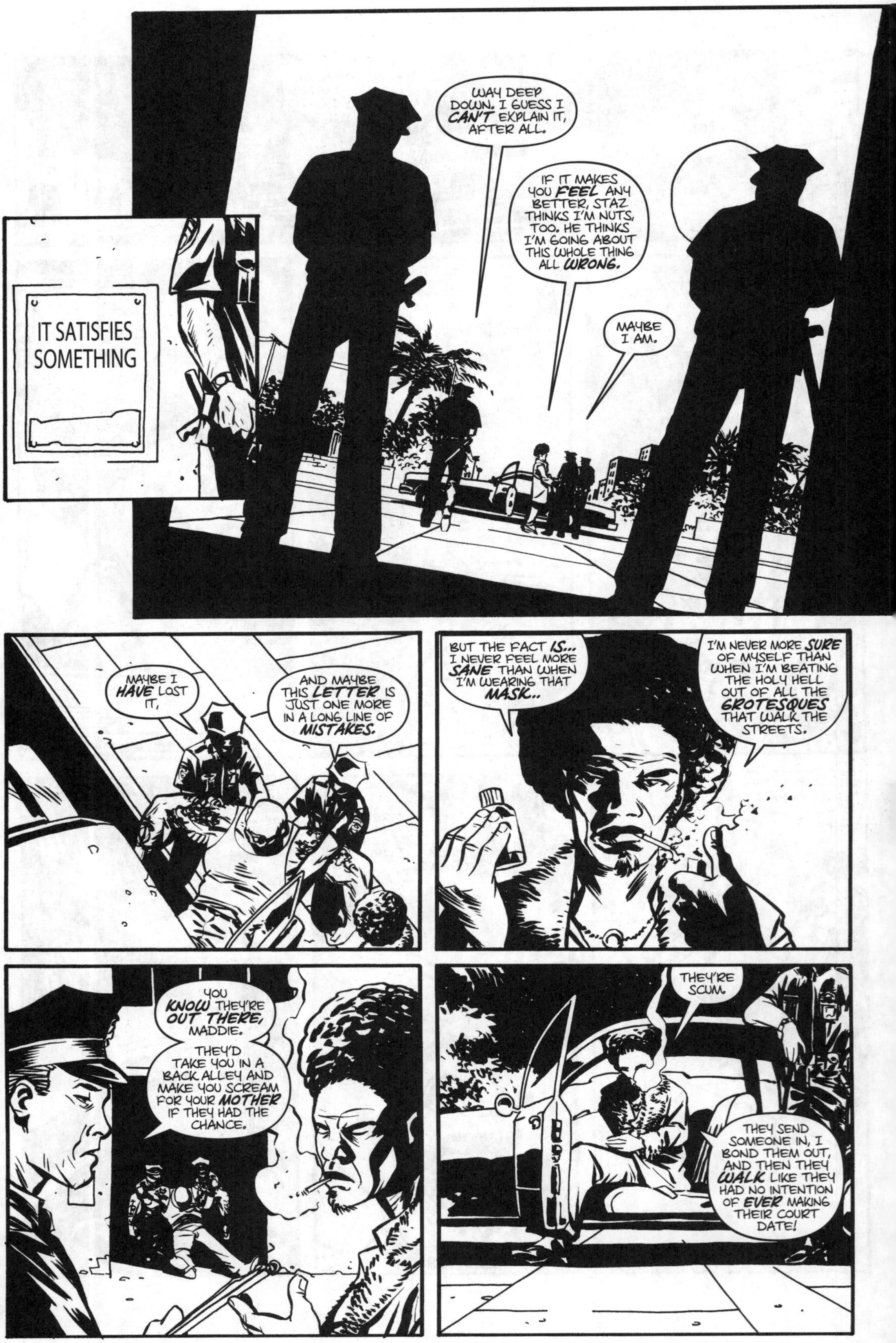
IT SATISFIES SOMETHING
WAY DEEP DOWN. I GUESS I CAN'T EXPLAIN IT, AFTER ALL.
IF IT MAKES YOU FEEL ANY BETTER, STAZ THINKS I'M NUTS, TOO. HE THINKS I'M GOING ABOUT THIS WHOLE THING ALL WRONG.
MAYBE I AM.
MAYBE I HAVE LOST IT,
AND MAYBE THIS LETTER IS JUST ONE MORE IN A LONG LINE OF MISTAKES.
BUT THE FACT IS... I NEVER FEEL MORE SANE THAN WHEN I'M WEARING THAT MASK...
I'M NEVER MORE SURE OF MYSELF THAN WHEN I'M BEATING THE HOLY HELL OUT OF ALL THE GROTESQUES THAT WALK THE STREETS.
YOU KNOW THEY'RE OUT THERE, MADDIE.
THEY'D TAKE YOU IN A BACK ALLEY AND MAKE YOU SCREAM FOR YOUR MOTHER IF THEY HAD THE CHANCE.
THEY'RE SCUM.
THEY SEND SOMEONE IN, I BOND THEM OUT, AND THEN THEY WALK LIKE THEY HAD NO INTENTION OF EVER MAKING THEIR COURT DATE!

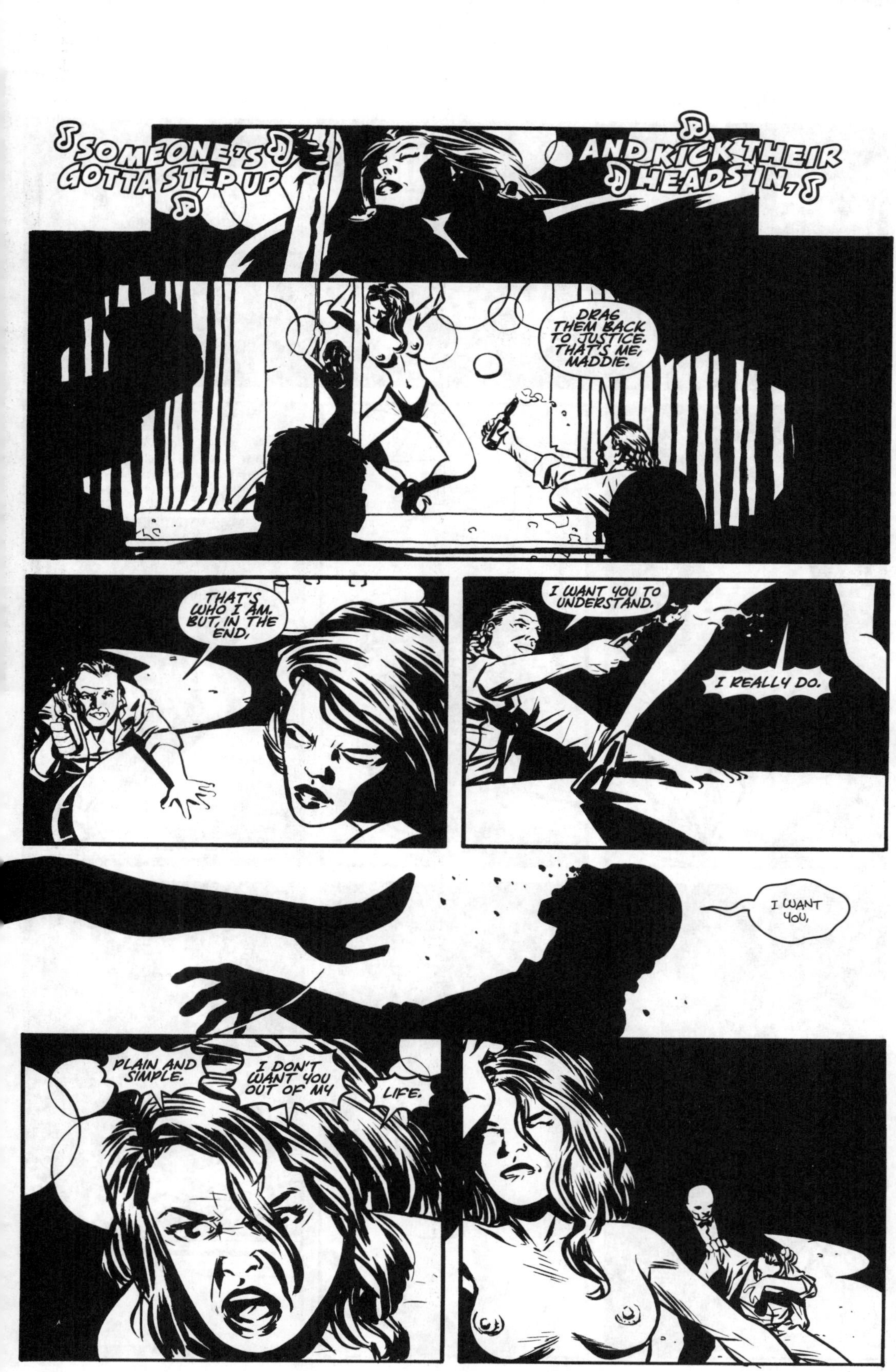
SOMEONE'S GOTTA STEP UP
AND KICK THEIR HEADS IN,
DRAG THEM BACK TO JUSTICE. THAT'S ME, MADDIE.
THAT'S WHO I AM. BUT, IN THE END,
I WANT YOU TO UNDERSTAND.
I REALLY DO.
I WANT YOU,
PLAIN AND SIMPLE.
I DON'T WANT YOU OUT OF MY
LIFE.

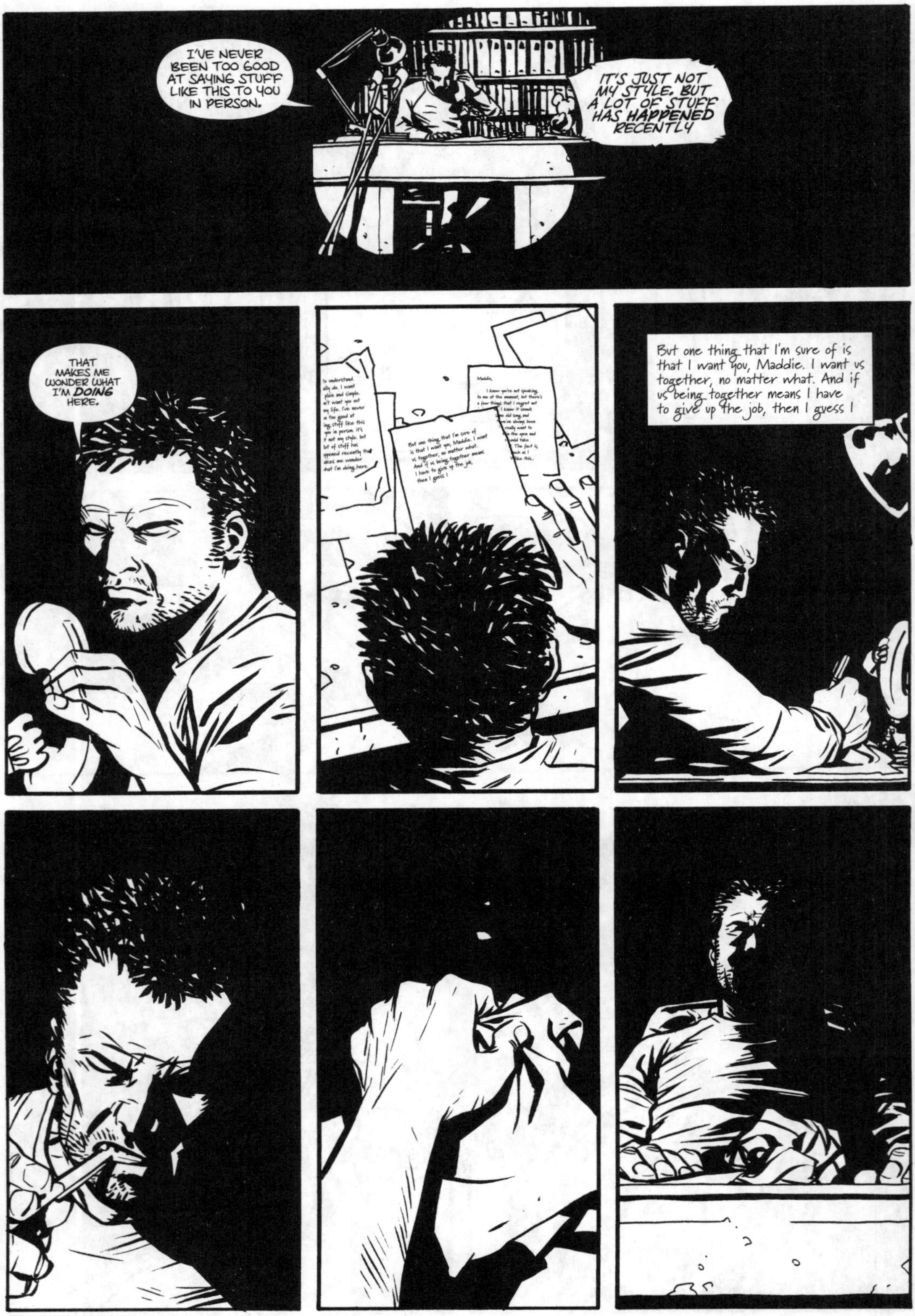

I'VE NEVER BEEN TOO GOOD AT SAYING STUFF LIKE THIS TO YOU IN PERSON.
IT'S JUST NOT MY STYLE. BUT A LOT OF STUFF HAS HAPPENED RECENTLY
THAT MAKES ME WONDER WHAT I'M DOING HERE.
But one thing that I'm sure of is that I want you, Maddie. I want us together, no matter what. And if us being together means I have to give up the job, then I guess I

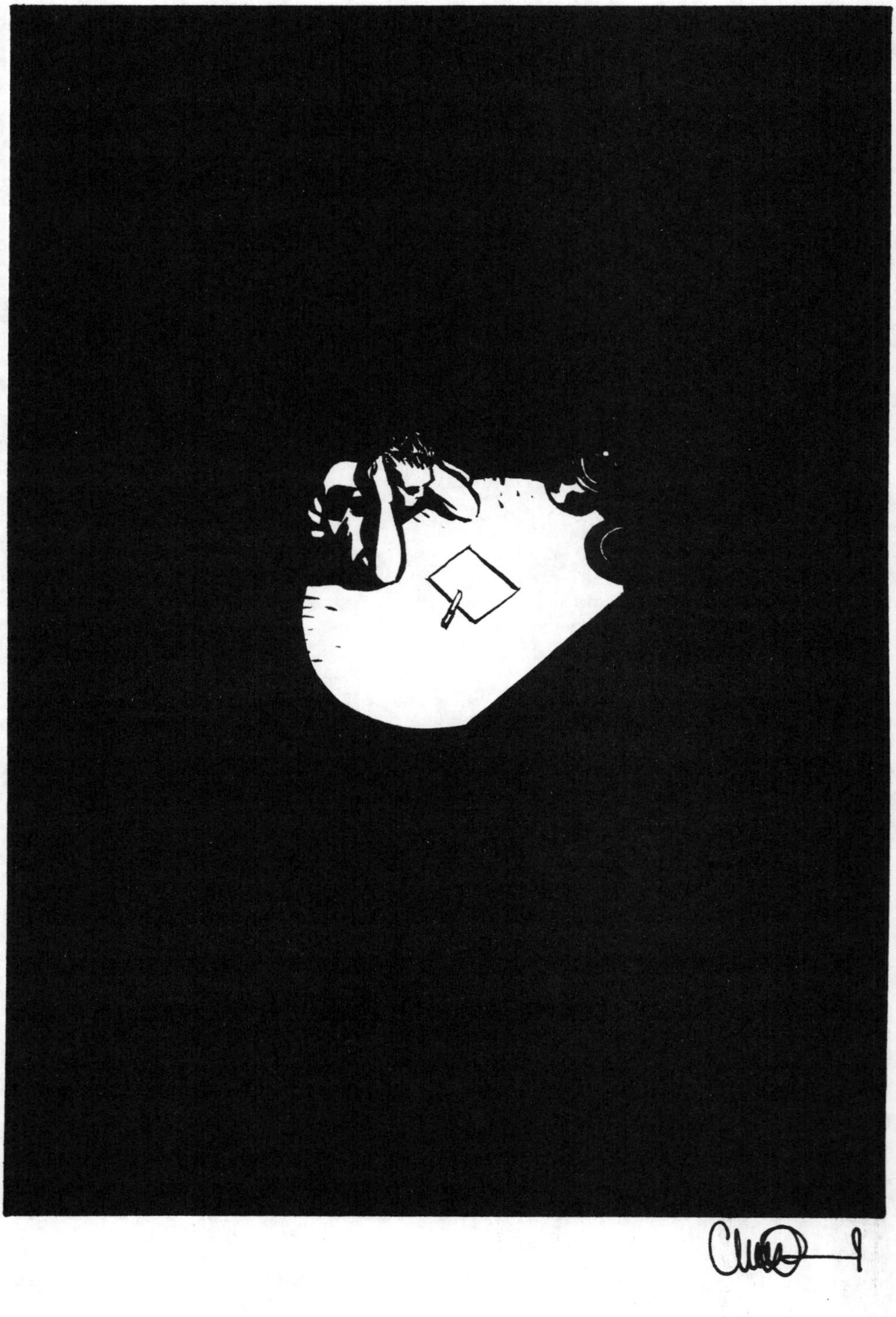

"There's nothing I can write in a letter to really convey all this shit. This is my life now. I've backed myself into a corner that I know I can't get out of. To be honest, I don't know if I want to get out of it. It just feels too good to stop now..."

END

behind the scenes

ISBN 1-932051-15-5

51295

9 781932 051155

codeflesh

CODEFLESH — VERSION #1

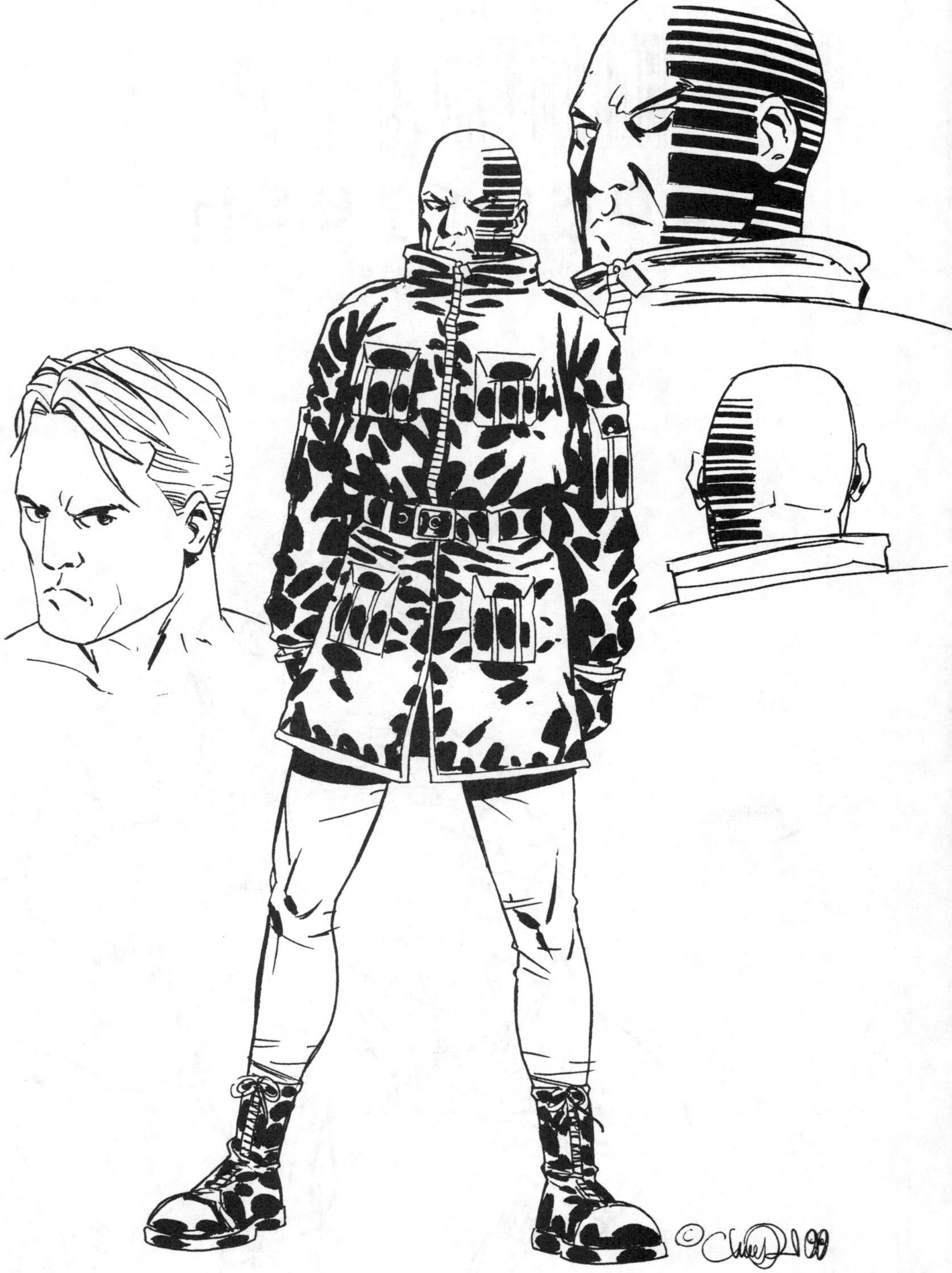

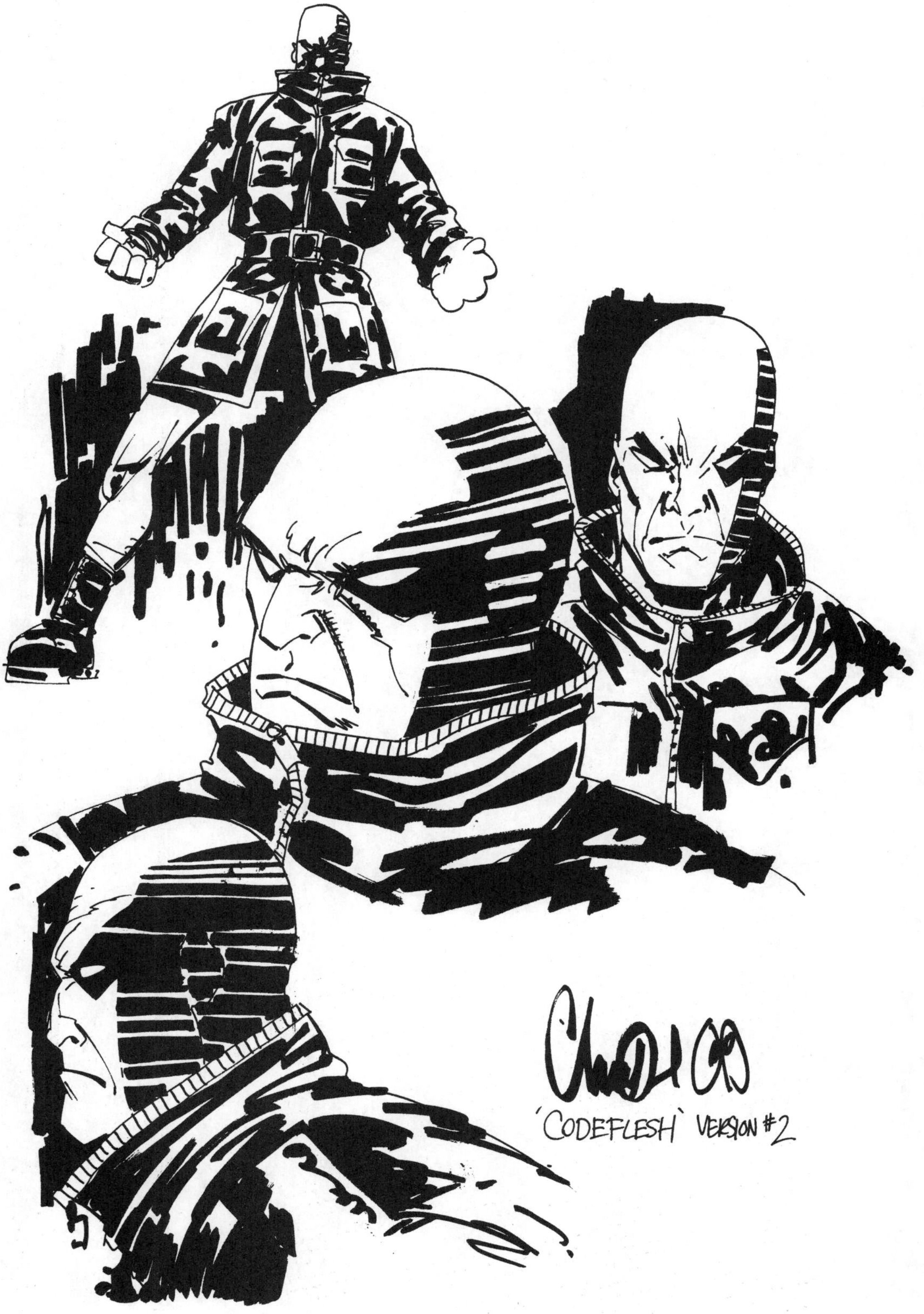
'CODEFLESH' VERSION #2